PENGUIN BOOKS

WEAPONS OF MATH DESTRUCTION

'In today's world, if you want to change your fate you've got to pray at the altar of the algorithm . . . As math guru Cathy O'Neil argues in her newest book, these models are just the latest way America's institutions perpetuate bias and prejudice to reward the rich and keep the poor, well, poor. It's a nuanced reminder that big data is only as good as the people wielding it' *Wired*

'In an era when many people uncritically applaud the power of big data, O'Neil argues for the dark side of the deluge to be tackled through algorithm audits, transparency and legal reform' *Nature*

'O'Neil has become a whistle-blower for the world of Big Data . . . Her work makes particularly disturbing points about how being on the wrong side of an algorithmic decision can snowball in incredibly destructive ways' *Time*

'A fascinating and deeply disturbing book. O'Neil explains how authority is shifting from humans to big data algorithms, which now decide whether to give you a loan, offer you a job or even lock you in jail' Yuval Noah Harari, *Guardian*, Books of the Year

'Written in an exceedingly accessible, almost literary style; her fascinating case studies of WMDs fit neatly into the genre of dystopian literature. There's a little Philip K. Dick, a little Orwell, a little Kafka in her portrait of powerful bureaucracies ceding control of the most intimate decisions of our lives to hyper-empowered computer models riddled with all of our unresolved, atavistic human biases' Chris Jackson, *Paris Review*

'Even as a professional mathematician, I had no idea how insidious Big Data could be until I read *Weapons of Math Destruction*. Though terrifying, it's a surprisingly fun read: O'Neil's vision of a world run by algorithms is laced with dark humour and exasperation – like a modern-day *Dr Strangelove* or *Catch-22*. It is eye-opening, disturbing, and deeply important' Steven Strogatz, Cornell University, author of *The Joy of x*

'Her analysis is superb, her writing is enticing, and her findings are unsettling' Danah Boyd, founder of Data & Society and author of *It's Complicated*

'Next time you hear someone gushing uncritically about the wonders of Big Data, show them *Weapons of Math Destruction*. It'll be salutary' Felix Salmon, *Fusion*

'*Weapons of Math Destruction* is the Big Data story Silicon Valley proponents won't tell . . . [It] pithily exposes flaws in how information is used to assess everything from creditworthiness to policing tactics . . . A thought-provoking read for anyone inclined to believe that data doesn't lie' *Reuters*

'Often we don't even know where to look for those important algorithms, because by definition the most dangerous ones are also the most secretive. That's why the catalogue of case studies in O'Neil's book are so important; she's telling us where to look' *Guardian*

'O'Neil is an ideal person to write this book . . . She is one of the strongest voices speaking out for limiting the ways we allow algorithms to influence our lives and against the notion that an algorithm, because it is implemented by an unemotional machine, cannot perpetrate bias or injustice . . . While *Weapons of Math Destruction* is full of hard truths and grim statistics, it is also accessible and even entertaining. O'Neil's writing is direct and easy to read – I devoured it in an afternoon' Evelyn Lamb, *Scientific American*

'You don't need to be a nerd to appreciate the significance of [O'Neil's] message . . . *Weapons* is a must-read for anyone who is working to combat economic and racial discrimination' *Goop*

'Cathy O'Neil's book is important and covers issues everyone should care about. Bonus points: it's accessible, compelling, and – something I wasn't expecting – really fun to read' *Inside Higher Ed*

'O'Neil is passionate about exposing the harmful effects of Big Data-driven mathematical models (what she calls WMDs), and she's uniquely qualified for the task . . . an entertaining and timely book that gives readers the tools to cut through the ideological fog obscuring the dangers of the Big Data revolution' *In These Times*

'An unusually lucid and readable look at the daunting algorithms that govern so many aspects of our lives' *Kirkus Reviews*

'Unlike some other recent books on data collection, hers is not hysterical; she offers more of a chilly wake-up call as she walks readers through the ways the 'big data' industry has facilitated social ills such as skyrocketing college tuitions, policing based on racial profiling, and high unemployment rates invulnerable communities . . . eerily prescient' *Publishers Weekly*

'Combating secrecy with clarity and confusion with understanding, this book can help us change course before it's too late' Astra Taylor, author of *The People's Platform: Taking Back Power and Culture in the Digital Age*

'Read *Weapons of Math Destruction* by Cathy O'Neil to deconstruct the latest growing tyranny of an arrogant establishment' Ralph Nader, author of *Unsafe at Any Speed*

'From getting a job to finding a spouse, predictive algorithms are silently shaping and controlling our destinies. Cathy O'Neil takes us on a journey of outrage and wonder, with prose that makes you feel like it's just a conversation' Linda Tirado, author of *Hand to Mouth: Living in Bootstrap America*

ABOUT THE AUTHOR

Cathy O'Neil is a data scientist and author of the blog mathbabe.org. She earned a PhD in mathematics from Harvard and taught at Barnard College before moving to the private sector, where she worked for the hedge fund D. E. Shaw. She then worked as a data scientist at various start-ups, building models that predict people's purchases and clicks. O'Neil started the Lede Program in Data Journalism at Columbia and is the author of *Doing Data Science*. She appears weekly on the *Slate Money* podcast.

CATHY O'NEIL

Weapons of Math Destruction

How Big Data Increases Inequality and
Threatens Democracy

PENGUIN BOOKS

PENGUIN BOOKS

UK | USA | Canada | Ireland | Australia
India | New Zealand | South Africa

Penguin Books is part of the Penguin Random House group of companies
whose addresses can be found at global.penguinrandomhouse.com.

First published in the United States of America by Crown, an imprint of the Crown
Publishing Group, a division of Penguin Random House LLC 2016
First published in Great Britain by Allen Lane 2016
Published in Penguin Books 2017

007

Printed in Great Britain by Clays Ltd, Elcograf S.p.A.

A CIP catalogue record for this book is available from the British Library

ISBN: 978–0–141–98541–1

THIS BOOK IS DEDICATED TO

ALL THE UNDERDOGS

ACKNOWLEDGMENTS

Thanks to my husband and kids for their incredible support. Thanks also to John Johnson, Steve Waldman, Maki Inada, Becky Jaffe, Aaron Abrams, Julie Steele, Karen Burnes, Matt LaMantia, Martha Poon, Lisa Radcliffe, Luis Daniel, and Melissa Bilski. Finally, thanks to the people without whom this book would not exist: Laura Strausfeld, Amanda Cook, Emma Berry, Jordan Ellenberg, Stephen Baker, Jay Mandel, Sam Kanson-Benanav, and Ernie Davis.

CONTENTS

WEAPONS OF MATH DESTRUCTION

INTRODUCTION

When I was a little girl, I used to gaze at the traffic out the car window and study the numbers on license plates. I would reduce each one to its basic elements—the prime numbers that made it up. $45 = 3 \times 3 \times 5$. That's called factoring, and it was my favorite investigative pastime. As a budding math nerd, I was especially intrigued by the primes.

My love for math eventually became a passion. I went to math camp when I was fourteen and came home clutching a Rubik's Cube to my chest. Math provided a neat refuge from the messiness of the real world. It marched forward, its field of knowledge expanding relentlessly, proof by proof. And I could add to it. I majored in math in college and went on to get my PhD. My thesis was on algebraic number theory, a field with roots in all that factoring I did as a child. Eventually, I became a tenure-track professor at Barnard, which had a combined math department with Columbia University.

And then I made a big change. I quit my job and went to work as a quant for D. E. Shaw, a leading hedge fund. In leaving academia for finance, I carried mathematics from abstract theory into practice. The operations we performed on numbers translated into trillions of dollars sloshing from one account to another. At first I was excited and amazed by working in this new laboratory, the global economy. But in the autumn of 2008, after I'd been there for a bit more than a year, it came crashing down.

The crash made it all too clear that mathematics, once my refuge, was not only deeply entangled in the world's problems but also fueling many of them. The housing crisis, the collapse of major financial institutions, the rise of unemployment—all had been aided and abetted by mathematicians wielding magic formulas. What's more, thanks to the extraordinary powers that I loved so much, math was able to combine with technology to multiply the chaos and misfortune, adding efficiency and scale to systems that I now recognized as flawed.

If we had been clear-headed, we all would have taken a step back at this point to figure out how math had been misused and how we could prevent a similar catastrophe in the future. But instead, in the wake of the crisis, new mathematical techniques were hotter than ever, and expanding into still more domains. They churned 24/7 through petabytes of information, much of it scraped from social media or e-commerce websites. And increasingly they focused not on the movements of global financial markets but on human beings, on us. Mathematicians and statisticians were studying our desires, movements, and spending power. They were predicting our trustworthiness and calculating our potential as students, workers, lovers, criminals.

This was the Big Data economy, and it promised spectacular gains. A computer program could speed through thousands of résumés or loan applications in a second or two and sort them into neat lists, with the most promising candidates on top. This not only saved time but also was marketed as fair and objective. After all, it didn't involve prejudiced humans digging through reams of paper, just machines processing cold numbers. By 2010 or so, mathematics was asserting itself as never before in human affairs, and the public largely welcomed it.

Yet I saw trouble. The math-powered applications powering the data economy were based on choices made by fallible human beings. Some of these choices were no doubt made with the best intentions. Nevertheless, many of these models encoded human prejudice, misunderstanding, and bias into the software systems that increasingly managed our lives. Like gods, these mathematical models were opaque, their workings invisible to all but the highest priests in their domain: mathematicians and computer scientists. Their verdicts, even when wrong or harmful, were beyond dispute or appeal. And they tended to punish the poor and the oppressed in our society, while making the rich richer.

I came up with a name for these harmful kinds of models: Weapons of Math Destruction, or WMDs for short. I'll walk you through an example, pointing out its destructive characteristics along the way.

As often happens, this case started with a laudable goal. In 2007, Washington, D.C.'s new mayor, Adrian Fenty, was determined to turn around the city's underperforming schools. He had his work cut out for him: at the time, barely one out of every two high school students was surviving to graduation after ninth grade, and only 8 percent of eighth graders were performing at grade level in math. Fenty hired an education reformer named Michelle Rhee to fill a powerful new post, chancellor of Washington's schools.

The going theory was that the students weren't learning enough because their teachers weren't doing a good job. So in 2009, Rhee implemented a plan to weed out the low-performing teachers. This is the trend in troubled school districts around the country, and from a systems engineering perspective the thinking makes perfect sense: Evaluate the teachers. Get rid of the worst ones, and place the best ones where they can do the most good. In the language of data scientists, this "optimizes" the school system, presumably ensuring better results for the kids. Except for "bad" teachers, who could argue with that? Rhee developed a teacher assessment tool called IMPACT, and at the end of the 2009–10 school year the district fired all the teachers whose scores put them in the bottom 2 percent. At the end of the following year, another 5 percent, or 206 teachers, were booted out.

Sarah Wysocki, a fifth-grade teacher, didn't seem to have any reason to worry. She had been at MacFarland Middle School for only two years but was already getting excellent reviews from her principal and her students' parents. One evaluation praised her attentiveness to the children; another called her "one of the best teachers I've ever come into contact with."

Yet at the end of the 2010–11 school year, Wysocki received a miserable score on her IMPACT evaluation. Her problem was a new scoring system known as value-added modeling, which purported to measure her effectiveness in teaching math and language skills. That score, generated by an algorithm, represented half of her overall evaluation, and it outweighed the positive reviews from school administrators and the community. This left the district with no choice but to fire her, along with 205 other teachers who had IMPACT scores below the minimal threshold.

This didn't seem to be a witch hunt or a settling of scores. Indeed, there's a logic to the school district's approach. Administrators, after all, could be friends with terrible teachers. They could admire their style or their apparent dedication. Bad teachers can *seem* good. So Washington, like many other school systems, would minimize this human bias and pay more attention to scores based on hard results: achievement scores in math and reading. The numbers would speak clearly, district officials promised. They would be more fair.

Wysocki, of course, felt the numbers were horribly unfair, and she wanted to know where they came from. "I don't think anyone understood them," she later told me. How could a good teacher get such dismal scores? What was the value-added model measuring?

Well, she learned, it was complicated. The district had hired a consultancy, Princeton-based Mathematica Policy Research, to come up with the evaluation system. Mathematica's challenge was to measure the educational progress of the students in the district and then to calculate how much of their advance or decline could be attributed to their teachers. This wasn't easy, of course. The researchers knew that many variables, from students' socioeconomic backgrounds to the effects of learning disabilities, could affect student outcomes. The algorithms had to make allowances for such differences, which was one reason they were so complex.

Indeed, attempting to reduce human behavior, performance, and potential to algorithms is no easy job. To understand what Mathematica was up against, picture a ten-year-old girl living in a poor neighborhood in southeastern Washington, D.C. At the end of one school year, she takes her fifth-grade standardized test. Then life goes on. She may have family issues or money problems. Maybe she's moving from one house to another or worried about an older brother who's in trouble with the law. Maybe she's unhappy about her weight or frightened by a bully at school. In any case, the following year she takes another standardized test, this one designed for sixth graders.

If you compare the results of the tests, the scores should stay stable, or hopefully, jump up. But if her results sink, it's easy to calculate the gap between her performance and that of the successful students.

But how much of that gap is due to her teacher? It's hard to know, and Mathematica's models have only a few numbers to compare. At Big Data companies like Google, by contrast, researchers run constant tests and monitor thousands of variables. They can change the font on a single advertisement from blue to red, serve each version to ten million people, and keep track of which one gets more clicks. They use this feedback to hone their algorithms and fine-tune their operation. While I have plenty of issues with Google, which we'll get to, this type of testing is an effective use of statistics.

Attempting to calculate the impact that one person may have on another over the course of a school year is much more complex. "There are so many factors that go into learning and teaching that it would be very difficult to measure them all," Wysocki says. What's more, attempting to score a teacher's effectiveness by analyzing the test results of only twenty-five or thirty students is statistically unsound, even laughable. The numbers are far too small given all the things that could go wrong. Indeed, if we were to analyze teachers with the statistical rigor of a search engine, we'd have to test them on thousands or even millions of randomly selected students. Statisticians count on large numbers to balance out exceptions and anomalies. (And WMDs, as we'll see, often punish individuals who happen to *be* the exception.)

Equally important, statistical systems require feedback—something to tell them when they're off track. Statisticians use errors to train their models and make them smarter. If Amazon.com, through a faulty correlation, started recommending lawn care books to teenage girls, the clicks would plummet, and the algorithm would be tweaked until it got it right. Without feedback, however, a statistical engine can continue spinning out faulty and damaging analysis while never learning from its mistakes.

Many of the WMDs I'll be discussing in this book, including the Washington school district's value-added model, behave like that. They define their own reality and use it to justify their results. This type of model is self-perpetuating, highly destructive— and very common.

When Mathematica's scoring system tags Sarah Wysocki and 205 other teachers as failures, the district fires them. But how does it ever learn if it was right? It doesn't. The system itself has determined that they were failures, and that is how they are viewed. Two hundred and six "bad" teachers are gone. That fact alone appears to demonstrate how effective the value-added model is. It is cleansing the district of underperforming teachers. Instead of searching for the truth, the score comes to embody it.

This is one example of a WMD feedback loop. We'll see many of them throughout this book. Employers, for example, are increasingly using credit scores to evaluate potential hires. Those who pay their bills promptly, the thinking goes, are more likely to show up to work on time and follow the rules. In fact, there are plenty of responsible people and good workers who suffer misfortune and see their credit scores fall. But the belief that bad credit correlates with bad job performance leaves those with low scores less likely to find work. Joblessness pushes them toward poverty, which further worsens their scores, making it even harder for them to land a job. It's a downward spiral. And employers never learn how many good employees they've missed out on by focusing on credit scores. In WMDs, many poisonous assumptions are camouflaged by math and go largely untested and unquestioned.

This underscores another common feature of WMDs. They tend to punish the poor. This is, in part, because they are engineered to evaluate large numbers of people. They specialize in bulk, and they're cheap. That's part of their appeal. The wealthy, by contrast, often benefit from personal input. A white-shoe law firm or an exclusive prep school will lean far more on recommendations and face-to-face interviews than will a fast-food chain or a cash-strapped urban school district. The privileged, we'll see time and again, are processed more by people, the masses by machines.

Wysocki's inability to find someone who could explain her appalling score, too, is telling. Verdicts from WMDs land like dictates from the algorithmic gods. The model itself is a black box, its contents a fiercely guarded corporate secret. This allows consultants like Mathematica to charge more, but it serves another purpose as well: if the people being evaluated are kept in the dark, the thinking goes, they'll be less likely to attempt to game the system. Instead, they'll simply have to work hard, follow the rules, and pray that the model registers and appreciates their efforts. But if the details are hidden, it's also harder to question the score or to protest against it.

For years, Washington teachers complained about the arbitrary scores and clamored for details on what went into them. It's an algorithm, they were told. It's very complex. This discouraged many from pressing further. Many people, unfortunately, are intimidated by math. But a math teacher named Sarah Bax continued to push the district administrator, a former colleague named Jason Kamras, for details. After a back-and-forth that extended for months, Kamras told her to wait for an upcoming technical report. Bax responded: "How do you justify evaluating people by a measure for which you are unable to provide explanation?" But that's the nature of WMDs. The analysis is outsourced to coders and statisticians. And as a rule, they let the machines do the talking.

Even so, Sarah Wysocki was well aware that her students' standardized test scores counted heavily in the formula. And here she had some suspicions. Before starting what would be her final year at MacFarland Middle School, she had been pleased to see that her incoming fifth graders had scored surprisingly well on their year-end tests. At Barnard Elementary School, where many of Sarah's students came from, 29 percent of the students were ranked at an "advanced reading level." This was five times the average in the school district.

Yet when classes started she saw that many of her students struggled to read even simple sentences. Much later, investigations by the *Washington Post* and *USA Today* revealed a high level of erasures on the standardized tests at forty-one schools in the district, including Barnard. A high rate of corrected answers points to a greater likelihood of cheating. In some of the schools, as many as 70 percent of the classrooms were suspected.

What does this have to do with WMDs? A couple of things. First, teacher evaluation algorithms are a powerful tool for behavioral modification. That's their purpose, and in the Washington schools they featured both a stick and a carrot. Teachers knew that if their students stumbled on the test their own jobs were at risk. This gave teachers a strong motivation to ensure their students passed, especially as the Great Recession battered the labor market. At the same time, if their students outperformed their peers, teachers and administrators could receive bonuses of up to $8,000. If you add those powerful incentives to the evidence in the case—the high number of erasures and the abnormally high test scores—there were grounds for suspicion that fourth-grade teachers, bowing either to fear or to greed, had corrected their students' exams.

It is conceivable, then, that Sarah Wysocki's fifth-grade students started the school year with artificially inflated scores. If so, their results the following year would make it appear that they'd lost ground in fifth grade—and that their teacher was an under-performer. Wysocki was convinced that this was what had happened to her. That explanation would fit with the observations from parents, colleagues, and her principal that she was indeed a good teacher. It would clear up the confusion. Sarah Wysocki had a strong case to make.

But you cannot appeal to a WMD. That's part of their fearsome power. They do not listen. Nor do they bend. They're deaf not only to charm, threats, and cajoling but also to logic—even when there is good reason to question the data that feeds their conclusions. Yes, if it becomes clear that automated systems are screwing up on an embarrassing and systematic basis, programmers will go back in and tweak the algorithms. But for the most part, the programs deliver unflinching verdicts, and the human beings employing them can only shrug, as if to say, "Hey, what can you do?"

And that is precisely the response Sarah Wysocki finally got from the school district. Jason Kamras later told the *Washington Post* that the erasures were "suggestive" and that the numbers might have been wrong in her fifth-grade class. But the evidence was not conclusive. He said she had been treated fairly.

Do you see the paradox? An algorithm processes a slew of statistics and comes up with a probability that a certain person *might* be a bad hire, a risky borrower, a terrorist, or a miserable teacher. That probability is distilled into a score, which can turn someone's life upside down. And yet when the person fights back, "suggestive" countervailing evidence simply won't cut it. The case must be ironclad. The human victims of WMDs, we'll see time and again, are held to a far higher standard of evidence than the algorithms themselves.

After the shock of her firing, Sarah Wysocki was out of a job for only a few days. She had plenty of people, including her principal, to vouch for her as a teacher, and she promptly landed a position at a school in an affluent district in northern Virginia. So thanks to a highly questionable model, a poor school lost a good teacher, and a rich school, which didn't fire people on the basis of their students' scores, gained one.

• • •

Following the housing crash, I woke up to the proliferation of WMDs in banking and to the danger they posed to our economy. In early 2011 I quit my job at the hedge fund. Later, after rebranding myself as a data scientist, I joined an e-commerce start-up. From that vantage point, I could see that legions of other WMDs were churning away in every conceivable industry, many of them exacerbating inequality and punishing the poor. They were at the heart of the raging data economy.

To spread the word about WMDs, I launched a blog, Math-Babe. My goal was to mobilize fellow mathematicians against the use of sloppy statistics and biased models that created their own toxic feedback loops. Data specialists, in particular, were drawn to the blog, and they alerted me to the spread of WMDs in new domains. But in mid-2011, when Occupy Wall Street sprang to life in Lower Manhattan, I saw that we had work to do among the broader public. Thousands had gathered to demand economic justice and accountability. And yet when I heard interviews with the Occupiers, they often seemed ignorant of basic issues related to finance. They clearly hadn't been reading my blog. (I should add, though, that you don't need to understand all the details of a system to know that it has failed.)

I could either criticize them or join them, I realized, so I joined them. Soon I was facilitating weekly meetings of the Alternative

Banking Group at Columbia University, where we discussed financial reform. Through this process, I came to see that my two ventures outside academia, one in finance, the other in data science, had provided me with fabulous access to the technology and culture powering WMDs.

Ill-conceived mathematical models now micromanage the economy, from advertising to prisons. These WMDs have many of the same characteristics as the value-added model that derailed Sarah Wysocki's career in Washington's public schools. They're opaque, unquestioned, and unaccountable, and they operate at a scale to sort, target, or "optimize" millions of people. By confusing their findings with on-the-ground reality, most of them create pernicious WMD feedback loops.

But there's one important distinction between a school district's value-added model and, say, a WMD that scouts out prospects for extortionate payday loans. They have different payoffs. For the school district, the payoff is a kind of political currency, a sense that problems are being fixed. But for businesses it's just the standard currency: money. For many of the businesses running these rogue algorithms, the money pouring in seems to prove that their models are working. Look at it through their eyes and it makes sense. When they're building statistical systems to find customers or manipulate desperate borrowers, growing revenue appears to show that they're on the right track. The software is doing its job. The trouble is that profits end up serving as a stand-in, or proxy, for truth. We'll see this dangerous confusion crop up again and again.

This happens because data scientists all too often lose sight of the folks on the receiving end of the transaction. They certainly understand that a data-crunching program is bound to misinterpret people a certain percentage of the time, putting them in the wrong groups and denying them a job or a chance at their dream house. But as a rule, the people running the WMDs don't dwell on those errors. Their feedback is money, which is also their incentive. Their systems are engineered to gobble up more data and fine-tune their analytics so that more money will pour in. Investors, of course, feast on these returns and shower WMD companies with more money.

And the victims? Well, an internal data scientist might say, no statistical system can be *perfect*. Those folks are collateral damage. And often, like Sarah Wysocki, they are deemed unworthy and expendable. Forget about them for a minute, they might say, and focus on all the people who get helpful suggestions from recommendation engines or who find music they love on Pandora, the ideal job on LinkedIn, or perhaps the love of their life on Match.com. Think of the astounding scale, and ignore the imperfections.

Big Data has plenty of evangelists, but I'm not one of them. This book will focus sharply in the other direction, on the damage inflicted by WMDs and the injustice they perpetuate. We will explore harmful examples that affect people at critical life moments: going to college, borrowing money, getting sentenced to prison, or finding and holding a job. All of these life domains are increasingly controlled by secret models wielding arbitrary punishments.

Welcome to the dark side of Big Data.

1

BOMB PARTS

What Is a Model?

It was a hot August afternoon in 1946. Lou Boudreau, the player-manager of the Cleveland Indians, was having a miserable day. In the first game of a doubleheader, Ted Williams had almost single-handedly annihilated his team. Williams, perhaps the game's greatest hitter at the time, had smashed three home runs and driven home eight. The Indians ended up losing 11 to 10.

Boudreau had to take action. So when Williams came up for the first time in the second game, players on the Indians' side started moving around. Boudreau, the shortstop, jogged over to where the second baseman would usually stand, and the second baseman backed into short right field. The third baseman moved to his left, into the shortstop's hole. It was clear that Boudreau, perhaps out of desperation, was shifting the entire orientation of his defense in an attempt to turn Ted Williams's hits into outs.

In other words, he was thinking like a data scientist. He had analyzed crude data, most of it observational: Ted Williams *usually* hit the ball to right field. Then he adjusted. And it worked. Fielders caught more of Williams's blistering line drives than before (though they could do nothing about the home runs sailing over their heads).

If you go to a major league baseball game today, you'll see that defenses now treat nearly every player like Ted Williams. While Boudreau merely observed where Williams usually hit the ball, managers now know precisely where every player has hit every ball over the last week, over the last month, throughout his career, against left-handers, when he has two strikes, and so on. Using this historical data, they analyze their current situation and calculate the positioning that is associated with the highest probability of success. And that sometimes involves moving players far across the field.

Shifting defenses is only one piece of a much larger question: What steps can baseball teams take to maximize the probability that they'll win? In their hunt for answers, baseball statisticians have scrutinized every variable they can quantify and attached it to a value. How much more is a double worth than a single? When, if ever, is it worth it to bunt a runner from first to second base?

The answers to all of these questions are blended and combined into mathematical models of their sport. These are parallel universes of the baseball world, each a complex tapestry of probabilities. They include every measurable relationship among every one of the sport's components, from walks to home runs to the players themselves. The purpose of the model is to run different scenarios at every juncture, looking for the optimal combinations. If the Yankees bring in a right-handed pitcher to face Angels slugger Mike Trout, as compared to leaving in the current pitcher, how much more likely are they to get him out? And how will that affect their overall odds of winning?

Baseball is an ideal home for predictive mathematical modeling. As Michael Lewis wrote in his 2003 bestseller, *Moneyball*, the sport has attracted data nerds throughout its history. In decades past, fans would pore over the stats on the back of baseball cards, analyzing Carl Yastrzemski's home run patterns or comparing Roger Clemens's and Dwight Gooden's strikeout totals. But starting in the 1980s, serious statisticians started to investigate what these figures, along with an avalanche of new ones, really meant: how they translated into wins, and how executives could maximize success with a minimum of dollars.

"Moneyball" is now shorthand for any statistical approach in domains long ruled by the gut. But baseball represents a healthy case study—and it serves as a useful contrast to the toxic models, or WMDs, that are popping up in so many areas of our lives. Baseball models are fair, in part, because they're transparent. Everyone has access to the stats and can understand more or less how they're interpreted. Yes, one team's model might give more value to home run hitters, while another might discount them a bit, because sluggers tend to strike out a lot. But in either case, the numbers of home runs and strikeouts are there for everyone to see.

Baseball also has statistical rigor. Its gurus have an immense data set at hand, almost all of it directly related to the performance of players in the game. Moreover, their data is highly relevant to the outcomes they are trying to predict. This may sound obvious, but as we'll see throughout this book, the folks building WMDs routinely lack data for the behaviors they're most interested in. So they substitute stand-in data, or proxies. They draw statistical correlations between a person's zip code or language patterns and her potential to pay back a loan or handle a job. These correlations are discriminatory, and some of them are illegal. Baseball models, for the most part, don't use proxies because they use pertinent inputs like balls, strikes, and hits.

Most crucially, that data is constantly pouring in, with new statistics from an average of twelve or thirteen games arriving daily from April to October. Statisticians can compare the results of these games to the predictions of their models, and they can see where they were wrong. Maybe they predicted that a left-handed reliever would give up lots of hits to right-handed batters—and yet he mowed them down. If so, the stats team has to tweak their model and also carry out research on why they got it wrong. Did the pitcher's new screwball affect his statistics? Does he pitch better at night? Whatever they learn, they can feed back into the model, refining it. That's how trustworthy models operate. They maintain a constant back-and-forth with whatever in the world they're trying to understand or predict. Conditions change, and so must the model.

Now, you may look at the baseball model, with its thousands of changing variables, and wonder how we could even be comparing it to the model used to evaluate teachers in Washington, D.C., schools. In one of them, an entire sport is modeled in fastidious detail and updated continuously. The other, while cloaked in mystery, appears to lean heavily on a handful of test results from one year to the next. Is that really a model?

The answer is yes. A model, after all, is nothing more than an abstract representation of some process, be it a baseball game, an oil company's supply chain, a foreign government's actions, or a movie theater's attendance. Whether it's running in a computer program or in our head, the model takes what we know and uses it to predict responses in various situations. All of us carry thousands of models in our heads. They tell us what to expect, and they guide our decisions.

Here's an informal model I use every day. As a mother of three, I cook the meals at home—my husband, bless his heart, cannot remember to put salt in pasta water. Each night when I begin to cook a family meal, I internally and intuitively model everyone's appetite. I know that one of my sons loves chicken (but hates hamburgers), while another will eat only the pasta (with extra grated parmesan cheese). But I also have to take into account that people's appetites vary from day to day, so a change can catch my model by surprise. There's some unavoidable uncertainty involved.

The input to my internal cooking model is the information I have about my family, the ingredients I have on hand or I know are available, and my own energy, time, and ambition. The output is how and what I decide to cook. I evaluate the success of a meal by how satisfied my family seems at the end of it, how much they've eaten, and how healthy the food was. Seeing how well it is received and how much of it is enjoyed allows me to update my model for the next time I cook. The updates and adjustments make it what statisticians call a "dynamic model."

Over the years I've gotten pretty good at making meals for my family, I'm proud to say. But what if my husband and I go away for a week, and I want to explain my system to my mom so she can fill in for me? Or what if my friend who has kids wants to know my methods? That's when I'd start to formalize my model, making it much more systematic and, in some sense, mathematical. And if I were feeling ambitious, I might put it into a computer program.

Ideally, the program would include all of the available food options, their nutritional value and cost, and a complete database of my family's tastes: each individual's preferences and aversions. It would be hard, though, to sit down and summon all that information off the top of my head. I've got loads of memories of people grabbing seconds of asparagus or avoiding the string beans. But they're all mixed up and hard to formalize in a comprehensive list.

The better solution would be to train the model over time, entering data every day on what I'd bought and cooked and noting the responses of each family member. I would also include parameters, or constraints. I might limit the fruits and vegetables to what's in season and dole out a certain amount of Pop-Tarts, but only enough to forestall an open rebellion. I also would add a number of rules. This one likes meat, this one likes bread and pasta, this one drinks lots of milk and insists on spreading Nutella on everything in sight.

If I made this work a major priority, over many months I might come up with a very good model. I would have turned the food management I keep in my head, my informal internal model, into a formal external one. In creating my model, I'd be extending my power and influence in the world. I'd be building an automated me that others can implement, even when I'm not around.

There would always be mistakes, however, because models are, by their very nature, simplifications. No model can include all of the real world's complexity or the nuance of human communication. Inevitably, some important information gets left out. I might have neglected to inform my model that junk-food rules are relaxed on birthdays, or that raw carrots are more popular than the cooked variety.

To create a model, then, we make choices about what's important enough to include, simplifying the world into a toy version that can be easily understood and from which we can infer important facts and actions. We expect it to handle only one job and accept that it will occasionally act like a clueless machine, one with enormous blind spots.

Sometimes these blind spots don't matter. When we ask Google Maps for directions, it models the world as a series of roads, tunnels, and bridges. It ignores the buildings, because they aren't relevant to the task. When avionics software guides an airplane, it models the wind, the speed of the plane, and the landing strip below, but not the streets, tunnels, buildings, and people.

A model's blind spots reflect the judgments and priorities of its creators. While the choices in Google Maps and avionics software appear cut and dried, others are far more problematic. The value-added model in Washington, D.C., schools, to return to that example, evaluates teachers largely on the basis of students' test scores, while ignoring how much the teachers engage the students, work on specific skills, deal with classroom management, or help students with personal and family problems. It's overly simple, sacrificing accuracy and insight for efficiency. Yet from the administrators' perspective it provides an effective tool to ferret out hundreds of apparently underperforming teachers, even at the risk of misreading some of them.

Here we see that models, despite their reputation for impartiality, reflect goals and ideology. When I removed the possibility of eating Pop-Tarts at every meal, I was imposing my ideology on the meals model. It's something we do without a second thought. Our own values and desires influence our choices, from the data we choose to collect to the questions we ask. Models are opinions embedded in mathematics.

Whether or not a model works is also a matter of opinion. After all, a key component of every model, whether formal or informal, is its definition of success. This is an important point that we'll return to as we explore the dark world of WMDs. In each case, we must ask not only who designed the model but also what that person or company is trying to accomplish. If the North Korean government built a model for my family's meals, for example, it might be optimized to keep us above the threshold of starvation at the lowest cost, based on the food stock available. Preferences would count for little or nothing. By contrast, if my kids were creating the model, success might feature ice cream at every meal. My own model attempts to blend a bit of the North Koreans' resource management with the happiness of my kids, along with my own priorities of health, convenience, diversity of experience, and sustainability. As a result, it's much more complex. But it still reflects my own personal reality. And a model built for today will work a bit worse tomorrow. It will grow stale if it's not constantly updated. Prices change, as do people's preferences. A model built for a six-year-old won't work for a teenager.

This is true of internal models as well. You can often see troubles when grandparents visit a grandchild they haven't seen for a while. On their previous visit, they gathered data on what the child knows, what makes her laugh, and what TV show she likes and (unconsciously) created a model for relating to this particular four-year-old. Upon meeting her a year later, they can suffer a few awkward hours because their models are out of date. Thomas the Tank Engine, it turns out, is no longer cool. It takes some time to gather new data about the child and adjust their models.

This is not to say that good models cannot be primitive. Some very effective ones hinge on a single variable. The most common model for detecting fires in a home or office weighs only one strongly correlated variable, the presence of smoke. That's usually enough. But modelers run into problems—or subject *us* to problems—when they focus models as simple as a smoke alarm on their fellow humans.

Racism, at the individual level, can be seen as a predictive model whirring away in billions of human minds around the world. It is built from faulty, incomplete, or generalized data. Whether it comes from experience or hearsay, the data indicates that certain types of people have behaved badly. That generates a binary prediction that all people of that race will behave that same way.

Needless to say, racists don't spend a lot of time hunting down reliable data to train their twisted models. And once their model morphs into a belief, it becomes hardwired. It generates poisonous assumptions, yet rarely tests them, settling instead for data that seems to confirm and fortify them. Consequently, racism is the most slovenly of predictive models. It is powered by haphazard data gathering and spurious correlations, reinforced by institutional inequities, and polluted by confirmation bias. In this way, oddly enough, racism operates like many of the WMDs I'll be describing in this book.

. . .

In 1997, a convicted murderer, an African American man named Duane Buck, stood before a jury in Harris County, Texas. Buck had killed two people, and the jury had to decide whether he would be sentenced to death or to life in prison with the chance of parole. The prosecutor pushed for the death penalty, arguing that if Buck were let free he might kill again.

Buck's defense attorney brought forth an expert witness, a psychologist named Walter Quijano, who didn't help his client's case one bit. Quijano, who had studied recidivism rates in the Texas prison system, made a reference to Buck's race, and during cross-examination the prosecutor jumped on it.

"You have determined that the . . . the race factor, black, increases the future dangerousness for various complicated reasons. Is that correct?" the prosecutor asked.

"Yes," Quijano answered. The prosecutor stressed that testimony in her summation, and the jury sentenced Buck to death.

Three years later, Texas attorney general John Cornyn found

that the psychologist had given similar race-based testimony in six other capital cases, most of them while he worked for the prosecution. Cornyn, who would be elected in 2002 to the US Senate, ordered new race-blind hearings for the seven inmates. In a press release, he declared: "It is inappropriate to allow race to be considered as a factor in our criminal justice system. . . . The people of Texas want and deserve a system that affords the same fairness to everyone."

Six of the prisoners got new hearings but were again sentenced to death. Quijano's prejudicial testimony, the court ruled, had not been decisive. Buck never got a new hearing, perhaps because it was his own witness who had brought up race. He is still on death row.

Regardless of whether the issue of race comes up explicitly at trial, it has long been a major factor in sentencing. A University of Maryland study showed that in Harris County, which includes Houston, prosecutors were three times more likely to seek the death penalty for African Americans, and four times more likely for Hispanics, than for whites convicted of the same charges. That pattern isn't unique to Texas. According to the American Civil Liberties Union, sentences imposed on black men in the federal system are nearly 20 percent longer than those for whites convicted of similar crimes. And though they make up only 13 percent of the population, blacks fill up 40 percent of America's prison cells.

So you might think that computerized risk models fed by data would reduce the role of prejudice in sentencing and contribute to more even-handed treatment. With that hope, courts in twenty-four states have turned to so-called recidivism models. These help judges assess the danger posed by each convict. And by many measures they're an improvement. They keep sentences more consistent and less likely to be swayed by the moods and biases of judges. They also save money by nudging down the length of the average sentence. (It costs an average of $31,000 a year to house an inmate, and double that in expensive states like Connecticut and New York.)

The question, however, is whether we've eliminated human bias or simply camouflaged it with technology. The new recidivism models are complicated and mathematical. But embedded within these models are a host of assumptions, some of them prejudicial. And while Walter Quijano's words were transcribed for the record, which could later be read and challenged in court, the workings of a recidivism model are tucked away in algorithms, intelligible only to a tiny elite.

One of the more popular models, known as LSI–R, or Level of Service Inventory–Revised, includes a lengthy questionnaire for the prisoner to fill out. One of the questions—"How many prior convictions have you had?"—is highly relevant to the risk of recidivism. Others are also clearly related: "What part did others play in the offense? What part did drugs and alcohol play?"

But as the questions continue, delving deeper into the person's life, it's easy to imagine how inmates from a privileged background would answer one way and those from tough inner-city streets another. Ask a criminal who grew up in comfortable suburbs about "the first time you were ever involved with the police," and he might not have a single incident to report other than the one that brought him to prison. Young black males, by contrast, are likely to have been stopped by police dozens of times, even when they've done nothing wrong. A 2013 study by the New York Civil Liberties Union found that while black and Latino males between the ages of fourteen and twenty-four made up only 4.7 percent of the city's population, they accounted for 40.6 percent of the stop-and-frisk checks by police. More than 90 percent of those stopped were innocent. Some of the others might have been drinking underage or carrying a joint. And unlike most rich kids, they got in trouble for it. So if early "involvement" with the police signals recidivism, poor people and racial minorities look far riskier.

The questions hardly stop there. Prisoners are also asked about whether their friends and relatives have criminal records. Again, ask that question to a convicted criminal raised in a middle-class neighborhood, and the chances are much greater that the answer will be no. The questionnaire does avoid asking about race, which is illegal. But with the wealth of detail each prisoner provides, that single illegal question is almost superfluous.

The LSI–R questionnaire has been given to thousands of inmates since its invention in 1995. Statisticians have used those results to devise a system in which answers highly correlated to recidivism weigh more heavily and count for more points. After answering the questionnaire, convicts are categorized as high, medium, and low risk on the basis of the number of points they accumulate. In some states, such as Rhode Island, these tests are used only to target those with high-risk scores for antirecidivism programs while incarcerated. But in others, including Idaho and Colorado, judges use the scores to guide their sentencing.

This is unjust. The questionnaire includes circumstances of a criminal's birth and upbringing, including his or her family, neighborhood, and friends. These details should not be relevant to a criminal case or to the sentencing. Indeed, if a prosecutor attempted to tar a defendant by mentioning his brother's criminal record or the high crime rate in his neighborhood, a decent defense attorney would roar, "Objection, Your Honor!" And a serious judge would sustain it. This is the basis of our legal system. We are judged by what we do, not by who we are. And although we don't know the exact weights that are attached to these parts of the test, any weight above zero is unreasonable.

Many would point out that statistical systems like the LSI–R are effective in gauging recidivism risk—or at least more accurate than a judge's random guess. But even if we put aside, ever so briefly, the crucial issue of fairness, we find ourselves descending into a pernicious WMD feedback loop. A person who scores as "high risk" is likely to be unemployed and to come from a neighborhood where many of his friends and family have had run-ins with the law. Thanks in part to the resulting high score on the evaluation, he gets a longer sentence, locking him away for more years in a prison where he's surrounded by fellow criminals— which raises the likelihood that he'll return to prison. He is finally released into the same poor neighborhood, this time with a crim-' inal record, which makes it that much harder to find a job. If he commits another crime, the recidivism model can claim another success. But in fact the model itself contributes to a toxic cycle and helps to sustain it. That's a signature quality of a WMD.

• • •

In this chapter, we've looked at three kinds of models. The baseball models, for the most part, are healthy. They are transparent and continuously updated, with both the assumptions and the conclusions clear for all to see. The models feed on statistics from the game in question, not from proxies. And the people being modeled understand the process and share the model's objective: winning the World Series. (Which isn't to say that many players, come contract time, won't quibble with a model's valuations: "Sure I struck out two hundred times, but look at my *home runs* . . .")

From my vantage point, there's certainly nothing wrong with the second model we discussed, the hypothetical family meal model. If my kids were to question the assumptions that under-lie it, whether economic or dietary, I'd be all too happy to provide them. And even though they sometimes grouse when facing something green, they'd likely admit, if pressed, that they share the goals of convenience, economy, health, and good taste—though they might give them different weights in their own models. (And they'll be free to create them when they start buying their own food.)

I should add that my model is highly unlikely to scale. I don't see Walmart or the US Agriculture Department or any other titan embracing my app and imposing it on hundreds of millions of people, like some of the WMDs we'll be discussing. No, my model is benign, especially since it's unlikely ever to leave my head and be formalized into code.

The recidivism example at the end of the chapter, however, is a different story entirely. It gives off a familiar and noxious odor. So let's do a quick exercise in WMD taxonomy and see where it fits.

The first question: Even if the participant is aware of being modeled, or what the model is used for, is the model opaque, or even invisible? Well, most of the prisoners filling out mandatory questionnaires aren't stupid. They at least have reason to suspect that information they provide will be used against them to control them while in prison and perhaps lock them up for longer. They know the game. But prison officials know it, too. And they keep quiet about the purpose of the LSI–R questionnaire. Otherwise, they know, many prisoners will attempt to game it, providing answers to make them look like model citizens the day they leave the joint. So the prisoners are kept in the dark as much as possible and do not learn their risk scores.

In this, they're hardly alone. Opaque and invisible models are the rule, and clear ones very much the exception. We're modeled as shoppers and couch potatoes, as patients and loan applicants, and very little of this do we see—even in applications we happily sign up for. Even when such models behave themselves, opacity can lead to a feeling of unfairness. If you were told by an usher, upon entering an open-air concert, that you couldn't sit in the first ten rows of seats, you might find it unreasonable. But if it were explained to you that the first ten rows were being reserved for people in wheelchairs, then it might well make a difference. Transparency matters.

And yet many companies go out of their way to hide the results of their models or even their existence. One common justification is that the algorithm constitutes a "secret sauce" crucial to their business. It's *intellectual property*, and it must be defended, if need be, with legions of lawyers and lobbyists. In the case of web giants like Google, Amazon, and Facebook, these precisely tailored algorithms alone are worth hundreds of billions of dollars. WMDs are, by design, inscrutable black boxes. That makes it extra hard to definitively answer the second question: Does the model work against the subject's interest? In short, is it unfair? Does it damage or destroy lives?

Here, the LSI–R again easily qualifies as a WMD. The people putting it together in the 1990s no doubt saw it as a tool to bring evenhandedness and efficiency to the criminal justice system. It could also help nonthreatening criminals land lighter sentences. This would translate into more years of freedom for them and enormous savings for American taxpayers, who are footing a $70 billion annual prison bill. However, because the questionnaire judges the prisoner by details that would not be admissible in court, it is unfair. While many may benefit from it, it leads to suffering for others.

A key component of this suffering is the pernicious feedback loop. As we've seen, sentencing models that profile a person by his or her circumstances help to create the environment that justifies their assumptions. This destructive loop goes round and round, and in the process the model becomes more and more unfair.

The third question is whether a model has the capacity to grow exponentially. As a statistician would put it, can it scale? This might sound like the nerdy quibble of a mathematician. But scale is what turns WMDs from local nuisances into tsunami forces, ones that define and delimit our lives. As we'll see, the developing WMDs in human resources, health, and banking, just to name a few, are quickly establishing broad norms that exert upon us something very close to the power of law. If a bank's model of a high-risk borrower, for example, is applied to you, the world will treat you as just that, a deadbeat—even if you're horribly mis-understood. And when that model scales, as the credit model has, it affects your whole life—whether you can get an apartment or a job or a car to get from one to the other.

When it comes to scaling, the potential for recidivism model-ing continues to grow. It's already used in the majority of states, and the LSI–R is the most common tool, used in at least twenty-four of them. Beyond LSI–R, prisons host a lively and crowded market for data scientists. The penal system is teeming with data, especially since convicts enjoy even fewer privacy rights than the rest of us. What's more, the system is so miserable, overcrowded, inefficient, expensive, and inhumane that it's crying out for im-provements. Who wouldn't want a cheap solution like this?

Penal reform is a rarity in today's polarized political world, an issue on which liberals and conservatives are finding common ground. In early 2015, the conservative Koch brothers, Charles and David, teamed up with a liberal think tank, the Center for American Progress, to push for prison reform and drive down the incarcerated population. But my suspicion is this: their bipartisan effort to reform prisons, along with legions of others, is almost certain to lead to the efficiency and perceived fairness of a data-fed solution. That's the age we live in. Even if other tools supplant LSI–R as its leading WMD, the prison system is likely to be a powerful incubator for WMDs on a grand scale.

So to sum up, these are the three elements of a WMD: Opacity, Scale, and Damage. All of them will be present, to one degree or another, in the examples we'll be covering. Yes, there will be room for quibbles. You could argue, for example, that the recidivism scores are not totally opaque, since they spit out scores that prisoners, in some cases, can see. Yet they're brimming with mystery, since the prisoners cannot see how their answers produce their score. The scoring algorithm is hidden. A couple of the other WMDs might not seem to satisfy the prerequisite for scale. They're not huge, at least not yet. But they represent dangerous species that are primed to grow, perhaps exponentially. So I count them. And finally, you might note that not all of these WMDs are universally damaging. After all, they send some people to Harvard, line others up for cheap loans or good jobs, and reduce jail sentences for certain lucky felons. But the point is not whether some people benefit. It's that so many suffer. These models, powered by algorithms, slam doors in the face of millions of people, often for the flimsiest of reasons, and offer no appeal. They're unfair.

And here's one more thing about algorithms: they can leap from one field to the next, and they often do. Research in epidemiology can hold insights for box office predictions; spam filters are being retooled to identify the AIDS virus. This is true of WMDs as well. So if mathematical models in prisons appear to succeed at their job—which really boils down to efficient management of people—they could spread into the rest of the economy along with the other WMDs, leaving us as collateral damage.

That's my point. This menace is rising. And the world of finance provides a cautionary tale.

2

SHELL SHOCKED

My Journey of Disillusionment

Imagine you have a routine. Every morning before catching the train from Joliet to Chicago's LaSalle Street station, you feed $2 into the coffee machine. It returns two quarters and a cup of coffee. But one day it returns four quarters. Three times in the next month the same machine delivers the same result. A pattern is developing.

Now, if this were a tiny anomaly in financial markets, and not a commuter train, a quant at a hedge fund—someone like me— could zero in on it. It would involve going through years of data, even decades, and then training an algorithm to predict this one recurring error—a fifty-cent swing in price—and to place bets on it. Even the smallest patterns can bring in millions to the first investor who unearths them. And they'll keep churning out profits until one of two things happens: either the phenomenon comes to an end or the rest of the market catches on to it, and the opportunity vanishes. By that point, a good quant will be hot on the trail of dozens of other tiny wrinkles.

The quest for what quants call market inefficiencies is like a treasure hunt. It can be fun. And as I got used to my new job at D. E. Shaw, I found it a welcome change from academia. While I had loved teaching at Barnard, and had loved my research on algebraic number theory, I found progress agonizingly slow. I wanted to be part of the fast-paced real world.

At that point, I considered hedge funds morally neutral—scavengers in the financial system, at worst. I was proud to go to Shaw, known as the Harvard of the hedge funds, and show the people there that my smarts could translate into money. Plus, I would be earning three times what I had earned as a professor. I could hardly suspect, as I began my new job, that it would give me a front-row seat during the financial crisis and a terrifying tutorial on how insidious and destructive math could be. At the hedge fund, I got my first up-close look at a WMD.

In the beginning, there was plenty to like. Everything at Shaw was powered by math. At a lot of firms, the traders run the show, making big deals, barking out orders, and landing multimillion-dollar bonuses. Quants are their underlings. But at Shaw the traders are little more than functionaries. They're called executioners. And the mathematicians reign supreme. My ten-person team was the "futures group." In a business in which everything hinges on what will happen tomorrow, what could be bigger than that?

We had about fifty quants in total. In the early days, it was entirely men, except for me. Most of them were foreign born. Many of them had come from abstract math or physics; a few, like me, had come from number theory. I didn't get much of a chance to talk shop with them, though. Since our ideas and algorithms were the foundation of the hedge fund's business, it was clear that we quants also represented a risk: if we walked away, we could quickly use our knowledge to fuel a fierce competitor.

To keep this from happening on a large, firm-threatening scale, Shaw mostly prohibited us from talking to colleagues in other groups—or sometimes even our own office mates—about what we were doing. In a sense, information was cloistered in a networked cell structure, not unlike that of Al Qaeda. That way, if one cell collapsed—if one of us hightailed it to Bridgewater or J.P. Morgan, or set off on our own—we'd take with us only our own knowledge. The rest of Shaw's business would carry on unaffected. As you can imagine, this wasn't terrific for camaraderie.

Newcomers were required to be on call every thirteen weeks in the futures group. This meant being ready to respond to computer problems whenever any of the world's markets were open, from Sunday evening our time, when the Asian markets came to life, to New York's closing bell at 4 p.m. on Friday. Sleep deprivation was an issue. But worse was the powerlessness to respond to issues in a shop that didn't share information. Say an algorithm appeared to be misbehaving. I'd have to locate it and then find the person responsible for it, at any time of the day or night, and tell him (and it was always a him) to fix it. It wasn't always a friendly encounter.

Then there were panics. Over holidays, when few people were working, weird things tended to happen. We had all sorts of things in our huge portfolio, including currency forwards, which were promises to buy large amounts of a foreign currency in a couple of days. Instead of actually buying the foreign currency, though, a trader would "roll over" the position each day so the promise would be put off for one more day. This way, our bet on the direction of the market would be sustained but we'd never have to come up with loads of cash. One time over Christmas I noticed a large position in Japanese yen that was coming due. Someone had to roll that contract over. This was a job typically handled by a colleague in Europe, who presumably was home with his family. I saw that if it didn't happen soon someone theoretically would have to show up in Tokyo with $50 million in yen. Ironing out that problem added a few frantic hours to the holiday.

All of those issues might fit into the category of occupational hazard. But the real problem came from a nasty feeling I started to have in my stomach. I had grown accustomed to playing in these oceans of currency, bonds, and equities, the trillions of dollars flowing through international markets. But unlike the numbers in my academic models, the figures in my models at the hedge fund stood for something. They were people's retirement funds and mortgages. In retrospect, this seems blindingly obvious. And of course, I knew it all along, but I hadn't truly appreciated the nature of the nickels, dimes, and quarters that we pried loose with our mathematical tools. It wasn't found money, like nuggets from a mine or coins from a sunken Spanish galleon. This wealth was coming out of people's pockets. For hedge funds, the smuggest of the players on Wall Street, this was "dumb money."

It was when the markets collapsed in 2008 that the ugly truth struck home in a big way. Even worse than filching dumb money from people's accounts, the finance industry was in the business of creating WMDs, and I was playing a small part.

The troubles had actually started a year earlier. In July of 2007, "interbank" interest rates spiked. After the recession that followed the terrorist attacks in 2001, low interest rates had fueled a housing boom. Anyone, it seemed, could get a mortgage, builders were turning exurbs, desert, and prairie into vast new housing developments, and banks gambled billions on all kinds of financial instruments tied to the building bonanza.

But these rising interest rates signaled trouble. Banks were losing trust in each other to pay back overnight loans. They were slowly coming to grips with the dangerous junk they held in their own portfolios and judged, wisely, that others were sitting on just as much risk, if not more. Looking back, you could say the interest rate spikes were actually a sign of sanity, although they obviously came too late.

At Shaw, these jitters dampened the mood a bit. Lots of companies were going to struggle, it was clear. The industry was going to take a hit, perhaps a very big one. But still, it might not be our problem. We didn't plunge headlong into risky markets. Hedge funds, after all, hedged. That was our nature. Early on, we called the market turbulence "the kerfuffle." For Shaw, it might cause some discomfort, maybe even an embarrassing episode or two, like when a rich man's credit card is denied at a fancy restaurant. But there was a good chance we'd be okay.

Hedge funds, after all, didn't make these markets. They just played in them. That meant that when the market crashed, as it would, rich opportunities would emerge from the wreckage. The game for hedge funds was not so much to ride markets up as to predict the movements within them. Down could be every bit as lucrative.

To understand how hedge funds operate at the margins, picture a World Series game at Chicago's Wrigley Field. With a dramatic home run in the bottom of the ninth inning, the Cubs win their first championship since 1908, back when Teddy Roosevelt was president. The stadium explodes in celebration. But a single row of fans stays seated, quietly analyzing a slew of results. These gamblers don't hold the traditional win-or-lose bets. Instead they may have bet that Yankees relievers would give up more walks than strikeouts, that the game would feature at least one bunt but no more than two, or that the Cubs' starter would last at least six innings. They even hold bets that other gamblers will win or lose their own bets. These people wager on many movements associated with the game, but not as much on the game itself. In this, they behave like hedge funds.

That made us feel safe, or at least safer. I remember a gala event to celebrate the architects of the system that would soon crash. The firm welcomed Alan Greenspan, the former Fed chairman, and Robert Rubin, the former Treasury secretary and Goldman Sachs executive. Rubin had pushed for a 1999 revision of the Depression-era Glass-Steagall Act. This removed the glass wall between banking and investment operations, which facilitated the orgy of speculation over the following decade. Banks were free to originate loans (many of them fraudulent) and sell them to their customers in the form of securities. That wasn't so unusual and could be considered a service they did for their customers. However, now that Glass Steagall was gone, the banks could, and sometimes did, bet against the very same securities that they'd sold to customers. This created mountains of risk—and endless investment potential for hedge funds. We placed our bets, after all, on market movements, up or down, and those markets were frenetic.

At the D. E. Shaw event, Greenspan warned us about problems in mortgage-backed securities. That memory nagged me when I realized a couple of years later that Rubin, who at the time worked at Citigroup, had been instrumental in collecting a massive portfolio of these exact toxic contracts—a major reason Citigroup later had to be bailed out at taxpayer expense.

Sitting with these two was Rubin's protégé and our part-time partner, Larry Summers. He had followed Rubin in Treasury and had gone on to serve as president of Harvard University. Summers had troubles with faculty, though. And professors had risen up against him in part because he suggested that the low numbers of women in math and the hard sciences might be due to genetic inferiority—what he called the unequal distribution of "intrinsic aptitude."

After Summers left the Harvard presidency, he landed at Shaw. And I remember that when it came time for our founder, David Shaw, to address the prestigious trio, he joked that Summers's move from Harvard to Shaw had been a "promotion." The markets might be rumbling, but Shaw was still on top of the world.

Yet as the crisis deepened the partners at Shaw lost a bit of their swagger. Troubled markets, after all, were entwined. For example, rumors were already circulating about the vulnerability of Lehman Brothers, which owned 20 percent of D. E. Shaw and handled many of our transactions. As the markets continued to rattle and shake, the internal mood turned fretful. We could crunch numbers with the best of the best. But what if the frightening tomorrow on the horizon didn't resemble any of the yesterdays? What if it was something entirely new and different?

That was a concern, because mathematical models, by their nature, are based on the past, and on the assumption that patterns will repeat. Before long, the equities group liquidated its holdings, at substantial cost. And the hiring spree for new quants, which had brought me to the firm, ended. Although people tried to laugh off this new climate, there was a growing fear. All eyes were on securitized products, especially the mortgage-backed securities Greenspan had warned us about.

For decades, mortgage securities had been the opposite of scary. They were boring financial instruments that individuals and investment funds alike used to diversify their portfolios. The idea behind them was that quantity could offset risk. Each single mortgage held potential for default: the home owner could declare bankruptcy, meaning the bank would never be able to recover all of the money it had loaned. At the other extreme, the borrower could pay back the mortgage ahead of schedule, bringing the flow of interest payments to a halt.

And so in the 1980s, investment bankers started to buy thousands of mortgages and package them into securities—a kind of bond, which is to say an instrument that pays regular dividends, often at quarterly intervals. A few of the home owners would default, of course. But most people would stay afloat and keep paying their mortgages, generating a smooth and predictable flow of revenue. In time, these bonds grew into an entire industry, a pillar of the capital markets. Experts grouped the mortgages into different classes, or tranches. Some were considered rock solid. Others carried more risk—and higher interest rates. Investors had reason to feel confident because the credit-rating agencies, Standard & Poor's, Moody's, and Fitch, had studied the securities and scored them for risk. They considered them sensible investments. But consider the opacity. Investors remained blind to the quality of the mortgages in the securities. Their only glimpse of what lurked inside came from analyst ratings. And these analysts collected fees from the very companies whose products they were rating. Mortgage-backed securities, needless to say, were an ideal platform for fraud.

If you want a metaphor, one commonly used in this field comes from sausages. Think of the mortgages as little pieces of meat of varying quality, and think of the mortgage-backed securities as bundles of the sausage that result from throwing everything together and adding a bunch of strong spices. Of course, sausages can vary in quality, and it's hard to tell from the outside what went into them, but since they have a stamp from the USDA saying they're safe to eat, our worries are put aside.

As the world later learned, mortgage companies were making

rich profits during the boom by loaning money to people for homes they couldn't afford. The strategy was simply to write unsustainable mortgages, snarf up the fees, and then unload the resulting securities—the sausages—into the booming mortgage security market. In one notorious case, a strawberry picker named Alberto Ramirez, who made $14,000 a year, managed to finance a $720,000 house in Rancho Grande, California. His broker apparently told him that he could refinance in a few months and later flip the house and make a tidy profit. Months later, he defaulted on the loan.

In the run-up to the housing collapse, mortgage banks were not only offering unsustainable deals but actively prospecting for victims in poor and minority neighborhoods. In a federal lawsuit, Baltimore officials charged Wells Fargo with targeting black neighborhoods for so-called ghetto loans. The bank's "emerging markets" unit, according to a former bank loan officer, Beth Jacobson, focused on black churches. The idea was that trusted pastors would steer their congregants toward loans. These turned out to be subprime loans carrying the highest interest rates. The bank sold these even to borrowers with rock-solid credit, who should have qualified for loans with far better terms. By the time Baltimore filed the suit, in 2009, more than half of the properties subject to foreclosure on Well Fargo loans were empty, and 71 percent of them were in largely African American neighborhoods. (In 2012, Wells Fargo settled the suit, agreeing to pay $175 million to thirty thousand victims around the country.)

To be clear, the subprime mortgages that piled up during the housing boom, whether held by strawberry pickers in California or struggling black congregants in Baltimore, were not WMDs. They were financial instruments, not models, and they had little to do with math. (In fact, the brokers went to great lengths to ignore inconvenient numbers.)

But when banks started loading mortgages like Alberto Ramirez's into classes of securities and selling them, they were relying on flawed mathematical models to do it. The risk model attached to mortgage-backed securities was a WMD. The banks were aware that some of the mortgages were sure to default. But banks held on to two false assumptions, which sustained their confidence in the system.

The first false assumption was that crack mathematicians in all of these companies were crunching the numbers and ever so carefully balancing the risk. The bonds were marketed as products whose risk was assessed by specialists using cutting-edge algorithms. Unfortunately, this just wasn't the case. As with so many WMDs, the math was directed against the consumer as a smoke screen. Its purpose was only to optimize short-term profits for the sellers. And those sellers trusted that they'd manage to unload the securities before they exploded. Smart people would win. And dumber people, the providers of dumb money, would wind up holding billions (or trillions) of unpayable IOUs. Even rigorous mathematicians—and there were a few—were working with numbers provided by people carrying out wide-scale fraud. Very few people had the expertise and the information required to know what was actually going on statistically, and most of the people who did lacked the integrity to speak up. The risk ratings on the securities were designed to be opaque and mathematically intimidating, in part so that buyers wouldn't perceive the true level of risk associated with the contracts they owned.

The second false assumption was that not many people would default at the same time. This was based on the theory, soon to be disproven, that defaults were largely random and unrelated events. This led to a belief that solid mortgages would offset the losers in each tranche. The risk models were assuming that the future would be no different from the past.

In order to sell these mortgage-backed bonds, the banks needed AAA ratings. For this, they looked to the three credit-rating agencies. As the market expanded, rating the growing billion-dollar market in mortgage bonds turned into a big business for the agencies, bringing in lucrative fees. They grew addicted to those fees. And they understood all too clearly that if they provided anything less than AAA ratings, the banks would take the work to their competitors. So the agencies played ball. They paid more attention to customer satisfaction than to the accuracy of their models. These risk models also created their own pernicious feedback loop. The AAA ratings on defective products turned into dollars. The dollars in turn created confidence in the products and in the cheating-and-lying process that manufactured them. The resulting cycle of mutual back-scratching and pocket-filling was how the whole sordid business operated until it blew up.

Of all the WMD qualities, the one that turned these risk models into a monstrous force of global dimension was scale. Snake oil vendors, of course, are as old as history, and in previous real estate bubbles unwitting buyers ended up with swampland and stacks of false deeds. But this time the power of modern computing fueled fraud at a scale unequaled in history. The damage was compounded by other vast markets that had grown up around the mortgage-backed securities: credit default swaps and synthetic collateralized debt obligations, or CDOs. Credit default swaps were small insurance policies that transferred the risk on a bond. The swaps gave banks and hedge funds alike a sense of security, since they could supposedly use them to balance risk. But if the entities holding these insurance policies go belly up, as many did, the chain reaction blows holes through the global economy. Synthetic CDOs went one step further: they were contracts whose value depended on the performance of credit default swaps and mortgage-backed securities. They allowed financial engineers to leverage up their bets even more.

The overheated (and then collapsing) market featured $3 trillion of subprime mortgages by 2007, and the market around it—including the credit default swaps and synthetic CDOs, which magnified the risks—was twenty times as big. No national economy could compare.

Paradoxically, the supposedly powerful algorithms that created the market, the ones that analyzed the risk in tranches of debt and sorted them into securities, turned out to be useless when it came time to clean up the mess and calculate what all the paper was actually worth. The math could multiply the horseshit, but it could not decipher it. This was a job for human beings. Only people could sift through the mortgages, picking out the false promises and wishful thinking and putting real dollar values on the loans. It was a painstaking process, because people—unlike WMDs—cannot scale their work exponentially, and for much of the industry it was a low priority. During this lengthy detox, of course, the value of the debt—and the homes that the debt relied on—kept falling. And as the economy took a nosedive, even home owners who could afford their mortgages when the crisis began were suddenly at risk of defaulting, too.

As I've mentioned, Shaw was a step or two removed from the epicenter of the market collapse. But as other players started to go under, they were frantically undoing trades that affected the ones we had on our books. It had a cascading effect, and as we entered the second half of 2008 we were losing money left and right.

Over the following months, disaster finally hit the mainstream. That's when everyone finally saw the people on the other side of the algorithms. They were desperate home owners losing their homes and millions of Americans losing their jobs. Credit card defaults leapt to record highs. The human suffering, which had been hidden from view behind numbers, spreadsheets, and risk scores, became palpable.

The chatter at Shaw was nervous. After the fall of Lehman Brothers in September of 2008, people discussed the political fallout. Barack Obama looked likely to win the election in November. Would he hammer the industry with new regulations? Raise taxes on carried interest? These people weren't losing their houses or maxing out their credit cards just to stay afloat. But they found plenty to worry about, just the same. The only choice was to wait it out, let the lobbyists do their work, and see if we'd be allowed to continue as usual.

By 2009, it was clear that the lessons of the market collapse had brought no new direction to the world of finance and had instilled no new values. The lobbyists succeeded, for the most part, and the game remained the same: to rope in dumb money. Except for a few regulations that added a few hoops to jump through, life went on.

This drama pushed me quickly along in my journey of disillusionment. I was especially disappointed in the part that mathematics had played. I was forced to confront the ugly truth: people had deliberately wielded formulas to impress rather than clarify. It was the first time I had been directly confronted with this toxic concept, and it made me want to escape, to go back in time to the world of proofs and Rubik's Cubes.

And so I left the hedge fund in 2009 with the conviction that I would work to fix the financial WMDs. New regulations were forcing banks to hire independent experts to analyze their risk. I went to work for one of the companies providing that analysis, RiskMetrics Group, one block north of Wall Street. Our product was a blizzard of numbers, each of them predicting the likelihood that a certain tranche of securities or commodities would go poof within the next week, the next year, or the next five years. When everyone is betting on everything that moves in the market, a smart read on risk is worth gold.

To calculate risk, our team employed the Monte Carlo method. To picture it, just imagine spinning the roulette wheel at a casino ten thousand times, taking careful notes all the while. Using Monte Carlo, you'd typically start with historical market data and run through thousands of test scenarios. How would the portfolio we're studying fare on each trading day since 2010, or 2005? Would it survive the very darkest days of the crash? How likely is it that a mortal threat will arise in the next year or two? To come up with these odds, scientists run thousands upon thousands of simulations. There was plenty to complain about with this method, but it was a simple way to get some handle on your risk.

My job was to act as a liaison between our risk management business and the largest and most discerning connoisseurs of risk, the quantitative hedge funds. I'd call the hedge funds, or they'd call me, and we'd discuss any questions they had about our numbers. As often as not, though, they'd notify me only when we'd made a mistake. The fact was, the hedge funds always considered themselves the smartest of the smart, and since understanding risk was fundamental to their existence, they would never rely entirely on outsiders like us. They had their own risk teams, and they bought our product mostly to look good for investors.

I also answered the hotline and would sometimes find myself answering questions from clients at big banks. Eager to repair their tattered image, they wanted to be viewed as responsible, which is why they were calling in the first place. But, unlike the hedge funds, they showed little interest in our analysis. The risk in their portfolios was something they almost seemed to ignore. Throughout my time at the hotline, I got the sense that the people warning about risk were viewed as party poopers or, worse, a threat to the bank's bottom line. This was true even after the cataclysmic crash of 2008, and it's not hard to understand why. If they survived that one—because they were too big to fail—why were they going to fret over risk in their portfolio now?

The refusal to acknowledge risk runs deep in finance. The culture of Wall Street is defined by its traders, and risk is something they actively seek to underestimate. This is a result of the way we define a trader's prowess, namely by his "Sharpe ratio," which is calculated as the profits he generates divided by the risks in his portfolio. This ratio is crucial to a trader's career, his annual bonus, his very sense of being. If you disembody those traders and consider them as a set of algorithms, those algorithms are relentlessly focused on optimizing the Sharpe ratio. Ideally, it will climb, or at least never fall too low. So if one of the risk reports on credit default swaps bumped up the risk calculation on one of a trader's key holdings, his Sharpe ratio would tumble. This could cost him hundreds of thousands of dollars when it came time to calculate his year-end bonus.

I soon realized that I was in the rubber-stamp business. In 2011 it was time to move again, and I saw a huge growth market for mathematicians like me. In the time it took me to type two words into my résumé, I was a newly proclaimed Data Scientist, and ready to plunge into the Internet economy. I landed a job at a New York start-up called Intent Media.

I started out building models to anticipate the behavior of visitors to various travel websites. The key question was whether someone showing up at the Expedia site was just browsing or looking to spend money. Those who weren't planning to buy were worth very little in potential revenue. So we would show them comparison ads for competing services such as Travelocity or Orbitz. If they clicked on the ad, it brought in a few pennies, which was better than nothing. However, we didn't want to feed these ads to serious shoppers. In the worst case, we'd gain a dime of ad revenue while sending potential customers to rivals, where perhaps they'd spend thousands of dollars on hotel rooms in London or Tokyo. It would take thousands of ad views to make up for even a few hundred dollars in lost fees. So it was crucial to keep those people in house.

My challenge was to design an algorithm that would distinguish window shoppers from buyers. There were a few obvious signals. Were they logged into the service? Had they bought there before? But I also scoured for other hints. What time of day was it, and what day of the year? Certain weeks are hot for buyers. The Memorial Day "bump," for example, occurs in mid-spring, when large numbers of people make summer plans almost in unison. My algorithm would place a higher value on shoppers during these periods, since they were more likely to buy.

The statistical work, as it turned out, was highly transferable from the hedge fund to e-commerce—the biggest difference was that, rather than the movement of markets, I was now predicting people's clicks.

In fact, I saw all kinds of parallels between finance and Big Data. Both industries gobble up the same pool of talent, much of it from elite universities like MIT, Princeton, or Stanford. These new hires are ravenous for success and have been focused on external metrics—like SAT scores and college admissions— their entire lives. Whether in finance or tech, the message they've received is that they will be rich, that they will run the world. Their productivity indicates that they're on the right track, and it translates into dollars. This leads to the fallacious conclusion that whatever they're doing to bring in more money is good. It "adds value." Otherwise, why would the market reward it?

In both cultures, wealth is no longer a means to get by. It becomes directly tied to personal worth. A young suburbanite with every advantage—the prep school education, the exhaustive coaching for college admissions tests, the overseas semester in Paris or Shanghai—still flatters himself that it is his skill, hard work, and prodigious problem-solving abilities that have lifted him into a world of privilege. Money vindicates all doubts. And the rest of his circle plays along, forming a mutual admiration society. They're eager to convince us all that Darwinism is at work, when it looks very much to the outside like a combination of gaming a system and dumb luck.

In both of these industries, the real world, with all of its messiness, sits apart. The inclination is to replace people with data trails, turning them into more effective shoppers, voters, or workers to optimize some objective. This is easy to do, and to justify, when success comes back as an anonymous score and when the people affected remain every bit as abstract as the numbers dancing across the screen.

I was already blogging as I worked in data science, and I was also getting more involved with the Occupy movement. More and more, I worried about the separation between technical models and real people, and about the moral repercussions of that separation. In fact, I saw the same pattern emerging that I'd witnessed in finance: a false sense of security was leading to widespread use of imperfect models, self-serving definitions of success, and growing feedback loops. Those who objected were regarded as nostalgic Luddites.

I wondered what the analogue to the credit crisis might be in Big Data. Instead of a bust, I saw a growing dystopia, with inequality rising. The algorithms would make sure that those deemed losers would remain that way. A lucky minority would gain ever more control over the data economy, raking in outrageous fortunes and convincing themselves all the while that they deserved it.

After a couple of years working and learning in the Big Data space, my journey to disillusionment was more or less complete, and the misuse of mathematics was accelerating. In spite of blogging almost daily, I could barely keep up with all the ways I was hearing of people being manipulated, controlled, and intimidated by algorithms. It started with teachers I knew struggling under the yoke of the value-added model, but it didn't end there. Truly alarmed, I quit my job to investigate the issue in earnest.

3

ARMS RACE

Going to College

If you sit down to dinner with friends in certain cities—San Francisco and Portland, to name two—you'll likely find that sharing plates is an impossibility. No two people can eat the same things. They're all on different diets. These range from vegan to various strains of Paleo, and people swear by them (if only for a month or two). Now imagine if one of those regimes, say the caveman diet, became the national standard: if 330 million people all followed its dictates.

The effects would be dramatic. For starters, a single national diet would put the agricultural economy through the wringer. Demand for the approved meats and cheeses would skyrocket, pushing prices up. Meanwhile, the diet's no-no sectors, like soybeans and potatoes, would go begging. Diversity would shrivel. Suffering bean farmers would turn over their fields to cows and pigs, even on land unsuited for it. The additional livestock would slurp up immense quantities of water. And needless to say, a single diet would make many of us extremely unhappy.

What does a single national diet have to do with WMDs? Scale. A formula, whether it's a diet or a tax code, might be perfectly innocuous in theory. But if it grows to become a national or global standard, it creates its own distorted and dystopian economy. This is what has happened in higher education.

The story starts in 1983. That was the year a struggling newsmagazine, *U.S. News & World Report*, decided to undertake an ambitious project. It would evaluate 1,800 colleges and universities throughout the United States and rank them for excellence. This would be a useful tool that, if successful, would help guide millions of young people through their first big life decision. For many, that single choice would set them on a career path and introduce them to lifelong friends, often including a spouse. What's more, a college-ranking issue, editors hoped, might turn into a newsstand sensation. Perhaps for that one week, *U.S. News* could match its giant rivals, *Time* and *Newsweek*.

But what information would feed this new ranking? In the beginning, the staff at *U.S. News* based its scores entirely on the results of opinion surveys it sent to university presidents. Stanford came out as the top national university, and Amherst as the best liberal arts college. While popular with readers, the ratings drove many college administrators crazy. Complaints poured into the magazine that the rankings were unfair. Many college presidents, students, and alumni insisted that they deserved a higher ranking. All the magazine had to do was look at the *data*.

In the following years, editors at *U.S. News* tried to figure out what they could measure. This is how many models start out, with a series of hunches. The process is not scientific and has scant grounding in statistical analysis. In this case, it was just people wondering what matters most in education, then figuring out which of those variables they could count, and finally deciding how much weight to give each of them in the formula.

In most disciplines, the analysis feeding a model would demand far more rigor. In agronomy, for example, researchers might compare the inputs—the soil, the sunshine, and fertilizer—and the outputs, which would be specific traits in the resulting crops. They could then experiment and optimize according to their objectives, whether price, taste, or nutritional value. This is not to say that agronomists cannot create WMDs. They can and do (especially when they neglect to consider long-term and wide-ranging effects of pesticides). But because their models, for the most part, are tightly focused on clear outcomes, they are ideal for scientific experimentation.

The journalists at U.S. News, though, were grappling with "educational excellence," a much squishier value than the cost of corn or the micrograms of protein in each kernel. They had no direct way to quantify how a four-year process affected one single student, much less tens of millions of them. They couldn't measure learning, happiness, confidence, friendships, or other aspects of a student's four-year experience. President Lyndon Johnson's ideal for higher education—"a way to deeper personal fulfillment, greater personal productivity and increased personal reward"—didn't fit into their model.

Instead they picked proxies that seemed to correlate with success. They looked at SAT scores, student-teacher ratios, and acceptance rates. They analyzed the percentage of incoming freshmen who made it to sophomore year and the percentage of those who graduated. They calculated the percentage of living alumni who contributed money to their alma mater, surmising that if they gave a college money there was a good chance they appreciated the education there. Three-quarters of the ranking would be produced by an algorithm—an opinion formalized in code—that incorporated these proxies. In the other quarter, they would factor in the subjective views of college officials throughout the country.

U.S. News's first data-driven ranking came out in 1988, and the results seemed sensible. However, as the ranking grew into a national standard, a vicious feedback loop materialized. The trouble was that the rankings were self-reinforcing. If a college fared badly in U.S. News, its reputation would suffer, and conditions would deteriorate. Top students would avoid it, as would top professors. Alumni would howl and cut back on contributions. The ranking would tumble further. The ranking, in short, was destiny.

In the past, college administrators had had all sorts of ways to gauge their success, many of them anecdotal. Students raved about certain professors. Some graduates went on to illustrious careers as diplomats or entrepreneurs. Others published award-winning novels. This all led to good word of mouth, which boosted a college's reputation. But was Macalester better than Reed, or Iowa better than Illinois? It was hard to say. Colleges were like different types of music, or different diets. There was room for varying opinions, with good arguments on both sides. Now the vast reputational ecosystem of colleges and universities was overshadowed by a single column of numbers.

If you look at this development from the perspective of a university president, it's actually quite sad. Most of these people no doubt cherished their own college experience—that's part of what motivated them to climb the academic ladder. Yet here they were at the summit of their careers dedicating enormous energy toward boosting performance in fifteen areas defined by a group of journalists at a second-tier newsmagazine. They were almost like students again, angling for good grades from a taskmaster. In fact, they were trapped by a rigid model, a WMD.

If the U.S. News list had turned into a moderate success, there would be no trouble. But instead it grew into a titan, quickly establishing itself as a national standard. It has been tying our education system into knots ever since, establishing a rigid to-do list for college administrators and students alike. The U.S. News college ranking has great scale, inflicts widespread damage, and generates an almost endless spiral of destructive feedback loops. While it's not as opaque as many other models, it is still a bona fide WMD.

Some administrators have gone to desperate lengths to drive up their rank. Baylor University paid the fee for admitted students to *retake* the SAT, hoping another try would boost their scores—and Baylor's ranking. Elite small schools, including Bucknell University in Pennsylvania and California's Claremont McKenna, sent false data to U.S. News, inflating the SAT scores of their incoming freshmen. And Iona College, in New York, acknowledged in 2011 that its employees had fudged numbers about nearly everything: test scores, acceptance and graduation rates, freshman retention, student-faculty ratio, and alumni giving. The lying paid off, at least for a while. U.S. News estimated that the false data had lifted Iona from fiftieth to thirtieth place among regional colleges in the Northeast.

The great majority of college administrators looked for less egregious ways to improve their rankings. Instead of cheating, they worked hard to improve each of the metrics that went into their score. They could argue that this was the most efficient use of resources. After all, if they worked to satisfy the U.S. News algorithm, they'd raise more money, attract brighter students and professors, and keep rising on the list. Was there really any choice?

Robert Morse, who has worked at the company since 1976 and heads up the college rankings, argued in interviews that the rankings pushed the colleges to set meaningful goals. If they could improve graduation rates or put students in smaller classes, that was a good thing. Education benefited from the focus. He admitted that the most relevant data—what the students had learned at each school—was inaccessible. But the U.S. News model, constructed from proxies, was the next best thing.

However, when you create a model from proxies, it is far simpler for people to game it. This is because proxies are easier to manipulate than the complicated reality they represent. Here's an example. Let's say a website is looking to hire a social media maven. Many people apply for the job, and they send information about the various marketing campaigns they've run. But it takes way too much time to track down and evaluate all of their work. So the hiring manager settles on a proxy. She gives strong consideration to applicants with the most followers on Twitter. That's a sign of social media engagement, isn't it?

Well, it's a reasonable enough proxy. But what happens when word leaks out, as it surely will, that assembling a crowd on Twitter is key for getting a job at this company? Candidates soon do everything they can to ratchet up their Twitter numbers. Some pay $19.95 for a service that populates their feed with thousands of followers, most of them generated by robots. As people game the system, the proxy loses its effectiveness. Cheaters wind up as false positives.

In the case of the U.S. News rankings, everyone from prospective students to alumni to human resources departments quickly accepted the score as a measurement of educational quality. So the colleges played along. They pushed to improve in each of the areas the rankings measured. Many, in fact, were most frustrated by the 25 percent of the ranking they had no control over—the reputational score, which came from the questionnaires filled out by college presidents and provosts.

This part of the analysis, like any collection of human opinion, was sure to include old-fashioned prejudice and ignorance. It tended to protect the famous schools at the top of the list, because they were the ones people knew about. And it made it harder for up-and-comers.

In 2008, Texas Christian University in Fort Worth, Texas, was tumbling in the *U.S. News* ranking. Its score, which had been 97 three years earlier, had fallen to 105, 108, and now 113. This agitated alumni and boosters and put the chancellor, Victor Boschini, in the hot seat. "The whole thing is very frustrating to me," Boschini told the campus news site, TCU 360. He insisted that TCU was advancing in every indicator. "Our retention rate is improving, our fundraising, all the things they go on."

There were two problems with Boschini's analysis. First, the U.S. News ranking model didn't judge the colleges in isolation. Even schools that improved their numbers would fall behind if others advanced faster. To put it in academic terms, the U.S. News model graded colleges on a curve. And that fed what amounted to a growing arms race.

The other problem was the reputational score, the 25 percent TCU couldn't control. Raymond Brown, the dean of admissions, noted that reputation was the most heavily weighted variable, "which is absurd because it is entirely subjective." Wes Waggoner, director of freshman admissions, added that colleges marketed themselves to each other to boost their reputational score. "I get stuff in the mail from other colleges trying to convince [us] that they're a good school," Waggoner said.

Despite this grousing, TCU set out to improve the 75 percent of the score it could control. After all, if the university's score rose, its reputation would eventually follow. With time, its peers would note the progress and give it higher numbers. The key was to get things moving in the right direction.

TCU launched a $250 million fund-raising drive. It far surpassed its goal and brought in $434 million by 2009. That alone boosted TCU's ranking, since fund-raising is one of the metrics. The university spent much of the money on campus improvements, including $100 million on the central mall and a new student union, in an effort to make TCU a more attractive destination for students. While there's nothing wrong with that, it conveniently feeds the U.S. News algorithm. The more students apply, the more selective the school can be.

Perhaps more important, TCU built a state-of-the-art sports training facility and pumped resources into its football program. In the following years, TCU's football team, the Horned Frogs, became a national powerhouse. In 2010, they went undefeated, beating Wisconsin in the Rose Bowl.

That success allowed TCU to benefit from what's called "the Flutie effect." In 1984, in one of the most exciting college football games in history, a quarterback at Boston College, Doug Flutie, completed a long last-second "Hail Mary" pass to defeat the University of Miami. Flutie became a legend. Within two years, applications to BC were up by 30 percent. The same boost occurred for Georgetown University when its basketball team, anchored by Patrick Ewing, played in three national championship games. Winning athletic programs, it turns out, are the most effective promotions for some applicants. To legions of athletically oriented high school seniors watching college sports on TV, schools with great teams look appealing. Students are proud to wear the school's name. They paint their faces and celebrate. Applications shoot up. With more students seeking admission, administrators can lift the bar, raising the average test scores of incoming freshmen. That helps the rating. And the more applicants the school rejects, the lower (and, for the ranking, better) its acceptance rate.

TCU's strategy worked. By 2013, it was the second most selective university in Texas, trailing only prestigious Rice University in Houston. That same year, it registered the highest SAT and

ACT scores in its history. Its rank in the *U.S. News* list climbed. In 2015, it finished in seventy-sixth place, a climb of thirty-seven places in just seven years.

Despite my issues with the *U.S. News* model and its status as a WMD, it's important to note that this dramatic climb up the rankings may well have benefited TCU as a university. After all, most of the proxies in the *U.S. News* model reflect a school's overall quality to some degree, just as many dieters thrive by following the caveman regime. The problem isn't the *U.S. News* model but its scale. It forces everyone to shoot for exactly the same goals, which creates a rat race—and lots of harmful unintended consequences.

In the years before the rankings, for example, college-bound students could sleep a bit better knowing that they had applied to a so-called safety school, a college with lower entrance standards. If students didn't get into their top choices, including the long shots (stretch schools) and solid bets (target schools), they'd get a perfectly fine education at the safety school—and maybe transfer to one of their top choices after a year or two.

The concept of a safety school is now largely extinct, thanks in great part to the *U.S. News* ranking. As we saw in the example of TCU, it helps in the rankings to be selective. If an admissions office is flooded with applications, it's a sign that something is going right there. It speaks to the college's reputation. And if a college can reject the vast majority of those candidates, it'll probably end up with a higher caliber of students. Like many of the proxies, this metric seems to make sense. It follows market movements.

But that market can be manipulated. A traditional safety school, for example, can look at historical data and see that only a small fraction of the top applicants ended up going there. Most of them got into their target or stretch schools and didn't need what amounted to an insurance policy. With the objective of boosting its selectivity score, the safety school can now reject the excellent candidates that, according to its own algorithm, are most likely not to matriculate. This process is far from exact. And the college, despite the work of the data scientists in its admissions office, no doubt loses a certain number of top students who would have chosen to attend. Those are the ones who learn, to their dismay, that so-called safety schools are no longer a sure bet.

The convoluted process does nothing for education. The college suffers. It loses the top students—the stars who enhance the experience for everyone, including the professors. In fact, the former safety school may now have to allocate some precious financial aid to enticing some of those stars to its campus. And that may mean less money for the students who need it the most.

...

It's here that we find the greatest shortcoming of the *U.S. News* college ranking. The proxies the journalists chose for educational excellence make sense, after all. Their spectacular failure comes, instead, from what they chose *not* to count: tuition and fees. Student financing was left out of the model.

This brings us to the crucial question we'll confront time and again. What is the objective of the modeler? In this case, put yourself in the place of the editors at *U.S. News* in 1988. When they were building their first statistical model, how would they know when it worked? Well, it would start out with a lot more credibility if it reflected the established hierarchy. If Harvard, Stanford, Princeton, and Yale came out on top, it would seem to validate their model, replicating the informal models that they and their customers carried in their own heads. To build such a model, they simply had to look at those top universities and count what made them so special. What did they have in common, as opposed to the safety school in the next town? Well, their students had stratospheric SATs and graduated like clockwork. The alumni were rich and poured money back into the universities. By analyzing the virtues of the name-brand universities, the ratings team created an elite yardstick to measure excellence.

Now, if they incorporated the cost of education into the formula, strange things might happen to the results. Cheap universities could barge into the excellence hierarchy. This could create surprises and sow doubts. The public might receive the *U.S. News* rankings as something less than the word of God. It was much safer to start with the venerable champions on top. Of course they cost a lot. But maybe that was the price of excellence.

By leaving cost out of the formula, it was as if U.S. News had handed college presidents a gilded checkbook. They had a commandment to maximize performance in fifteen areas, and keeping costs low wasn't one of them. In fact, if they raised prices, they'd have more resources for addressing the areas where they were being measured.

Tuition has skyrocketed ever since. Between 1985 and 2013, the cost of higher education rose by more than 500 percent, nearly four times the rate of inflation. To attract top students, colleges, as we saw at TCU, have gone on building booms, featuring glass-walled student centers, luxury dorms, and gyms with climbing walls and whirlpool baths. This would all be wonderful for students and might enhance their college experience—if they weren't the ones paying for it, in the form of student loans that would burden them for decades. We cannot place the blame for this trend entirely on the U.S. News rankings. Our entire society has embraced not only the idea that a college education is essential but the idea that a degree from a highly ranked school can catapult a student into a life of power and privilege. The U.S. News WMD fed on these beliefs, fears, and neuroses. It created powerful incentives that have encouraged spending while turning a blind eye to skyrocketing tuitions and fees.

As colleges position themselves to move up the *U.S. News* charts, they manage their student populations almost like an investment portfolio. We'll see this often in the world of data, from advertising to politics. For college administrators, each prospective student represents a series of assets and usually a liability or two. A great athlete, for example, is an asset, but she might come with low test scores or a middling class rank. Those are liabilities. She might also need financial aid, another liability. To balance the portfolio, ideally, they'd find other candidates who can pay their way and have high test scores. But those ideal candidates, after being accepted, might choose to go elsewhere. That's a risk, which must be quantified. This is frighteningly complex, and an entire consulting industry has risen up to "optimize recruitment."

Noel-Levitz, an education consulting firm, offers a predictive analytics package called ForecastPlus, which allows administrators to rank enrollment prospects by geography, gender, ethnicity, field of study, academic standing, or "any other characteristic you desire." Another consultancy, RightStudent, gathers and sells data to help colleges target the most promising candidates for recruitment. These include students who can pay full tuition, as well as others who might be eligible for outside scholarships. For some of these, a learning disability is a plus.

All of this activity takes place within a vast ecosystem surrounding the *U.S. News* rankings, whose model functions as the de facto law of the land. If the editors rejigger the weightings on the model, paying less attention to SAT scores, for example, or more to graduation rates, the entire ecosystem of education must adapt. This extends from universities to consultancies, high school guidance departments, and, yes, the students.

Naturally, the rankings themselves are a growing franchise. The *U.S. News & World Report* magazine, long the company's sole business, has withered away, disappearing from print in 2010. But the rating business continues to grow, extending into medical schools, dental schools, and graduate programs in liberal arts and engineering. U.S. News even ranks high schools.

As the rankings grow, so do efforts to game them. In a 2014 U.S. News ranking of global universities, the mathematics department at Saudi Arabia's King Abdulaziz University landed in seventh place, right behind Harvard. The department had been around for only two years but had somehow leapfrogged ahead of several giants of mathematics, including Cambridge and MIT.

At first blush, this might look like a positive development. Perhaps MIT and Cambridge were coasting on their fame while a hardworking insurgent powered its way into the elite. With a pure reputational ranking, such a turnaround would take decades. But data can bring surprises to the surface in a hurry.

Algorithms, though, can also be gamed. Lior Pachter, a computational biologist at Berkeley, looked into it. He found that the Saudi university had contacted a host of mathematicians whose work was highly cited and had offered them $72,000 to serve as adjunct faculty. The deal, according to a recruiting letter Pachter posted on his blog, stipulated that the mathematicians had to work three weeks a year in Saudi Arabia. The university would fly them there in business class and put them up at a five-star hotel. Conceivably, their work in Saudi Arabia added value locally. But the university also required them to change their affiliation on the Thomson Reuters academic citation website, a key reference for the U.S. News rankings. That meant the Saudi university could claim the publications of their new adjunct faculty as its own. And since citations were one of the algorithm's primary inputs, King Abdulaziz University soared in the rankings.

. . .

Students in the Chinese city of Zhongxiang had a reputation for acing the national standardized test, or *gaokao*, and winning places in China's top universities. They did so well, in fact, that authorities began to suspect they were cheating. Suspicions grew in 2012, according to a report in Britain's *Telegraph*, when provincial authorities found ninety-nine identical copies of a single test.

The next year, as students in Zhongxiang arrived to take the exam, they were dismayed to be funneled through metal detectors and forced to relinquish their mobile phones. Some surrendered tiny transmitters disguised as pencil erasers. Once inside, the students found themselves accompanied by fifty-four investigators from different school districts. A few of these investigators crossed the street to a hotel, where they found groups positioned to communicate with the students through their transmitters.

The response to this crackdown on cheating was volcanic. Some two thousand stone-throwing protesters gathered in the street outside the school. They chanted, "We want fairness. There is no fairness if you don't let us cheat."

It sounds like a joke, but they were absolutely serious. The stakes for the students were sky high. As they saw it, they faced a chance either to pursue an elite education and a prosperous career or to stay stuck in their provincial city, a relative backwater. And whether or not it was the case, they had the perception that others were cheating. So preventing the students in Zhongxiang from cheating *was* unfair. In a system in which cheating is the norm, following the rules amounts to a handicap. Just ask the Tour de France cyclists who were annihilated for seven years straight by Lance Armstrong and his doping teammates.

The only way to win in such a scenario is to gain an advantage and to make sure that others aren't getting a bigger one. This is the case not only in China but also in the United States, where high school admissions officers, parents, and students find themselves caught in a frantic effort to game the system spawned by the U.S. News model.

An entire industry of coaches and tutors thrives on the model's feedback loop and the anxiety it engenders. Many of them cost serious money. A four-day "application boot camp," run by a company called Top Tier Admissions, costs $16,000 (plus room and board). During the sessions, the high school juniors develop their essays, learn how to "ace" their interviews, and create an "activity sheet" to sum up all the awards, sports, club activities, and community work that admissions officers are eager to see.

Sixteen thousand dollars may sound like a lot of money. But much like the Chinese protesters in Zhongxiang, many American families fret that their children's future success and fulfillment hinge upon acceptance to an elite university.

The most effective coaches understand the admissions models at each college so that they can figure out how a potential student might fit into their portfolios. A California-based entrepreneur, Steven Ma, takes this market-based approach to an extreme. Ma, founder of ThinkTank Learning, places the prospective students into his own model and calculates the likelihood that they'll get into their target colleges. He told Bloomberg BusinessWeek, for example, that an American-born senior with a 3.8 GPA, an SAT score of 2000, and eight hundred hours of extracurricular activities had a 20.4 percent shot of getting into New York University, and a 28.1 percent chance at the University of Southern California. ThinkTank then offers guaranteed consulting packages. If that hypothetical student follows the consultancy's coaching and gets into NYU, it will cost $25,931, or $18,826 for USC. If he's rejected, it costs nothing.

Each college's admissions model is derived, at least in part, from the U.S. News model, and each one is a mini-WMD. These models lead students and their parents to run in frantic circles and spend obscene amounts of money. And they're opaque. This leaves most of the participants (or victims) in the dark. But it creates a big business for consultants, like Steven Ma, who manage to learn their secrets, either by cultivating sources at the universities or by reverse-engineering their algorithms.

The victims, of course, are the vast majority of Americans, the poor and middle-class families who don't have thousands of dollars to spent on courses and consultants. They miss out on precious insider knowledge. The result is an education system that favors the privileged. It tilts against needy students, locking out the great majority of them—and pushing them down a path toward poverty. It deepens the social divide.

But even those who claw their way into a top college lose out. If you think about it, the college admissions game, while lucrative for some, has virtually no educational value. The complex and fraught production simply re-sorts and reranks the very same pool of eighteen-year-old kids in newfangled ways. They don't master important skills by jumping through many more hoops or writing meticulously targeted college essays under the watchful eye of professional tutors. Others scrounge online for cut-rate versions of those tutors. All of them, from the rich to the working class, are simply being trained to fit into an enormous machine—to satisfy a WMD. And at the end of the ordeal, many of them will be saddled with debt that will take decades to pay off. They're pawns in an arms race, and it's a particularly nasty one.

So is there a fix? During his second term, President Obama suggested coming up with a new college rankings model, one more in tune with national priorities and middle-class means than the U.S. News version. His secondary goal was to sap power from for-profit colleges (a money-sucking scourge that we'll discuss in the next chapter). Obama's idea would be to tie a college ranking system to a different set of metrics, including affordability, the percentage of poor and minority students, and postgraduation job placement. Like the *U.S. News* ranking, it would also consider graduation rate. If colleges dipped below the minimums in these categories, they'd get cut off from the $180 million-per-year federal student loan market (which the for-profit universities have been feasting on).

All of those sound like worthy goals, to be sure, but every ranking system can be gamed. And when that happens, it creates new and different feedback loops and a host of unintended consequences.

It's easy to raise graduation rates, for example, by lowering standards. Many students struggle with math and science prerequisites and foreign languages. Water down those requirements, and more students will graduate. But if one goal of our educational system is to produce more scientists and technologists for a global economy, how smart is that? It would also be a cinch to pump up the income numbers for graduates. All colleges would have to do is shrink their liberal arts programs, and get rid of education departments and social work departments while they're at it, since teachers and social workers make less money than engineers, chemists, and computer scientists. But they're no less valuable to society.

It also wouldn't be too hard to lower costs. One approach already gaining popularity is to lower the percentage of tenured faculty, replacing these expensive professors, as they retire, with cheaper instructors, or adjuncts. For some departments at some universities, this might make sense. But there are costs. Tenured faculty, working with graduate students, power important research and set the standards for their departments, whereas harried adjuncts, who might teach five courses at three colleges just to pay rent, rarely have the time or energy to deliver more than commodity education. Another possible approach, that of removing unnecessary administrative positions, seems all too rare.

The number of "graduates employed nine months after graduation" can be gamed too. A *New York Times* report in 2011 focused on law schools, which are already evaluated by their ability
to position their students for careers. Say a newly minted lawyer
with $150,000 in student loans is working as a barista. For some
unscrupulous law schools investigated by the *Times*, he counted
as employed. Some schools went further, hiring their own graduates for hourly temp jobs just as the crucial nine-month period approached. Others sent out surveys to recent alumni and counted
all those that didn't respond as "employed."

• • •

Perhaps it was just as well that the Obama administration failed to
come up with a rejiggered ranking system. The pushback by college presidents was fierce. After all, they had spent decades optimizing themselves to satisfy the *U.S. News* WMD. A new formula
based on graduation rates, class size, alumni employment and income, and other metrics could wreak havoc with their ranking
and reputation. No doubt they also made good points about the
vulnerabilities of any new model and the new feedback loops it
would generate.

So the government capitulated. And the result might be better.
Instead of a ranking, the Education Department released loads
of data on a website. The result is that students can ask their own
questions about the things that matter to them—including class
size, graduation rates, and the average debt held by graduating
students. They don't need to know anything about statistics or the
weighting of variables. The software itself, much like an online
travel site, creates individual models for each person. Think of it:
transparent, controlled by the user, and personal. You might call
it the opposite of a WMD.

4

PROPAGANDA MACHINE

Online Advertising

One day during my stint as a data scientist for the advertising start-up Intent Media, a prominent venture capitalist visited the office. He seemed to be mulling an investment in the company, which was eager to put on its best face. So all of us were summoned to hear him speak.

He outlined the brilliant future of targeted advertising. By contributing rivers of data, people would give advertisers the ability to learn about them in great detail. This would enable companies to target them with what they deemed valuable information, which would arrive at just the right time and place. A pizzeria, for example, might know that you're not only in the neighborhood but also likely to be hungry for the same deep dish double cheese with pepperoni that you had last week at halftime of the Dallas Cowboys game. Their system might see that people whose data follows patterns similar to yours are more likely to click on a discount coupon during that twenty-minute window.

The weakest part of his argument, it seemed to me, was its justification. He argued that the coming avalanche of personalized advertising would be so useful and timely that customers would welcome it. They would beg for more. As he saw it, most people objected to advertisements because they were irrelevant to them. In the future, they wouldn't be. Presumably, folks in his exclusive demo would welcome pitches tailored to them, perhaps featuring cottages in the Bahamas, jars of hand-pressed virgin olive oil, or time-shares for private jets. And he joked that he would never have to see another ad for the University of Phoenix—a for-profit education factory that appeals largely to the striving (and more easily cheated) underclasses.

It was strange, I thought, that he mentioned the University of Phoenix. Somehow he was seeing the ads, and I wasn't. Or maybe I didn't notice them. In any case, I knew quite a bit about for-profit universities, which had by that point become multimillion-dollar operations. These so-called diploma mills were often underwritten by government-financed loans, and the diplomas they awarded had scant value in the workplace. In many professions, they were no more valuable than a high school degree.

While the WMD in the U.S. News Best Colleges ranking made life miserable for rich and middle-class students (and their families), the for-profit colleges focused on the other, more vulnerable, side of the population. And the Internet gave them the perfect tool to do so. It's little surprise, therefore, that the industry's dramatic growth coincided with the arrival of the Internet as an always-on communications platform for the masses. While spending more than $50 million on Google ads alone, the University of Phoenix targeted poor people with the bait of upward mobility. Its come-on carried the underlying criticism that the struggling classes weren't doing enough to improve their lives. And it worked. Between 2004 and 2014, for-profit enrollment tripled, and the industry now accounts for 11 percent of the country's college and university students.

The marketing of these universities is a far cry from the early promise of the Internet as a great equalizing and democratizing force. If it was true during the early dot-com days that "nobody knows you're a dog," it's the exact opposite today. We are ranked, categorized, and scored in hundreds of models, on the basis of our revealed preferences and patterns. This establishes a powerful basis for legitimate ad campaigns, but it also fuels their predatory cousins: ads that pinpoint people in great need and sell them false or overpriced promises. They find inequality and feast on it. The result is that they perpetuate our existing social stratification, with all of its injustices. The greatest divide is between the winners in our system, like our venture capitalist, and the people his models prey upon.

Anywhere you find the combination of great need and ignorance, you'll likely see predatory ads. If people are anxious about their sex lives, predatory advertisers will promise them Viagra or Cialis, or even penis extensions. If they are short of money, offers will pour in for high-interest payday loans. If their computer is acting sludgy, it might be a virus inserted by a predatory advertiser, who will then offer to fix it. And as we'll see, the boom in for-profit colleges is fueled by predatory ads.

When it comes to WMDs, predatory ads practically define the genre. They zero in on the most desperate among us at enormous scale. In education, they promise what's usually a false road to prosperity, while also calculating how to maximize the dollars they draw from each prospect. Their operations cause immense and nefarious feedback loops and leave their customers buried under mountains of debt. And the targets have little idea how they were scammed, because the campaigns are opaque. They just pop up on the computer, and later call on the phone. The victims rarely learn how they were chosen or how the recruiters came to know so much about them.

Consider Corinthian College. Until recently, it was a giant in the industry. Its various divisions had more than eighty thousand students, the great majority of them receiving government-financed loans. In 2013, the for-profit college got busted by the attorney general of California for lying about job placement rates, overcharging students, and using unofficial military seals in predatory ads to reel in vulnerable people. The complaint pointed out that one of its divisions, Everest University Online's Brandon Campus, charged $68,800 in tuition for an online bachelor's degree in paralegal. (Such courses cost less than $10,000 at many traditional colleges around the country.)

Moreover, according to the complaint, Corinthian College targeted "isolated," "impatient" individuals with "low self esteem" who have "few people in their lives who care about them" and who are "stuck" and "unable to see and plan well for future." The complaint called Corinthian College's practices "unlawful, unfair, and fraudulent." In 2014, amid more reports of abuses, the Obama administration put a hold on the company's access to federal student loan funding. That was its lifeblood. In mid-2015, the company sold off most of its campuses and declared Chapter 11 bankruptcy.

But the industry marches on. Vatterott College, a career-training institute, is a particularly nasty example. A 2012 Senate committee report on for-profit colleges described Vatterott's recruiting manual, which sounds diabolical. It directs recruiters to target "Welfare Mom w/Kids. Pregnant Ladies. Recent Divorce. Low Self-Esteem. Low Income Jobs. Experienced a Recent Death. Physically/Mentally Abused. Recent Incarceration. Drug Rehabilitation. Dead-End Jobs—No Future."

Why, specifically, were they targeting these folks? Vulnerability is worth gold. It always has been. Picture an itinerant quack in an old western movie. He pulls into town with his wagon full of jangling jars and bottles. When he sits down with an elderly prospective customer, he seeks out her weaknesses. She covers her mouth when she smiles, indicating that she's sensitive about her bad teeth. She anxiously twirls her old wedding ring, which from the looks of her swollen knuckle will be stuck there till the end of her days. Arthritis. So when he pitches his products to her, he focuses on the ugliness of her teeth and her aching hands. He can promise to restore the beauty of her smile and wash away the pain from her joints. With this knowledge, he knows he's halfway to a sale before even clearing his throat to speak.

The playbook for predatory advertisers is similar, but they carry it out at massive scale, targeting millions of people every day. The customers' ignorance, of course, is a crucial piece of the puzzle. Many of the targeted students are immigrants who come to this country believing that private universities are more prestigious than public ones. This argument is plausible if the private universities happen to be Harvard and Princeton. But the idea that DeVry or the University of Phoenix would be preferable to any state university (much less public gems such as Berkeley, Michigan, or Virginia) is something only newcomers to the system could ever believe.

Once the ignorance is established, the key for the recruiter, just as for the snake-oil merchant, is to locate the most vulnerable people and then use their private information against them. This involves finding where they suffer the most, which is known as the "pain point." It might be low self-esteem, the stress of raising kids in a neighborhood of warring gangs, or perhaps a drug addiction. Many people unwittingly disclose their pain points when they look for answers on Google or, later, when they fill out college questionnaires. With that valuable nugget in hand, recruiters simply promise that an expensive education at their university will provide the solution and eliminate the pain. "We deal with people that live in the moment and for the moment," Vatterott's training materials explain. "Their decision to start, stay in school or quit school is based more on emotion than logic. Pain is the greater motivator in the short term." A recruiting team at ITT Technical Institute went so far as to draw up an image of a dentist bearing down on a patient in agony, with the words "Find Out Where Their Pain Is."

A potential student's first click on a for-profit college website comes only after a vast industrial process has laid the groundwork. Corinthian, for example, had a thirty-person marketing team that spent $120 million annually, much of it to generate and pursue 2.4 million leads, which led to sixty thousand new students and $600 million in annual revenue. These large marketing teams reach potential students through a wide range of channels, from TV ads and billboards on highways and bus stops to direct mail, search advertising on Google, and even recruiters visiting schools and knocking on doors. An analyst on the team designs the various promotions with the explicit goal of getting feedback. To optimize recruiting—and revenue—they need to know whom their messages reached and, if possible, what impact they had. Only with this data can they go on to optimize the operation.

The key for any optimization program, naturally, is to pick an objective. For diploma mills like the University of Phoenix, I think it's safe to say, the goal is to recruit the greatest number of students who can land government loans to pay most of their tuition and fees. With that objective in mind, the data scientists have to figure out how best to manage their various communication channels so that together they generate the most bang for each buck.

The data scientists start off with a Bayesian approach, which in statistics is pretty close to plain vanilla. The point of Bayesian analysis is to rank the variables with the most impact on the desired outcome. Search advertising, TV, billboards, and other promotions would each be measured as a function of their effectiveness per dollar. Each develops a different probability, which is expressed as a value, or a weight.

It gets complicated, though, because the various messaging campaigns all interact with each other, and much of their impact can't be measured. For example, do bus advertisements drive up the probability that a prospect will take a phone call? It's hard to say. It's easier to track online messaging, and for-profits can gather vital details about each prospect—where they live and what web pages they've surfed.

That's why much of the advertising money at for-profit universities goes to Google and Facebook. Each of these platforms allows advertisers to segment their target populations in meticulous detail. Publicists for a Judd Apatow movie, for example, could target males from age eighteen to twenty-eight in the fifty richest zip codes, perhaps zeroing in on those who have clicked on or "liked" links to Apatow's hit movie *Trainwreck*, have mentioned him on Twitter, or are friends with someone who has. But for-profit colleges hunt in the opposite direction. They're more likely to be targeting people in the poorest zip codes, with special attention to those who have clicked on an ad for payday loans or seem to be concerned with post-traumatic stress. (Combat veterans are highly recruited, in part because it's easier to get financing for them.)

The campaign proceeds to run an endless series of competing ads against each other to see which ones bring in the most prospects. This method, based on so-called A/B testing, is one that direct-mail marketers have been using for decades. They send a plethora of come-ons, measure the responses, and fine-tune their campaigns. Every time you discover another credit card offer in your mailbox, you're participating in one of these tests. By throwing out the letter unopened, you're providing the company with a valuable piece of data: that campaign didn't work for you. Next time they'll try a slightly different approach. It may seem fruitless, since so many of these offers wind up in the trash. But for many direct marketers, whether they're operating on the Internet or through the mail, a 1 percent response rate is the stuff of dreams. After all, they're working with huge numbers. One percent of the US population is more than three million people.

Once these campaigns move online, the learning accelerates. The Internet provides advertisers with the greatest laboratory ever for consumer research and lead generation. Feedback from each promotion arrives within seconds—a lot faster than the mail. Within hours (instead of months), each campaign can zero in on the most effective messages and come closer to reaching the glittering promise of all advertising: to reach a prospect at the right time, and with precisely the best message to trigger a decision, and thus succeed in hauling in another paying customer. This fine-tuning never stops.

And increasingly, the data-crunching machines are sifting through our data on their own, searching for our habits and hopes, fears and desires. With machine learning, a fast-growing domain of artificial intelligence, the computer dives into the data, following only basic instructions. The algorithm finds patterns on its own, and then, through time, connects them with outcomes. In a sense, it learns.

Compared to the human brain, machine learning isn't especially efficient. A child places her finger on the stove, feels pain, and masters for the rest of her life the correlation between the hot metal and her throbbing hand. And she also picks up the word for it: burn. A machine learning program, by contrast, will often require millions or billions of data points to create its statistical models of cause and effect. But for the first time in history, those petabytes of data are now readily available, along with powerful computers to process them. And for many jobs, machine learning proves to be more flexible and nuanced than the traditional programs governed by rules.

Language scientists, for example, spent decades, from the 1960s to the early years of this century, trying to teach computers how to read. During most of this time, they programmed definitions and grammatical rules into the code. But as any foreign-language student discovers all too quickly, languages teem with exceptions. They have slang and sarcasm. The meaning of certain words changes with time and geography. The complexity of language is a programmer's nightmare. Ultimately, coding it is hopeless.

But with the Internet, people across the earth have produced quadrillions of words about our lives and work, our shopping, and our friendships. By doing this, we have unwittingly built the greatest-ever training corpus for natural-language machines. As we turned from paper to e-mail and social networks, machines could study our words, compare them to others, and gather something about their context. The progress has been fast and dramatic. As late as 2011, Apple underwhelmed most of techdom with its natural-language "personal assistant," Siri. The technology was conversant only in certain areas, and it made laughable mistakes. Most people I know found it near useless. But now I hear people talking to their phones all the time, asking for the weather report, sports scores, or directions. Somewhere between 2008 and 2015, give or take, the linguistic skills of algorithms advanced from pre-K to middle school, and for some applications much higher.

These advances in natural language have opened up a mother lode of possibilities for advertisers. The programs "know" what a word means, at least enough to associate it with certain behaviors and outcomes, at least some of the time. Fueled in part by this growing linguistic mastery, advertisers can probe for deeper patterns. An advertising program might start out with the usual demographic and geographic details. But over the course of weeks and months it begins to learn the patterns of the people it's targeting and to make predictions about their next moves. It gets to know them. And if the program is predatory, it gauges their weaknesses and vulnerabilities and pursues the most efficient path to exploit them.

In addition to cutting-edge computer science, predatory advertisers often work with middlemen, who use much cruder methods to target prospects. In 2010, one effective ad featured a photo of President Obama and said: "Obama Asks Moms to Return to School: Finish Your Degree—Financial Aid Available to Those Who Qualify." The ad suggested that the president had signed a new bill aimed at getting mothers back in school. This was a lie. But if it spurred people to click, it served its purpose.

Behind this misleading headline, an entire dirty industry was beavering away. When a consumer clicked on the ad, according to a ProPublica investigation, she was asked a few questions, including her age and phone number, and was immediately contacted by a for-profit school. These callers didn't give her any more information about President Obama's new bill, because it never existed. Instead they offered to help her borrow money for enrollment.

This kind of online targeting is called "lead generation." Its goal is to come up with lists of prospects, which can be sold—in this case, to for-profit universities. According to the ProPublica report, between 20 and 30 percent of the promotional budgets at for-profit colleges go to lead generation. For the most promising leads, colleges will pay as much as $150 each.

One lead generator, Salt Lake City–based Neutron Interactive, posted fake jobs at websites like Monster.com, as well as ads promising to help people get food stamps and Medicaid coverage, according to David Halperin, a public policy researcher. Using the same optimization methods, they would roll out loads of different ads, measuring their effectiveness for each demographic.

The purpose of these ads was to lure desperate job seekers to provide their cell phone numbers. In follow-up calls, only 5 percent of the people showed interest in college courses. But those names were valuable leads. Each one was worth as much as $85 to for-profit colleges. And they would do everything in their power to make that investment pay off. Within five minutes of signing up, according to a US Government Accountability Office report, prospective students could expect to begin receiving calls. One target received more than 180 calls in a single month.

The for-profit colleges, of course, have their own methods for generating leads. One of their most valuable tools is the College Board website, the resource that many students use to sign up for SAT tests and research the next step in their lives. According to Mara Tucker, a college preparedness counselor for the Urban Assembly Institute of Math and Science for Young Women, a public school in Brooklyn, the search engine on the website is engineered to direct poor students toward for-profit universities. Once a student has indicated in an online questionnaire that she'll need financial aid, the for-profit colleges pop up at the top of her list of matching schools.

For-profit colleges also provide free services in exchange for face time with students. Cassie Magesis, another readiness counselor at the Urban Assembly, told me that the colleges provide free workshops to guide students in writing their résumés. These sessions help the students. But impoverished students who provide their contact information are subsequently stalked. The for-profit colleges do not bother targeting rich students. They and their parents know too much.

Recruiting in all of its forms is the heart of the for-profit business, and it accounts for far more of their spending, in most cases, than education. A Senate report on thirty for-profit systems found that they employed one recruiter for every forty-eight students. Apollo Group, the parent company for the University of Phoenix, spent more than a billion dollars on marketing in 2010, almost all of it focused on recruiting. That came out to $2,225 per student on marketing and only $892 per student on instruction. Compare that to Portland Community College in Oregon, which spends $5,953 per student on instruction and about 1.2 percent of its budget, or $185 per student, on marketing.

• • •

Math, in the form of complex models, fuels the predatory advertising that brings in prospects for these colleges. But by the time a recruiter is hounding prospective students on their cell phones, we've left the world of numbers behind. The sales pitches, with their promises of affordable tuition, bright career prospects, and upward mobility, aren't that different from the promotions for magic elixirs, baldness cures, and vibrating belts that reduce waistline fat. They're not new.

Yet a crucial component of a WMD is that it is damaging to many people's lives. And with these types of predatory ads, the damage doesn't begin until students start taking out big loans for their tuition and fees.

The crucial metric is the so-called 90-10 rule, included in the Higher Education Act of 1965. It stipulates that colleges cannot get more than 90 percent of their funding from federal aid. The thinking was that as long as the students had some "skin in the game" they would tend to take their education more seriously. But for-profit colleges quickly worked this ratio into their business plan. If students could scrape together a few thousand dollars, either from savings or bank loans, the universities could line them up for nine times that sum in government loans, making each student incredibly profitable.

To many of the students, the loans sound like free money, and the school doesn't take pains to correct this misconception. But it is debt, and many of them quickly find themselves up to their necks in it. The outstanding debt for students at the bankrupt Corinthian Colleges amounted to $3.5 billion. Almost all of it was backed by taxpayers and will never be repaid.

Some people no doubt attend for-profit colleges and emerge with knowledge and skills that serve them well. But do they fare better than graduates from community colleges, whose degrees cost a fraction as much? In 2014, investigators at CALDER/American Institutes for Research created nearly nine thousand fictitious résumés. Some of their fake job applicants held associate degrees from for-profit universities, others had similar diplomas from community colleges, while a third group had no college education at all. The researchers sent their résumés to job postings in seven major cities and then measured the response rate. They found that diplomas from for-profit colleges were worth less in the workplace than those from community colleges and about the same as a high school diploma. And yet these colleges cost on average 20 percent more than flagship public universities.

The feedback loop for this WMD is far less complicated than it is nefarious. The poorest 40 percent of the US population is in desperate straits. Many industrial jobs have disappeared, either replaced by technology or shipped overseas. Unions have lost their punch. The top 20 percent of the population controls 89 percent of the wealth in the country, and the bottom 40 percent controls none of it. Their assets are negative: the average household in this enormous and struggling underclass has a net debt of $14,800, much of it in extortionate credit card accounts. What these people need is money. And the key to earning more money, they hear again and again, is education.

Along come the for-profit colleges with their highly refined WMDs to target and fleece the population most in need. They sell them the promise of an education and a tantalizing glimpse of upward mobility—while plunging them deeper into debt. They take advantage of the pressing need in poor households, along with their ignorance and their aspirations, then they exploit it. And they do this at great scale. This leads to hopelessness and despair, along with skepticism about the value of education more broadly, and it exacerbates our country's vast wealth gap.

It's worth noting that these diploma mills drive inequality in both directions. The presidents of the leading for-profit universities make millions of dollars every year. For example, Gregory W. Cappelli, CEO of Apollo Education Group, the parent company of the University of Phoenix, took home $25.1 million in total compensation in 2011. At public universities, which have their own distortions, only football and basketball coaches can hope to make that much.

. . .

For-profit colleges, sadly, are hardly alone in deploying predatory ads. They have plenty of company. If you just think about where people are hurting, or desperate, you'll find advertisers wielding their predatory models. One of the biggest opportunities, naturally, is for loans. Everyone needs money, but some more urgently than others. These people are not hard to find. The neediest are far more likely to reside in impoverished zip codes. And from a

predatory advertiser's perspective, they practically shout out for
special attention with their queries on search engines and their
clicks on coupons.

Like for-profit colleges, the payday loan industry operates
WMDs. Some of them are run by legal operations, but the industry is fundamentally predatory, charging outrageous interest
rates that average 574 percent on short-term loans that are flipped
on average eight times—making them much more like long-term
loans. They are critically supported by legions of data brokers and
lead generators, many of them scam artists. Their advertisements
pop up on computers and phones, offering fast access to cash.
When the prospects fill out the applications, often including their
bank information, they open themselves to theft and abuse.

In 2015, the Federal Trade Commission charged two data
brokers for selling the loan applications of more than half a million consumers. According to the suit, the companies, Sequoia
One of Tampa, Florida, and Gen X Marketing Group of nearby
Clearwater, made off with customers' phone numbers, employer
details, social security numbers, and bank account information—
and then sold them for about fifty cents each. The companies
that bought the information, according to the regulators, raided
the consumers' bank accounts for "at least" $7.1 million. Many
of the victims were subsequently charged bank fees for emptying
out their account or bouncing checks.

If you think about the numbers involved, they're almost pathet-
ically low. Spread over a half million accounts, $7.1 million comes
to barely $14 each. Even if the thieves failed to access many of
these accounts, much of the money they stole was no doubt in
small numbers, the last $50 or $100 that some poor people keep
in their accounts.

Now regulators are pushing for new laws governing the market
for personal data—a crucial input for all sorts of WMDs. To date,

a couple of federal laws, such as the Fair Credit Reporting Act and the Health Insurance Portability and Accountability Act, or HIPAA, establish some limits on health and credit data. Maybe, with an eye on lead generators, they'll add more.

However, as we'll see in coming chapters, some of the most effective and nefarious WMDs manage to engineer work-arounds. They study everything from neighborhoods to Facebook friends to predict our behavior—and even lock us up.

5

CIVILIAN CASUALTIES

Justice in the Age of Big Data

The small city of Reading, Pennsylvania, has had a tough go of it in the postindustrial era. Nestled in the green hills fifty miles west of Philadelphia, Reading grew rich on railroads, steel, coal, and textiles. But in recent decades, with all of those industries in steep decline, the city has languished. By 2011, it had the highest poverty rate in the country, at 41.3 percent. (The following year, it was surpassed, if barely, by Detroit.) As the recession pummeled Reading's economy following the 2008 market crash, tax revenues fell, which led to a cut of forty-five officers in the police department—despite persistent crime.

Reading police chief William Heim had to figure out how to

get the same or better policing out of a smaller force. So in 2013 he invested in crime prediction software made by PredPol, a Big Data start-up based in Santa Cruz, California. The program processed historical crime data and calculated, hour by hour, where crimes were most likely to occur. The Reading policemen could view the program's conclusions as a series of squares, each one just the size of two football fields. If they spent more time patrolling these squares, there was a good chance they would discourage crime. And sure enough, a year later, Chief Heim announced that burglaries were down by 23 percent.

Predictive programs like PredPol are all the rage in budget-strapped police departments across the country. Departments from Atlanta to Los Angeles are deploying cops in the shifting squares and reporting falling crime rates. New York City uses a similar program, called CompStat. And Philadelphia police are using a local product called HunchLab that includes risk terrain analysis, which incorporates certain features, such as ATMs or convenience stores, that might attract crimes. Like those in the rest of the Big Data industry, the developers of crime prediction software are hurrying to incorporate any information that can boost the accuracy of their models.

If you think about it, hot-spot predictors are similar to the shifting defensive models in baseball that we discussed earlier. Those systems look at the history of each player's hits and then position fielders where the ball is most likely to travel. Crime prediction software carries out similar analysis, positioning cops where crimes appear most likely to occur. Both types of models optimize resources. But a number of the crime prediction models are more sophisticated, because they predict progressions that could lead to waves of crime. PredPol, for example, is based on seismic software: it looks at a crime in one area, incorporates it into historical patterns, and predicts when and where it might occur next.

(One simple correlation it has found: if burglars hit your next-door neighbor's house, batten down the hatches.)

Predictive crime models like PredPol have their virtues. Unlike the crime-stoppers in Steven Spielberg's dystopian movie *Minority Report* (and some ominous real-life initiatives, which we'll get to shortly), the cops don't track down people before they commit crimes. Jeffrey Brantingham, the UCLA anthropology professor who founded PredPol, stressed to me that the model is blind to race and ethnicity. And unlike other programs, including the recidivism risk models we discussed, which are used for sentencing guidelines, PredPol doesn't focus on the individual. Instead, it targets geography. The key inputs are the type and location of each crime and when it occurred. That seems fair enough. And if cops spend more time in the high-risk zones, foiling burglars and car thieves, there's good reason to believe that the community benefits.

But most crimes aren't as serious as burglary and grand theft auto, and that is where serious problems emerge. When police set up their PredPol system, they have a choice. They can focus exclusively on so-called Part 1 crimes. These are the violent crimes, including homicide, arson, and assault, which are usually reported to them. But they can also broaden the focus by including Part 2 crimes, including vagrancy, aggressive panhandling, and selling and consuming small quantities of drugs. Many of these "nuisance" crimes would go unrecorded if a cop weren't there to see them.

These nuisance crimes are endemic to many impoverished neighborhoods. In some places police call them antisocial behavior, or ASB. Unfortunately, including them in the model threatens to skew the analysis. Once the nuisance data flows into a predictive model, more police are drawn into those neighborhoods, where they're more likely to arrest more people. After all, even if their objective is to stop burglaries, murders, and rape, they're bound to have slow periods. It's the nature of patrolling. And if a patrolling cop sees a couple of kids who look no older than sixteen guzzling from a bottle in a brown bag, he stops them. These types of low-level crimes populate their models with more and more dots, and the models send the cops back to the same neighborhood.

This creates a pernicious feedback loop. The policing itself spawns new data, which justifies more policing. And our prisons fill up with hundreds of thousands of people found guilty of victimless crimes. Most of them come from impoverished neighborhoods, and most are black or Hispanic. So even if a model is color blind, the result of it is anything but. In our largely segregated cities, geography is a highly effective proxy for race.

If the purpose of the models is to prevent serious crimes, you might ask why nuisance crimes are tracked at all. The answer is that the link between antisocial behavior and crime has been an article of faith since 1982, when a criminologist named George Kelling teamed up with a public policy expert, James Q. Wilson, to write a seminal article in the *Atlantic Monthly* on so-called broken-windows policing. The idea was that low-level crimes and misdemeanors created an atmosphere of disorder in a neighborhood. This scared law-abiding citizens away. The dark and empty streets they left behind were breeding grounds for serious crime. The antidote was for society to resist the spread of disorder. This included fixing broken windows, cleaning up graffiti-covered subway cars, and taking steps to discourage nuisance crimes.

This thinking led in the 1990s to zero-tolerance campaigns, most famously in New York City. Cops would arrest kids for jumping the subway turnstiles. They'd apprehend people caught sharing a single joint and rumble them around the city in a paddy wagon for hours before eventually booking them. Some credited these energetic campaigns for dramatic falls in violent crimes.

Others disagreed. The authors of the bestselling book *Freakonomics* went so far as to correlate the drop in crime to the legalization of abortion in the 1970s. And plenty of other theories also surfaced, ranging from the falling rates of crack cocaine addiction to the booming 1990s economy. In any case, the zero-tolerance movement gained broad support, and the criminal justice system sent millions of mostly young minority men to prison, many of them for minor offenses.

But zero tolerance actually had very little to do with Kelling and Wilson's "broken-windows" thesis. Their case study focused on what appeared to be a successful policing initiative in Newark, New Jersey. Cops who walked the beat there, according to the program, were supposed to be *highly* tolerant. Their job was to adjust to the neighborhood's own standards of order and to help uphold them. Standards varied from one part of the city to another. In one neighborhood, it might mean that drunks had to keep their bottles in bags and avoid major streets but that side streets were okay. Addicts could sit on stoops but not lie down. The idea was only to make sure the standards didn't fall. The cops, in this scheme, were helping a neighborhood maintain its own order but not imposing their own.

You might think I'm straying a bit from PredPol, mathematics, and WMDs. But each policing approach, from broken windows to zero tolerance, represents a model. Just like my meal planning or the U.S. News Top College ranking, each crime-fighting model calls for certain input data, followed by a series of responses, and each is calibrated to achieve an objective. It's important to look at policing this way, because these mathematical models now dominate law enforcement. And some of them are WMDs.

That said, we can understand why police departments would choose to include nuisance data. Raised on the orthodoxy of zero tolerance, many have little more reason to doubt the link between small crimes and big ones than the correlation between smoke and fire. When police in the British city of Kent tried out PredPol, in 2013, they incorporated nuisance crime data into their model. It seemed to work. They found that the PredPol squares were ten times as efficient as random patrolling and twice as precise as analysis delivered by police intelligence. And what type of crimes did the model best predict? Nuisance crimes. This makes all the sense in the world. A drunk will pee on the same wall, day in and day out, and a junkie will stretch out on the same park bench, while a car thief or a burglar will move about, working hard to anticipate the movements of police.

Even as police chiefs stress the battle against violent crime, it would take remarkable restraint not to let loads of nuisance data flow into their predictive models. More data, it's easy to believe, is better data. While a model focusing only on violent crimes might produce a sparse constellation on the screen, the inclusion of nuisance data would create a fuller and more vivid portrait of lawlessness in the city.

And in most jurisdictions, sadly, such a crime map would track poverty. The high number of arrests in those areas would do nothing but confirm the broadly shared thesis of society's middle and upper classes: that poor people are responsible for their own shortcomings and commit most of a city's crimes.

But what if police looked for different kinds of crimes? That may sound counterintuitive, because most of us, including the police, view crime as a pyramid. At the top is homicide. It's followed by rape and assault, which are more common, and then shoplifting, petty fraud, and even parking violations, which happen all the time. Prioritizing the crimes at the top of the pyramid makes sense. Minimizing violent crime, most would agree, is and should be a central part of a police force's mission.

But how about crimes far removed from the boxes on the

PredPol maps, the ones carried out by the rich? In the 2000s, the kings of finance threw themselves a lavish party. They lied, they bet billions against their own customers, they committed fraud and paid off rating agencies. Enormous crimes were committed there, and the result devastated the global economy for the best part of five years. Millions of people lost their homes, jobs, and health care.

We have every reason to believe that more such crimes are occurring in finance right now. If we've learned anything, it's that the driving goal of the finance world is to make a huge profit, the bigger the better, and that anything resembling self-regulation is worthless. Thanks largely to the industry's wealth and powerful lobbies, finance is underpoliced.

Just imagine if police enforced their zero-tolerance strategy in finance. They would arrest people for even the slightest infraction, whether it was chiseling investors on 401ks, providing misleading guidance, or committing petty frauds. Perhaps SWAT teams would descend on Greenwich, Connecticut. They'd go undercover in the taverns around Chicago's Mercantile Exchange.

Not likely, of course. The cops don't have the expertise for that kind of work. Everything about their jobs, from their training to their bullet-proof vests, is adapted to the mean streets. Clamping down on white-collar crime would require people with different tools and skills. The small and underfunded teams who handle that work, from the FBI to investigators at the Securities and Exchange Commission, have learned through the decades that bankers are virtually invulnerable. They spend heavily on our politicians, which always helps, and are also viewed as crucial to our economy. That protects them. If their banks go south, our economy could go with them. (The poor have no such argument.) So except for a couple of criminal outliers, such as Ponzi-scheme master Bernard Madoff, financiers don't get arrested. As a group, they made it through the 2008 market crash practically unscathed. What could ever burn them now?

My point is that police make choices about where they direct their attention. Today they focus almost exclusively on the poor. That's their heritage, and their mission, as they understand it. And now data scientists are stitching this status quo of the social order into models, like PredPol, that hold ever-greater sway over our lives.

The result is that while PredPol delivers a perfectly useful and even high-minded software tool, it is also a do-it-yourself WMD. In this sense, PredPol, even with the best of intentions, empowers police departments to zero in on the poor, stopping more of them, arresting a portion of those, and sending a subgroup to prison. And the police chiefs, in many cases, if not most, think that they're taking the only sensible route to combating crime. That's where it is, they say, pointing to the highlighted ghetto on the map. And now they have cutting-edge technology (powered by Big Data) reinforcing their position there, while adding precision and "science" to the process.

The result is that we criminalize poverty, believing all the while that our tools are not only scientific but fair.

. . .

One weekend in the spring of 2011, I attended a data "hackathon" in New York City. The goal of such events is to bring together hackers, nerds, mathematicians, and software geeks and to mobilize this brainpower to shine light on the digital systems that wield so much power in our lives. I was paired up with the New York Civil Liberties Union, and our job was to break out the data on one of the NYPD's major anticrime policies, so-called stop, question, and frisk. Known simply as stop and frisk to most people, the practice had drastically increased in the data-driven age of CompStat.

The police regarded stop and frisk as a filtering device for crime. The idea is simple. Police officers stop people who look suspicious to them. It could be the way they're walking or dressed, or their tattoos. The police talk to them and size them up, often while they're spread-eagled against a wall or the hood of a car. They ask for their ID, and they frisk them. Stop enough people, the thinking goes, and you'll no doubt stop loads of petty crimes, and perhaps some big ones. The policy, implemented by Mayor Michael Bloomberg's administration, had loads of public support. Over the previous decade, the number of stops had risen by 600 percent, to nearly seven hundred thousand incidents. The great majority of those stopped were innocent. For them, these encounters were highly unpleasant, even infuriating. Yet many in the public associated the program with the sharp decline of crime in the city. New York, many felt, was safer. And statistics indicated as much. Homicides, which had reached 2,245 in 1990, were down to 515 (and would drop below 400 by 2014).

Everyone knew that an outsized proportion of the people the police stopped were young, dark-skinned men. But how many did they stop? And how often did these encounters lead to arrests or stop crimes? While this information was technically public, much of it was stored in a database that was hard to access. The software didn't work on our computers or flow into Excel spreadsheets. Our job at the hackathon was to break open that program and free the data so that we could all analyze the nature and effectiveness of the stop-and-frisk program.

What we found, to no great surprise, was that an overwhelming majority of these encounters—about 85 percent—involved young African American or Latino men. In certain neighborhoods, many of them were stopped repeatedly. Only 0.1 percent, or one of one thousand stopped, was linked in any way to a violent crime. Yet this filter captured many others for lesser crimes, from drug possession to underage drinking, that might have otherwise gone undiscovered. Some of the targets, as you might expect, got angry, and a good number of those found themselves charged with resisting arrest.

The NYCLU sued the Bloomberg administration, charging that the stop-and-frisk policy was racist. It was an example of uneven policing, one that pushed more minorities into the criminal justice system and into prison. Black men, they argued, were six times more likely to be incarcerated than white men and twenty-one times more likely to be killed by police, at least according to the available data (which is famously underreported).

Stop and frisk isn't exactly a WMD, because it relies on human judgment and is not formalized into an algorithm. But it is built upon a simple and destructive calculation. If police stop one thousand people in certain neighborhoods, they'll uncover, on average, one significant suspect and lots of smaller ones. This isn't so different from the long-shot calculations used by predatory advertisers or spammers. Even when the hit ratio is miniscule, if you give yourself enough chances you'll reach your target. And that helps to explain why the program grew so dramatically under Bloomberg's watch. If stopping six times as many people led to six times the number of arrests, the inconvenience and harassment suffered by thousands upon thousands of innocent people was justified. Weren't *they* interested in stopping crime?

Aspects of stop and frisk were similar to WMDs, though. For example, it had a nasty feedback loop. It ensnared thousands of black and Latino men, many of them for committing the petty crimes and misdemeanors that go on in college frats, unpunished, every Saturday night. But while the great majority of university students were free to sleep off their excesses, the victims of stop and frisk were booked, and some of them dispatched to the hell that is Rikers Island. What's more, each arrest created new data, further justifying the policy.

As stop and frisk grew, the venerable legal concept of probable cause was rendered virtually meaningless, because police were hunting not only people who might have already committed a crime but also those who might commit one in the future. Sometimes, no doubt, they accomplished this goal. By arresting a young man whose suspicious bulge turned out to be an unregistered gun, they might be saving the neighborhood from a murder or armed robbery, or even a series of them. Or maybe not. Whatever the case, there was a logic to stop and frisk, and many found it persuasive.

But was the policy constitutional? In August of 2013, federal judge Shira A. Scheindlin ruled that it was not. She said officers routinely "stopped blacks and Hispanics who would not have been stopped if they were white." Stop and frisk, she wrote, ran afoul of the Fourth Amendment, which protects against unreasonable searches and seizures by the government, and it also failed to provide the equal protection guaranteed by the Fourteenth Amendment. She called for broad reforms to the practice, including increased use of body cameras on patrolling policemen. This would help establish probable cause—or the lack of it—and remove some of the opacity from the stop-and-frisk model. But it would do nothing to address the issue of uneven policing.

While looking at WMDs, we're often faced with a choice between fairness and efficacy. Our legal traditions lean strongly toward fairness. The Constitution, for example, presumes innocence and is engineered to value it. From a modeler's perspective, the presumption of innocence is a constraint, and the result is that some guilty people go free, especially those who can afford good lawyers. Even those found guilty have the right to appeal their verdict, which chews up time and resources. So the system sacrifices enormous efficiencies for the promise of fairness. The Constitution's implicit judgment is that freeing someone who may well have committed a crime, for lack of evidence, poses less of a danger to our society than jailing or executing an innocent person.

WMDs, by contrast, tend to favor efficiency. By their very nature, they feed on data that can be measured and counted. But fairness is squishy and hard to quantify. It is a concept. And computers, for all of their advances in language and logic, still struggle mightily with concepts. They "understand" beauty only as a word associated with the Grand Canyon, ocean sunsets, and grooming tips in *Vogue* magazine. They try in vain to measure "friendship" by counting likes and connections on Facebook. And the concept of fairness utterly escapes them. Programmers don't know how to code for it, and few of their bosses ask them to.

So fairness isn't calculated into WMDs. And the result is massive, industrial production of *unfairness*. If you think of a WMD as a factory, unfairness is the black stuff belching out of the smoke stacks. It's an emission, a toxic one.

The question is whether we as a society are willing to sacrifice a bit of efficiency in the interest of fairness. Should we handicap the models, leaving certain data out? It's possible, for example, that adding gigabytes of data about antisocial behavior might help PredPol predict the mapping coordinates for serious crimes. But this comes at the cost of a nasty feedback loop. So I'd argue that we should discard the data.

It's a tough case to make, similar in many ways to the battles over wiretapping by the National Security Agency. Advocates of the snooping argue that it's important for our safety. And those running our vast national security apparatus will keep pushing for more information to fulfill their mission. They'll continue to encroach on people's privacy until they get the message that they must find a way to do their job within the bounds of the Constitution. It might be harder, but it's necessary.

The other issue is equality. Would society be so willing to sacrifice the concept of probable cause if everyone had to endure the harassment and indignities of stop and frisk? Chicago police have their own stop-and-frisk program. In the name of fairness, what if they sent a bunch of patrollers into the city's exclusive Gold Coast? Maybe they'd arrest joggers for jaywalking from the park across W. North Boulevard or crack down on poodle pooping along Lakeshore Drive. This heightened police presence would probably pick up more drunk drivers and perhaps uncover a few cases of insurance fraud, spousal abuse, or racketeering. Occasionally, just to give everyone a taste of the unvarnished experience, the cops might throw wealthy citizens on the trunks of their cruisers, wrench their arms, and snap on the handcuffs, perhaps while swearing and calling them hateful names.

In time, this focus on the Gold Coast would create data. It would describe an increase in crime there, which would draw even more police into the fray. This would no doubt lead to growing anger and confrontations. I picture a double parker talking back to police, refusing to get out of his Mercedes, and finding himself facing charges for resisting arrest. Yet another Gold Coast crime.

This may sound less than serious. But a crucial part of justice is equality. And that means, among many other things, experiencing criminal justice equally. People who favor policies like stop and frisk should experience it themselves. Justice cannot just be something that one part of society inflicts upon the other.

The noxious effects of uneven policing, whether from stop and frisk or predictive models like PredPol, do not end when the accused are arrested and booked in the criminal justice system. Once there, many of them confront another WMD that I discussed in chapter 1, the recidivism model used for sentencing guidelines. The biased data from uneven policing funnels right into this model. Judges then look to this supposedly scientific analysis, crystallized into a single risk score. And those who take this score seriously have reason to give longer sentences to prisoners who appear to pose a higher risk of committing other crimes.

And why are nonwhite prisoners from poor neighborhoods more likely to commit crimes? According to the data inputs for the recidivism models, it's because they're more likely to be jobless, lack a high school diploma, and have had previous run-ins with the law. And their friends have, too.

Another way of looking at the same data, though, is that these prisoners live in poor neighborhoods with terrible schools and scant opportunities. And they're highly policed. So the chance that an ex-convict returning to that neighborhood will have another brush with the law is no doubt larger than that of a tax fraudster who is released into a leafy suburb. In this system, the poor and nonwhite are punished more for being who they are and living where they live.

What's more, for supposedly scientific systems, the recidivism models are logically flawed. The unquestioned assumption is that locking away "high-risk" prisoners for more time makes society safer. It is true, of course, that prisoners don't commit crimes against society while behind bars. But is it possible that their time in prison has an effect on their behavior once they step out? Is there a chance that years in a brutal environment surrounded by felons might make them more likely, and not less, to commit another crime? Such a finding would undermine the very basis of the recidivism sentencing guidelines. But prison systems, which are awash in data, do not carry out this highly important research.

All too often they use data to justify the workings of the system but not to question or improve the system.

Compare this attitude to the one found at Amazon.com. The giant retailer, like the criminal justice system, is highly focused on a form of recidivism. But Amazon's goal is the opposite. It wants people to come back again and again to buy. Its software system targets recidivism and encourages it.

Now, if Amazon operated like the justice system, it would start by scoring shoppers as potential recidivists. Maybe more of them live in certain area codes or have college degrees. In this case, Amazon would market more to these people, perhaps offering them discounts, and if the marketing worked, those with high recidivist scores would come back to shop more. If viewed superficially, the results would appear to corroborate Amazon's scoring system.

But unlike the WMDs in criminal justice, Amazon does not settle for such glib correlations. The company runs a data laboratory. And if it wants to find out what drives shopping recidivism, it carries out research. Its data scientists don't just study zip codes and education levels. They also inspect people's experience within the Amazon ecosystem. They might start by looking at the patterns of all the people who shopped once or twice at Amazon and never returned. Did they have trouble at checkout? Did their packages arrive on time? Did a higher percentage of them post a bad review? The questions go on and on, because the future of the company hinges upon a system that learns continually, one that figures out what makes customers tick.

If I had a chance to be a data scientist for the justice system, I would do my best to dig deeply to learn what goes on inside those prisons and what impact those experiences might have on prisoners' behavior. I'd first look into solitary confinement. Hundreds of thousands of prisoners are kept for twenty-three hours a day in these prisons within prisons, most of them no bigger than a horse stall. Researchers have found that time in solitary produces deep feelings of hopelessness and despair. Could that have any impact on recidivism? That's a test I'd love to run, but I'm not sure the data is even collected.

How about rape? In *Unfair: The New Science of Criminal Injustice*, Adam Benforado writes that certain types of prisoners are targeted for rape in prisons. The young and small of stature are especially vulnerable, as are the mentally disabled. Some of these people live for years as sex slaves. It's another important topic for analysis that anyone with the relevant data and expertise could work out, but prison systems have thus far been uninterested in cataloging the long-term effects of this abuse.

A serious scientist would also search for positive signals from the prison experience. What's the impact of more sunlight, more sports, better food, literacy training? Maybe these factors will improve convicts' behavior after they go free. More likely, they'll have varying impact. A serious justice system research program would delve into the effects of each of these elements, how they work together, and which people they're most likely to help. The goal, if data were used constructively, would be to optimize prisons—much the way companies like Amazon optimize websites or supply chains—for the benefit of both the prisoners and society at large.

But prisons have every incentive to avoid this data-driven approach. The PR risks are too great—no city wants to be the subject of a scathing report in the *New York Times*. And, of course, there's big money riding on the overcrowded prison system. Privately run prisons, which house only 10 percent of the incarcerated population, are a $5 billion industry. Like airlines, the private prisons make profits only when running at high capacity. Too much poking and prodding might threaten that income source.

So instead of analyzing prisons and optimizing them, we deal with them as black boxes. Prisoners go in and disappear from our view. Nastiness no doubt occurs, but behind thick walls. What goes on in there? Don't ask. The current models stubbornly stick to the dubious and unquestioned hypothesis that more prison time for supposedly high-risk prisoners makes us safer. And if studies appear to upend that logic, they can be easily ignored.

And this is precisely what happens. Consider a recidivism study by Michigan economics professor Michael Mueller-Smith. After studying 2.6 million criminal court records in Harris County, Texas, he concluded that the longer inmates in Harris County, Texas, spent locked up, the greater the chance that they would fail to find employment upon release, would require food stamps and other public assistance, and would commit further crimes. But to turn those conclusions into smart policy and better justice, politicians will have to take a stand on behalf of a feared minority that many (if not most) voters would much prefer to ignore. It's a tough sell.

· · ·

Stop and frisk may seem intrusive and unfair, but in short time it will also be viewed as primitive. That's because police are bringing back tools and techniques from the global campaign against terrorism and focusing them on local crime fighting. In San Diego, for example, police are not only asking the people they stop for identification, or frisking them. On occasion, they also take photos of them with iPads and send them to a cloud-based facial recognition service, which matches them against a database of criminals and suspects. According to a report in the *New York Times*, San Diego police used this facial recognition program on 20,600 people between 2011 and 2015. They also probed many of them with mouth swabs to harvest DNA.

Advances in facial recognition technology will soon allow for much broader surveillance. Officials in Boston, for example, were considering using security cameras to scan thousands of faces at outdoor concerts. This data would be uploaded to a service that could match each face against a million others per second. In the end, officials decided against it. Concern for privacy, on that occasion, trumped efficiency. But this won't always be the case.

As technology advances, we're sure to see a dramatic growth of surveillance. The good news, if you want to call it that, is that once thousands of security cameras in our cities and towns are sending up our images for analysis, police won't have to discriminate as much. And the technology will no doubt be useful for tracking down suspects, as happened in the Boston Marathon bombing. But it means that we'll all be subject to a digital form of stop and frisk, our faces matched against databases of known criminals and terrorists.

The focus then may well shift toward spotting *potential* lawbreakers—not just neighborhoods or squares on a map but individuals. These preemptive campaigns, already well established in the fight against terrorism, are a breeding ground for WMDs.

In 2009, the Chicago Police Department received a $2 million grant from the National Institute of Justice to develop a predictive program for crime. The theory behind Chicago's winning application was that with enough research and data they might be able to demonstrate that the spread of crime, like epidemics, follows certain patterns. It can be predicted and, hopefully, prevented.

The scientific leader of the Chicago initiative was Miles Wernick, the director of the Medical Imaging Research Center at the Illinois Institute of Technology (IIT). Decades earlier, Wernick had helped the US military analyze data to pick out battlefield targets. He had since moved to medical data analysis, including the progression of dementia. But like most data scientists, he didn't see his expertise as tethered to a specific industry. He spotted patterns. And his focus in Chicago would be the patterns of crime, and of criminals.

The early efforts of Wernick's team focused on singling out hot spots for crime, much as PredPol does. But the Chicago team went much further. They developed a list of the approximately four hundred people most likely to commit a violent crime. And it ranked them on the probability that they would be involved in a homicide.

One of the people on the list, a twenty-two-year-old high school dropout named Robert McDaniel, answered his door one summer day in 2013 and found himself facing a police officer. McDaniel later told the *Chicago Tribune* that he had no history of gun violations and had never been charged with a violent crime. Like most of the young men in Austin, his dangerous West Side neighborhood, McDaniel had had brushes with the law, and he knew plenty of people caught up in the criminal justice system. The policewoman, he said, told him that the force had its eye on him and to watch out.

Part of the analysis that led police to McDaniel involved his social network. He knew criminals. And there is no denying that people are statistically more likely than not to behave like the people they spend time with. Facebook, for example, has found that friends who communicate often are far more likely to click on the same advertisement. Birds of a feather, statistically speaking, *do* fly together.

And to be fair to Chicago police, they're not arresting people like Robert McDaniel, at least not yet. The goal of the police in this exercise is to save lives. If the four hundred people who appear most likely to commit violent crimes receive a knock on the door and a warning, maybe some of them will think twice before packing a gun.

But let's consider McDaniel's case in terms of fairness. He happened to grow up in a poor and dangerous neighborhood. In this, he was unlucky. He has been surrounded by crime, and many of his acquaintances have gotten caught up in it. And largely because of these circumstances—and not his own actions—he has been deemed dangerous. Now the police have their eye on him. And if he behaves foolishly, as millions of other Americans do on a regular basis, if he buys drugs or gets into a barroom fight or carries an unregistered handgun, the full force of the law will fall down on him, and probably much harder than it would on most of us. After all, he's been warned.

I would argue that the model that led police to Robert McDaniel's door has the wrong objective. Instead of simply trying to eradicate crimes, police should be attempting to build relationships in the neighborhood. This was one of the pillars of the original "broken-windows" study. The cops were on foot, talking to people, trying to help them uphold their own community standards. But that objective, in many cases, has been lost, steamrollered by models that equate arrests with safety.

This isn't the case everywhere. I recently visited Camden, New Jersey, which was the murder capital of the country in 2011. I found that the police department in Camden, rebuilt and placed under state control in 2012, had a dual mandate: lowering crime and engendering community trust. If building trust is the objective, an arrest may well become a last resort, not the first. This more empathetic approach could lead to warmer relations between the police and the policed, and fewer of the tragedies we've seen in recent years—the police killings of young black men and the riots that follow them.

From a mathematical point of view, however, trust is hard to quantify. That's a challenge for people building models. Sadly, it's far simpler to keep counting arrests, to build models that assume we're birds of a feather and treat us as such. Innocent people surrounded by criminals get treated badly, and criminals surrounded by a law-abiding public get a pass. And because of the strong correlation between poverty and reported crime, the poor continue to get caught up in these digital dragnets. The rest of us barely have to think about them.

6

INELIGIBLE TO SERVE

Getting a Job

A few years ago, a young man named Kyle Behm took a leave from his studies at Vanderbilt University. He was suffering from bipolar disorder and needed time to get treatment. A year and a half later, Kyle was healthy enough to return to his studies at a different school. Around that time, he learned from a friend about a part-time job at Kroger. It was just a minimum-wage job at a supermarket, but it seemed like a sure thing. His friend, who was leaving the job, could vouch for him. For a high-achieving student like Kyle, the application looked like a formality.

But Kyle didn't get called back for an interview. When he inquired, his friend explained to him that he had been "red-lighted" by the personality test he'd taken when he applied for the job. The test was part of an employee selection program developed by Kronos, a workforce management company based outside of Boston. When Kyle told his father, Roland, an attorney, what had happened, his father asked him what kind of questions had appeared on the test. Kyle said that they were very much like the "Five Factor Model" test, which he'd been given at the hospital. That test grades people for extraversion, agreeableness, conscientiousness, neuroticism, and openness to ideas.

At first, losing one minimum-wage job because of a questionable test didn't seem like such a big deal. Roland Behm urged his son to apply elsewhere. But Kyle came back each time with the same news. The companies he was applying to were all using the same test, and he wasn't getting offers. Roland later recalled: "Kyle said to me, 'I had an almost perfect SAT and I was at Vanderbilt a few years ago. If I can't get a part-time minimum-wage job, how broken am I?' And I said, 'I don't think you're that broken.'"

But Roland Behm was bewildered. Questions about mental health appeared to be blackballing his son from the job market. He decided to look into it and soon learned that the use of personality tests for hiring was indeed widespread among large corporations. And yet he found very few legal challenges to this practice. As he explained to me, people who apply for a job and are redlighted rarely learn that they were rejected because of their test results. Even when they do, they're not likely to contact a lawyer.

Behm went on to send notices to seven companies—Finish Line, Home Depot, Kroger, Lowe's, PetSmart, Walgreen Co., and Yum Brands—informing them of his intent to file a class-action suit alleging that the use of the exam during the job application process was unlawful.

The suit, as I write this, is still pending. Arguments are likely to focus on whether the Kronos test can be considered a medical exam, the use of which in hiring is illegal under the Americans with Disabilities Act of 1990. If this turns out to be the case, the court will have to determine whether the hiring companies themselves are responsible for running afoul of the ADA, or if Kronos is.

The question for this book is how automatic systems judge us when we seek jobs and what criteria they evaluate. Already, we've seen WMDs poisoning the college admissions process, both for the rich and for the middle class. Meanwhile, WMDs in criminal justice rope in millions, the great majority of them poor, most of whom never had the chance to attend college at all. Members of each of these groups face radically different challenges. But they have something in common, too. They all ultimately need a job.

Finding work used to be largely a question of whom you knew. In fact, Kyle Behm was following the traditional route when he applied for work at Kroger. His friend had alerted him to the opening and put in a good word. For decades, that was how people got a foot in the door, whether at grocers, the docks, banks, or law firms. Candidates then usually faced an interview, where a manager would try to get a feel for them. All too often this translated into a single basic judgment: Is this person like me (or others I get along with)? The result was a lack of opportunity for job seekers without a friend inside, especially if they came from a different race, ethnic group, or religion. Women also found themselves excluded by this insider game.

Companies like Kronos brought science into corporate human resources in part to make the process fairer. Founded in the 1970s by MIT graduates, Kronos's first product was a new kind of punch clock, one equipped with a microprocessor, which added up employees' hours and reported them automatically. This may sound banal, but it was the beginning of the electronic push (now blazing along at warp speed) to track and optimize a workforce.

As Kronos grew, it developed a broad range of software tools for workforce management, including a software program, Workforce Ready HR, that promised to eliminate "the guesswork" in hiring, according to its web page: "We can help you screen, hire, and onboard candidates most likely to be productive—the best-fit employees who will perform better and stay on the job longer."

Kronos is part of a burgeoning industry. The hiring business is automating, and many of the new programs include personality tests like the one Kyle Behm took. It is now a $500 million annual business and is growing by 10 to 15 percent a year, according to Hogan Assessment Systems Inc., a testing company. Such tests now are used on 60 to 70 percent of prospective workers in the United States, up from 30 to 40 percent about five years ago, estimates Josh Bersin of the consulting firm Deloitte.

Naturally, these hiring programs can't incorporate information about how the candidate would actually perform at the company. That's in the future, and therefore unknown. So like many other Big Data programs, they settle for proxies. And as we've seen, proxies are bound to be inexact and often unfair. In fact, the Supreme Court ruled in a 1971 case, *Griggs v. Duke Power Company*, that intelligence tests for hiring were discriminatory and therefore illegal. One would think that case might have triggered some soul-searching. But instead the industry simply opted for replacements, including personality tests like one that red-flagged Kyle Behm.

Even putting aside the issues of fairness and legality, research suggests that personality tests are poor predictors of job performance. Frank Schmidt, a business professor at the University of Iowa, analyzed a century of workplace productivity data to measure the predictive value of various selection processes. Personality tests ranked low on the scale—they were only one-third as predictive as cognitive exams, and also far below reference checks. This is particularly galling because certain personality tests, research shows, can actually help employees gain insight into themselves. They can also be used for team building and for enhancing communication. After all, they create a situation in which people think explicitly about how to work together. That intention alone might end up creating a better working environment. In other words, if we define the goal as a happier worker, personality tests might end up being a useful tool.

But instead they're being used as a filter to weed out applicants. "The primary purpose of the test," said Roland Behm, "is not to find the best employee. It's to exclude as many people as possible as cheaply as possible."

You might think that personality tests would be easy to game. If you go online to take a Five Factor Personality Test, it looks like a cinch. One question asks: "Have frequent mood swings?" It would probably be smart to answer "very inaccurate." Another asks: "Get mad easily?" Again, check no. Not too many companies want to hire hotheads.

In fact, companies can get in trouble for screening out applicants on the basis of such questions. Regulators in Rhode Island found that CVS Pharmacy was illegally screening out applicants with mental illnesses when a personality test required respondents to agree or disagree to such statements as "People do a lot of things that make you angry" and "There's no use having close friends; they always let you down." More intricate questions, which are harder to game, are more likely to keep the companies out of trouble. Consequently, many of the tests used today force applicants to make difficult choices, likely leaving them with a sinking feeling of "Damned if I do, damned if I don't."

McDonald's, for example, asked prospective workers to choose which of the following best described them:

"It is difficult to be cheerful when there are many problems to take care of" *or* "Sometimes, I need a push to get started on my work."

The *Wall Street Journal* asked an industrial psychologist, Tomas Chamorro-Premuzic, to analyze thorny questions like these. The first item, Chamorro-Premuzic said, captured "individual differences in neuroticism and conscientiousness"; the second, "low ambition and drive." So the prospective worker is pleading guilty to being either high-strung or lazy.

A Kroger question was far simpler: Which adjective best describes you at work, unique or orderly?

Answering "unique," said Chamorro-Premuzic, captures "high self concept, openness and narcissism," while "orderly" expresses conscientiousness and self control.

Note that there's no option to answer "all of the above." Prospective workers must pick one option, without a clue as to how the program will interpret it. And some of the analysis will draw unflattering conclusions. If you go to a kindergarten class in much of the country, for example, you'll often hear teachers emphasize to the children that they're unique. It's an attempt to boost their self-esteem and, of course, it's true. Yet twelve years later, when that student chooses "unique" on a personality test while applying for a minimum-wage job, the program might read the answer as a red flag: Who wants a workforce peopled with narcissists?

Defenders of the tests note that they feature lots of questions and that no single answer can disqualify an applicant. Certain patterns of answers, however, can and do disqualify them. And we do not know what those patterns are. We're not told what the tests are looking for. The process is entirely opaque.

What's worse, after the model is calibrated by technical experts, it receives precious little feedback. Again, sports provide a good contrast here. Most professional basketball teams employ data geeks, who run models that analyze players by a series of metrics, including foot speed, vertical leap, free-throw percentage, and a host of other variables. When the draft comes, the Los Angeles Lakers might pass on a hotshot point guard from Duke because his assist statistics are low. Point guards have to be good passers. Yet in the following season they're dismayed to see that the rejected player goes on to win Rookie of the Year for the Utah Jazz and leads the league in assists. In such a case, the Lakers can return to their model to see what they got wrong. Maybe his college team was relying on him to score, which punished his assist numbers. Or perhaps he learned something important about passing in Utah. Whatever the case, they can work to improve their model.

Now imagine that Kyle Behm, after getting red-lighted at Kroger, goes on to land a job at McDonald's. He turns into a stellar employee. He's managing the kitchen within four months and the entire franchise a year later. Will anyone at Kroger go back to the personality test and investigate how they could have gotten it so wrong?

Not a chance, I'd say. The difference is this: Basketball teams are managing individuals, each one potentially worth millions of dollars. Their analytics engines are crucial to their competitive advantage, and they are hungry for data. Without constant feedback, their systems grow outdated and dumb. The companies hiring minimum-wage workers, by contrast, are managing herds. They slash expenses by replacing human resources professionals with machines, and those machines filter large populations into more manageable groups. Unless something goes haywire in the workforce—an outbreak of kleptomania, say, or plummeting productivity—the company has little reason to tweak the filtering model. It's doing its job—even if it misses out on potential stars.

The company may be satisfied with the status quo, but the victims of its automatic systems suffer. And as you might expect,

I consider personality tests in hiring departments to be WMDs. They check all the boxes. First, they are in widespread use and have enormous impact. The Kronos exam, with all of its flaws, is scaled across much of the hiring economy. Under the previous status quo, employers no doubt had biases. But those biases varied from company to company, which might have cracked open a door somewhere for people like Kyle Behm. That's increasingly untrue. And Kyle was, in some sense, lucky. Job candidates, especially those applying for minimum-wage work, get rejected all the time and rarely find out why. It was just chance that Kyle's friend happened to hear about the reason for his rejection and told him about it. Even then, the case against the big Kronos users would likely have gone nowhere if Kyle's father hadn't been a lawyer, one with enough time and money to mount a broad legal challenge. This is rarely the case for low-level job applicants.*

Finally, consider the feedback loop that the Kronos personality test engenders. Red-lighting people with certain mental health issues prevents them from having a normal job and leading a normal life, further isolating them. This is exactly what the Americans with Disabilities Act is supposed to prevent.

• • •

The majority of job applicants, thankfully, are not blackballed by automatic systems. But they still face the challenge of moving their application to the top of the pile and landing an interview. This has long been a problem for racial and ethnic minorities, as well as women.

In 2001 and 2002, before the expansion of automatic résumé

---

* Yes, it's true that many college-bound students labor for a summer or two in minimum-wage jobs. But if they have a miserable experience there, or are misjudged by an arbitrary WMD, it only reinforces the message that they should apply themselves at school and leave such hellish jobs behind.

readers, researchers from the University of Chicago and MIT sent out five thousand phony résumés for job openings advertised in the *Boston Globe* and the *Chicago Tribune*. The jobs ranged from clerical work to customer service and sales. Each of the résumés was modeled for race. Half featured typically white names like Emily Walsh and Brendan Baker, while the others with similar qualifications carried names like Lakisha Washington and Jamaal Jones, which would sound African American. The researchers found that the white names got 50 percent more callbacks than the black ones. But a secondary finding was perhaps even more striking. The white applicants with strong résumés got much more attention than whites with weaker ones; when it came to white applicants, it seemed, the hiring managers were paying attention. But among blacks, the stronger résumés barely made a difference. The hiring market, clearly, was still poisoned by prejudice.

The ideal way to circumvent such prejudice is to consider applicants blindly. Orchestras, which had long been dominated by men, famously started in the 1970s to hold auditions with the musician hidden behind a sheet. Connections and reputations suddenly counted for nothing. Nor did the musician's race or alma mater. The music from behind the sheet spoke for itself. Since then, the percentage of women playing in major orchestras has leapt by a factor of five—though they still make up only a quarter of the musicians.

The trouble is that few professions can engineer such an even-handed tryout for job applicants. Musicians behind the sheet can actually perform the job they're applying for, whether it's a Dvorak cello concerto or bossa nova on guitar. In other professions, employers have to hunt through résumés, looking for qualities that might predict success.

As you might expect, human resources departments rely on

automatic systems to winnow down piles of résumés. In fact, some 72 percent of résumés are never seen by human eyes. Computer programs flip through them, pulling out the skills and experiences that the employer is looking for. Then they score each résumé as a match for the job opening. It's up to the people in the human resources department to decide where the cutoff is, but the more candidates they can eliminate with this first screening, the fewer human-hours they'll have to spend processing the top matches.

So job applicants must craft their résumés with that automatic reader in mind. It's important, for example, to sprinkle the résumé liberally with words the specific job opening is looking for. This could include positions (sales manager, chief financial officer, software architect), languages (Mandarin, Java), or honors (summa cum laude, Eagle Scout).

Those with the latest information learn what machines appreciate and what tangles them up. Images, for example, are useless. Most résumé scanners don't yet process them. And fancy fonts do nothing but confuse the machines, says Mona Abdel-Halim. She's the cofounder of Resunate.com, a job application tool. The safe ones, she says, are plain vanilla fonts, like Ariel and Courier. And forget about symbols such as arrows. They only confuse things, preventing the automatic systems from correctly parsing the information.

The result of these programs, much as with college admissions, is that those with the money and resources to prepare their résumés come out on top. Those who don't take these steps may never know that they're sending their résumés into a black hole. It's one more example in which the wealthy and informed get the edge and the poor are more likely to lose out.

To be fair, the résumé business has always had one sort of bias or another. In previous generations, those in the know were careful to organize the résumé items clearly and consistently, type them on a quality computer, like an IBM Selectric, and print them on paper with a high rag content. Such résumés were more likely to make it past human screeners. More times than not, handwritten résumés, or ones with smudges from mimeograph machines, ended up in the circular file. So in this sense, the unequal paths to opportunity are nothing new. They have simply returned in a new incarnation, this time to guide society's winners past electronic gatekeepers.

The unequal treatment at the hands of these gatekeepers extends far beyond résumés. Our livelihoods increasingly depend on our ability to make our case to machines. The clearest example of this is Google. For businesses, whether it's a bed-and-breakfast or an auto repair shop, success hinges on showing up on the first page of search results. Now individuals face similar challenges, whether trying to get a foot in the door of a company, to climb the ranks—or even to survive waves of layoffs. The key is to learn what the machines are looking for. But here too, in a digital universe touted to be fair, scientific, and democratic, the insiders find a way to gain a crucial edge.

●●●

In the 1970s, the admissions office at St. George's Hospital Medical School, in the South London district of Tooting, saw an opportunity. They received more than twelve applications for each of their 150 openings each year. Combing through all those applications was a lot of work, requiring multiple screeners. And since each of those screeners had different ideas and predilections, the process was somewhat capricious. Would it be possible to program a computer to sort through the applications and reduce the field to a more manageable number?

Big organizations, like the Pentagon and IBM, were already using computers for such work. But for a medical school to come up with its own automated assessment program in the late '70s, just as Apple was releasing its first personal computer, represented a bold experiment.

It turned out, however, to be an utter failure. St. George was not only precocious in its use of mathematical modeling, it seemed, but also an unwitting pioneer in WMDs.

As with so many WMDs, the problem began at the get-go, when the administrators established the model's twin objectives. The first was to boost efficiency, letting the machine handle much of the grunt work. It would automatically cull down the two thousand applications to five hundred, at which point humans would take over with a lengthy interviewing process. The second objective was fairness. The computer would remain unswayed by administrators' moods or prejudices, or by urgent entreaties from lords or cabinet ministers. In this first automatic screening, each applicant would be judged by the same criteria.

And what would those criteria be? That looked like the easy part. St. George's already had voluminous records of screenings from the previous years. The job was to teach the computerized system how to replicate the same procedures that human beings had been following. As I'm sure you can guess, these inputs were the problem. The computer learned from the humans how to discriminate, and it carried out this work with breathtaking efficiency.

In fairness to the administrators at St. George's, not all of the discrimination in the training data was overtly racist. A good number of the applications with foreign names, or from foreign addresses, came from people who clearly had not mastered the English language. Instead of considering the possibility that great doctors could learn English, which is obvious today, the tendency was simply to reject them. (After all, the school had to discard three-quarters of the applications, and that seemed like an easy place to start.)

Now, while the human beings at St. George's had long tossed out applications littered with grammatical mistakes and misspellings, the computer—illiterate itself—could hardly follow suit. But it could correlate the rejected applications of the past with birthplaces and, to a lesser degree, surnames. So people from certain places, like Africa, Pakistan, and immigrant neighborhoods of the United Kingdom, received lower overall scores and were not invited to interviews. An outsized proportion of these people were nonwhite. The human beings had also rejected female applicants, with the all-too-common justification that their careers would likely be interrupted by the duties of motherhood. The machine, naturally, did the same.

In 1988, the British government's Commission for Racial Equality found the medical school guilty of racial and gender discrimination in its admissions policy. As many as sixty of the two thousand applicants every year, according to the commission, may have been refused an interview purely because of their race, ethnicity, or gender.

The solution for the statisticians at St. George's—and for those in other industries—would be to build a digital version of a blind audition eliminating proxies such as geography, gender, race, or name to focus only on data relevant to medical education. The key is to analyze the skills each candidate brings to the school, not to judge him or her by comparison with people who seem similar. What's more, a bit of creative thinking at St. George's could have addressed the challenges facing women and foreigners. The *British Medical Journal* report accompanying the commission's judgment said as much. If language and child care issues posed problems for otherwise solid candidates, the solution was not to reject those candidates but instead to provide them with help—whether English classes or onsite day care—to pull them through.

This is a point I'll be returning to in future chapters: we've seen time and again that mathematical models can sift through data to locate people who are likely to face great challenges, whether from crime, poverty, or education. It's up to society whether to use that intelligence to reject and punish them—or to reach out to them with the resources they need. We can use the scale and efficiency that make WMDs so pernicious in order to help people. It all depends on the objective we choose.

• • •

So far in this chapter, we've been looking at models that filter out job candidates. For most companies, those WMDs are designed to cut administrative costs and to reduce the risk of bad hires (or ones that might require more training). The objective of the filters, in short, is to save money.

HR departments, of course, are also eager to save money through the hiring choices they make. One of the biggest expenses for a company is workforce turnover, commonly called churn. Replacing a worker earning $50,000 a year costs a company about $10,000, or 20 percent of that worker's yearly pay, according to the Center for American Progress. Replacing a high-level employee can cost multiples of that—as much as two years of salary.

Naturally, many hiring models attempt to calculate the likelihood that each job candidate will stick around. Evolv, Inc., now a part of Cornerstone OnDemand, helped Xerox scout out prospects for its calling center, which employs more than forty thousand people. The churn model took into account some of the metrics you might expect, including the average time people stuck around on previous jobs. But they also found some intriguing correlations. People the system classified as "creative types" tended to stay longer at the job, while those who scored high on "inquisitiveness" were more likely to set their questioning minds toward other opportunities.

But the most problematic correlation had to do with geography. Job applicants who lived farther from the job were more likely to churn. This makes sense: long commutes are a pain. But Xerox managers noticed another correlation. Many of the people suffering those long commutes were coming from poor neighborhoods. So Xerox, to its credit, removed that highly correlated churn data from its model. The company sacrificed a bit of efficiency for fairness.

While churn analysis focuses on the candidates most likely to fail, the more strategically vital job for HR departments is to locate future stars, the people whose intelligence, inventiveness, and drive can change the course of an entire enterprise. In the higher echelons of the economy, companies are on the hunt for employees who think creatively and work well in teams. So the modelers' challenge is to pinpoint, in the vast world of Big Data, the bits of information that correlate with originality and social skills.

Résumés alone certainly don't cut it. Most of the items listed there—the prestigious university, the awards, even the skills— are crude proxies for high-quality work. While there's no doubt some correlation between tech prowess and a degree from a top school, it's far from perfect. Plenty of software talent comes from elsewhere—consider the high school hackers. What's more, résumés are full of puffery and sometimes even lies. With a quick search through LinkedIn or Facebook, a system can look further afield, identifying some of a candidate's friends and colleagues. But it's still hard to turn that data into a prediction that a certain engineer might be a perfect fit for a twelve-member consultancy in Palo Alto or Fort Worth. Finding the person to fill a role like that requires a far broader sweep of data and a more ambitious model.

A pioneer in this field is Gild, a San Francisco–based start-up. Extending far beyond a prospect's alma mater or résumé, Gild sorts through millions of job sites, analyzing what it calls each person's "social data." The company develops profiles of job candidates for its customers, mostly tech companies, keeping them up to date as the candidates add new skills. Gild claims that it can even predict when a star employee is likely to change jobs and can alert its customer companies when it's the right time to make an offer. But Gild's model attempts to quantify and also *qualify* each worker's "social capital." How integral is this person to the community of fellow programmers? Do they share and contribute code? Say a Brazilian coder—Pedro, let's call him—lives in São Paulo and spends every evening from dinner to one in the morning in communion with fellow coders the world over, solving cloud-computing problems or brainstorming gaming algorithms on sites like GitHub or Stack Overflow. The model could attempt to gauge Pedro's passion (which probably gets a high score) and his level of engagement with others. It would also evaluate the skill and social importance of his contacts. Those with larger followings would count for more. If his principal online contact happened to be Google's Sergey Brin, or Palmer Luckey, founder of the virtual reality maker Oculus VR, Pedro's social score would no doubt shoot through the roof.

But models like Gild's rarely receive such explicit signals from the data. So they cast a wider net, in search of correlations to workplace stardom wherever they can find them. And with more than six million coders in their database, the company can find all kinds of patterns. Vivienne Ming, Gild's chief scientist, said in an interview with *Atlantic Monthly* that Gild had found a bevy of talent frequenting a certain Japanese manga site. If Pedro spends time at that comic-book site, of course, it doesn't predict super-stardom. But it does nudge up his score.

That makes sense for Pedro. But certain workers might be doing something else offline, which even the most sophisticated algorithm couldn't infer—at least not today. They might be taking care of children, for example, or perhaps attending a book group. The fact that prospects don't spend six hours discussing manga every evening shouldn't be counted against them. And if, like most of techdom, that manga site is dominated by males and has a sexual tone, a good number of the women in the industry will probably avoid it.

Despites these issues, Gild is just one player. It doesn't have the clout of a global giant and is not positioned to set a single industry standard. Compared to some of the horrors we've seen—the predatory ads burying families in debt and the personality tests excluding people from opportunities—Gild is tame. Its category of predictive model has more to do with rewarding people than punishing them. No doubt the analysis is uneven: some potential stars are undoubtedly overlooked. But I don't think the talent miners yet rise to the level of a WMD.

Still, it's important to note that these hiring and "onboarding" models are ever-evolving. The world of data continues to expand, with each of us producing ever-growing streams of updates about our lives. All of this data will feed our potential employers, giving them insights into us.

Will those insights be tested, or simply used to justify the status quo and reinforce prejudices? When I consider the sloppy and self-serving ways that companies use data, I'm often reminded of phrenology, a pseudoscience that was briefly the rage in the nineteenth century. Phrenologists would run their fingers over the patient's skull, probing for bumps and indentations. Each one, they thought, was linked to personality traits that existed in twenty-seven regions of the brain. Usually, the conclusion of the phrenologist jibed with the observations he made. If a patient was morbidly anxious or suffering from alcoholism, the skull probe would usually find bumps and dips that correlated with that observation—which, in turn, bolstered faith in the science of phrenology.

Phrenology was a model that relied on pseudoscientific nonsense to make authoritative pronouncements, and for decades it went untested. Big Data can fall into the same trap. Models like the ones that red-lighted Kyle Behm and blackballed foreign medical students at St. George's can lock people out, even when the "science" inside them is little more than a bundle of untested assumptions.

SWEATING BULLETS

On the Job

Workers at major corporations in America recently came up with a new verb: *clopening*. That's when an employee works late one night to close the store or café and then returns a few hours later, before dawn, to open it. Having the same employee closing and opening, or clopening, often makes logistical sense for a company. But it leads to sleep-deprived workers and crazy schedules.

Wildly irregular schedules are becoming increasingly common, and they especially affect low-wage workers at companies like Starbucks, McDonald's, and Walmart. A lack of notice compounds the problem. Many employees find out only a day or two in advance that they'll have to work a Wednesday-night shift or handle rush hour on Friday. It throws their lives into chaos and wreaks havoc on child care plans. Meals are catch as catch can, as is sleep.

These irregular schedules are a product of the data economy. In the last chapter, we saw how WMDs sift through job candidates, blackballing some and ignoring many more. We saw how the software often encodes poisonous prejudices, learning from past records just how to be unfair. Here we continue the journey on to the job, where efficiency-focused WMDs treat workers as cogs in a machine. Clopening is just one product of this trend, which is likely to grow as surveillance extends into the workplace, providing more grist for the data economy.

For decades, before companies were swimming in data, scheduling was anything but a science. Imagine a family-owned hardware store whose clerks work from 9 to 5, six days a week. One year, the daughter goes to college. And when she comes back for the summer she sees the business with fresh eyes. She notices that practically no one comes to the store on Tuesday mornings. The clerk web-surfs on her phone, uninterrupted. That's a revenue drain. Meanwhile, on Saturdays, muttering customers wait in long lines.

These observations provide valuable data, and she helps her parents model the business to it. They start by closing the store on Tuesday mornings, and they hire a part-timer to help with the Saturday crush. These changes add a bit of intelligence to the dumb and inflexible status quo.

With Big Data, that college freshman is replaced by legions of PhDs with powerful computers in tow. Businesses can now analyze customer traffic to calculate exactly how many employees they will need each hour of the day. The goal, of course, is to spend as little money as possible, which means keeping staffing at the bare minimum while making sure that reinforcements are on hand for the busy times.

You might think that these patterns would repeat week after week, and that companies could simply make adjustments to their fixed schedules, just like the owners of our hypothetical hardware store. But new software scheduling programs offer far more sophisticated options. They process new streams of ever-changing data, from the weather to pedestrian patterns. A rainy afternoon, for example, will likely drive people from the park into cafés. So they'll need more staffing, at least for an hour or two. High school football on Friday night might mean more foot traffic on Main Street, but only before and after the game, not during it. Twitter volume suggests that 26 percent more shoppers will rush out to tomorrow's Black Friday sales than did last year. Conditions change, hour by hour, and the workforce must be deployed to match the fluctuating demand. Otherwise the company is wasting money.

The money saved, naturally, comes straight from employees' pockets. Under the inefficient status quo, workers had not only predictable hours but also a certain amount of downtime. You could argue that they benefited from inefficiency: some were able to read on the job, even study. Now, with software choreographing the work, every minute should be busy. And these minutes will come whenever the program demands it, even if it means clopening from Friday to Saturday.

In 2014, the *New York Times* ran a story about a harried single mother named Jannette Navarro, who was trying to work her way through college as a barista at Starbucks while caring for her four-year-old. The ever-changing schedule, including the occasional clopening, made her life almost impossible and put regular day care beyond reach. She had to put school on hold. The only thing she could schedule was work. And her story was typical. According to US government data, two-thirds of food service workers and more than half of retail workers find out about scheduling changes with notice of a week or less—often just a day or two, which can leave them scrambling to arrange transportation or child care.

Within weeks of the article's publication, the major corporations it mentioned announced that they would adjust their scheduling practices. Embarrassed by the story, the employers promised to add a single constraint to their model. They would eliminate clopenings and learn to live with slightly less robust optimization. Starbucks, whose brand hinges more than most on fair treatment of workers, went further, saying that the company would adjust the software to reduce the scheduling nightmares for its 130,000 baristas. All work hours would be posted at least one week in advance.

A year later, however, Starbucks was failing to meet these targets, or even to eliminate the clopenings, according to a follow-up report in the *Times*. The trouble was that minimal staffing was baked into the culture. In many companies, managers' pay is contingent upon the efficiency of their staff as measured by revenue per employee hour. Scheduling software helps them boost these numbers and their own compensation. Even when executives tell managers to loosen up, they often resist. It goes against everything they've been taught. What's more, at Starbucks, if a manager exceeds his or her "labor budget," a district manager is alerted, said one employee. And that could lead to a write-up. It's usually easier just to change someone's schedule, even if it means violating the corporate pledge to provide one week's notice.

In the end, the business models of publicly traded companies like Starbucks are built to feed the bottom line. That's reflected in their corporate cultures and their incentives, and, increasingly, in their operational software. (And if that software allows for tweaks, as Starbucks does, the ones that are made are likely to be ones that boost profits.)

Much of the scheduling technology has its roots in a powerful discipline of applied mathematics called "operations research," or OR. For centuries, mathematicians used the rudiments of OR to help farmers plan crop plantings and help civil engineers map highways to move people and goods efficiently. But the discipline didn't really take off until World War II, when the US and British military enlisted teams of mathematicians to optimize their use of resources. The Allies kept track of various forms of an "exchange ratio," which compared Allied resources spent versus enemy resources destroyed. During Operation Starvation, which took place between March and August 1945, the Twenty-first Bomber Command was tasked with destroying Japanese merchant ships in order to prevent food and other goods from arriving safely on Japanese shores. OR teams worked to minimize the number of mine-laying aircraft for each Japanese merchant ship that was sunk. They managed an "exchange ratio" of over 40 to 1—only 15 aircraft were lost in sinking 606 Japanese ships. This was considered highly efficient, and was due, in part, to the work of the OR team.

Following World War II, major companies (as well as the Pentagon) poured enormous resources into OR. The science of logistics radically transformed the way we produce goods and bring them to market.

In the 1960s, Japanese auto companies made another major leap, devising a manufacturing system called Just in Time. The idea was that instead of storing mountains of steering wheels or transmission blocks and retrieving them from vast warehouses, the assembly plant would order parts as they were needed rather than paying for them to sit idle. Toyota and Honda established complex chains of suppliers, each of them constantly bringing in parts on call. It was as if the industry were a single organism, with its own homeostatic control systems.

Just in Time was highly efficient, and it quickly spread across the globe. Companies in many geographies can establish just-in-time supply chains in a snap. These models likewise constitute the mathematical underpinnings of companies like Amazon, Federal Express, and UPS.

Scheduling software can be seen as an extension of the just-in-time economy. But instead of lawn mower blades or cell phone screens showing up right on cue, it's people, usually people who badly need money. And because they need money so desperately, the companies can bend their lives to the dictates of a mathematical model.

I should add that companies take steps not to make people's lives *too* miserable. They all know to the penny how much it costs to replace a frazzled worker who finally quits. Those numbers are in the data, too. And they have other models, as we discussed in the last chapter, to reduce churn, which drains profits and efficiency.

The trouble, from the employees' perspective, is an oversupply of low-wage labor. People are hungry for work, which is why so many of them cling to jobs that pay barely eight dollars per hour. This oversupply, along with the scarcity of effective unions, leaves workers with practically no bargaining power. This means the big retailers and restaurants can twist the workers' lives to ever-more-absurd schedules without suffering from excessive churn. They make more money while their workers' lives grow hellish. And because these optimization programs are everywhere, the workers know all too well that changing jobs isn't likely to improve their lot. Taken together, these dynamics provide corporations with something close to a captive workforce.

I'm sure it comes as no surprise that I consider scheduling software one of the more appalling WMDs. It's massive, as we've discussed, and it takes advantage of people who are already struggling to make ends meet. What's more, it is entirely opaque. Workers often don't have a clue about when they'll be called to work. They are summoned by an arbitrary program.

Scheduling software also creates a poisonous feedback loop. Consider Jannette Navarro. Her haphazard scheduling made it impossible for her to return to school, which dampened her employment prospects and kept her in the oversupplied pool of low-wage workers. The long and irregular hours also make it hard for workers to organize or to protest for better conditions. Instead, they face heightened anxiety and sleep deprivation, which causes dramatic mood swings and is responsible for an estimated 13 percent of highway deaths. Worse yet, since the software is designed to save companies money, it often limits workers' hours to fewer than thirty per week, so that they are not eligible for company health insurance. And with their chaotic schedules, most find it impossible to make time for a second job. It's almost as if the software were designed expressly to punish low-wage workers and to keep them down.

The software also condemns a large percentage of our children to grow up without routines. They experience their mother bleary eyed at breakfast, or hurrying out the door without dinner, or arguing with *her* mother about who can take care of them on Sunday morning. This chaotic life affects children deeply. According to a study by the Economic Policy Institute, an advocacy group, "Young children and adolescents of parents working unpredictable schedules or outside standard daytime working hours are more likely to have inferior cognition and behavioral outcomes." The parents might blame themselves for having a child who acts out or fails in school, but in many cases the real culprit is the poverty that leads workers to take jobs with haphazard schedules—and the scheduling models that squeeze struggling families even harder.

The root of the trouble, as with so many other WMDs, is the modelers' choice of objectives. The model is optimized for efficiency and profitability, not for justice or the good of the "team." This is, of course, the nature of capitalism. For companies, revenue is like oxygen. It keeps them alive. From their perspective, it would be profoundly stupid, even unnatural, to turn away from potential savings. That's why society needs countervailing forces, such as vigorous press coverage that highlights the abuses of efficiency and shames companies into doing the right thing. And when they come up short, as Starbucks did, it must expose them again and again. It also needs regulators to keep them in line, strong unions to organize workers and amplify their needs and complaints, and politicians willing to pass laws to restrain corporations' worst excesses. Following the *New York Times* report in 2014, Democrats in Congress promptly drew up bills to rein in scheduling software. But facing a Republican majority fiercely opposed to government regulations, the chances that their bill would become law were nil. The legislation died.

• • •

In 2008, just as the great recession was approaching, a San Francisco company called Cataphora marketed a software system that rated tech workers on a number of metrics, including their generation of ideas. This was no easy task. Software programs, after all, are hard-pressed to distinguish between an idea and a simple string of words. If you think about it, the difference is often just a matter of context. Yesterday's ideas—that the earth is round, or even that people might like to share photos in social networks— are today's facts. We humans each have a sense for when an idea becomes an established fact and know when it has been debunked or discarded (though we often disagree). However, that distinction flummoxes even the most sophisticated AI. So Cataphora's system needed to look to humans themselves for guidance.

Cataphora's software burrowed into corporate e-mail and messaging in its hunt for ideas. Its guiding hypothesis was that the best ideas would tend to spread more widely through the network. If people cut and pasted certain groups of words and shared them, those words were likely ideas, and the software could quantify them.

But there were complications. Ideas were not the only groups of words that were widely shared on social networks. Jokes, for example, were wildly viral and equally befuddling to software systems. Gossip also traveled like a rocket. However, jokes and gossip followed certain patterns, so it was possible to teach the program to filter out at least some of them. With time, the system identified the groups of words most likely to represent ideas. It tracked them through the network, counting the number of times they were copied, measuring their distribution, and identifying their source.

Very soon, the roles of the employees appeared to come into focus. Some people were idea generators, the system concluded. On its chart of employees, Cataphora marked idea generators with circles, which were bigger and darker if they produced lots of ideas. Other people were connectors. Like neurons in a distributed network, they transmitted information. The most effective connectors made snippets of words go viral. The system painted those people in dark colors as well.

Now, whether or not this system effectively measured the flow of ideas, the concept itself was not nefarious. It can make sense to use this type of analysis to identify what people know and to match them with their most promising colleagues and collaborators. IBM and Microsoft use in-house programs to do just this. It's very similar to a dating algorithm (and often, no doubt, has similarly spotty results). Big Data has also been used to study the productivity of call center workers.

A few years ago, MIT researchers analyzed the behavior of call center employees for Bank of America to find out why some teams were more productive than others. They hung a so-called socio-metric badge around each employee's neck. The electronics in these badges tracked the employees' location and also measured, every sixteen milliseconds, their tone of voice and gestures. It recorded when people were looking at each other and how much each person talked, listened, and interrupted. Four teams of call center employees—eighty people in total—wore these badges for six weeks.

These employees' jobs were highly regimented. Talking was discouraged because workers were supposed to spend as many of their minutes as possible on the phone, solving customers' problems. Coffee breaks were scheduled one by one.

The researchers found, to their surprise, that the fastest and most efficient call center team was also the most social. These employees pooh-poohed the rules and gabbed much more than the others. And when all of the employees were encouraged to socialize more, call center productivity soared.

But data studies that track employees' behavior can also be used to cull a workforce. As the 2008 recession ripped through the economy, HR officials in the tech sector started to look at those Cataphora charts with a new purpose. They saw that some workers were represented as big dark circles, while others were smaller and dimmer. If they had to lay off workers, and most companies did, it made sense to start with the small and dim ones on the chart.

Were those workers really expendable? Again we come to digital phrenology. If a system designates a worker as a low idea generator or weak connector, that verdict becomes its own truth. That's her score.

Perhaps someone can come in with countervailing evidence. The worker with the dim circle might generate fabulous ideas but not share them on the network. Or perhaps she proffers priceless advice over lunch or breaks up the tension in the office with a joke. Maybe everybody likes her. That has great value in the workplace. But computing systems have trouble finding digital proxies for these kinds of soft skills. The relevant data simply isn't collected, and anyway it's hard to put a value on them. They're usually easier to leave out of a model.

So the system identifies apparent losers. And a good number of them lost their jobs during the recession. That alone is unjust. But what's worse is that systems like Cataphora's receive minimal feedback data. Someone identified as a loser, and subsequently fired, may have found another job and generated a fistful of patents. That data usually isn't collected. The system has no inkling that it got one person, or even a thousand people, entirely wrong.

That's a problem, because scientists need this error feedback—in this case the presence of false negatives—to delve into forensic analysis and figure out what went wrong, what was misread, what data was ignored. It's how systems learn and get smarter. Yet as we've seen, loads of WMDs, from recidivism models to teacher scores, blithely generate their own reality. Managers assume that the scores are true enough to be useful, and the algorithm makes tough decisions easy. They can fire employees and cut costs and blame their decisions on an objective number, whether it's accurate or not.

Cataphora remained small, and its worker evaluation model was a sideline—much more of its work was in identifying patterns of fraud or insider trading within companies. The company went out of business in 2012, and its software was sold to a start-up, Chenope. But systems like Cataphora's have the potential to become true WMDs. They can misinterpret people, and punish them, without any proof that their scores correlate to the quality of their work.

This type of software signals the rise of WMDs in a new realm.

For a few decades, it may have seemed that industrial workers and service workers were the only ones who could be modeled and optimized, while those who trafficked in ideas, from lawyers to chemical engineers, could steer clear of WMDs, at least at work. Cataphora was an early warning that this will not be the case. Indeed, throughout the tech industry, many companies are busy trying to optimize their white-collar workers by looking at the patterns of their communications. The tech giants, including Google, Facebook, Amazon, IBM, and many others, are hot on this trail.

For now, at least, this diversity is welcome. It holds out the hope, at least, that workers rejected by one model might be appreciated by another. But eventually, an industry standard will emerge, and then we'll all be in trouble.

• • •

In 1983, the Reagan administration issued a lurid alarm about the state of America's schools. In a report called *A Nation at Risk*, a presidential panel warned that a "rising tide of mediocrity" in the schools threatened "our very future as a Nation and a people." The report added that if "an unfriendly foreign power" had attempted to impose these bad schools on us, "we might well have viewed it as an act of war."

The most noteworthy signal of failure was what appeared to be plummeting scores on the SATs. Between 1963 and 1980, verbal scores had fallen by 50 points, and math scores were down 40 points. Our ability to compete in a global economy hinged on our skills, and they seemed to be worsening.

Who was to blame for this sorry state of affairs? The report left no doubt about that. Teachers. The *Nation at Risk* report called for action, which meant testing the students—and using the results to zero in on the underperforming teachers. As we saw in the Introduction, this practice can cost teachers their jobs. Sarah Wysocki, the teacher in Washington who was fired after her class posted surprisingly low scores, was the victim of such a test. My point in telling that story was to show a WMD in action, how it can be arbitrary, unfair, and deaf to appeals.

But along with being educators and caretakers of children, teachers are obviously workers, and here I want to delve a bit deeper into the models that score their performance, because they might spread to other parts of the workforce. Consider the case of Tim Clifford. He's a middle school English teacher in New York City, with twenty-six years of experience. A few years ago, Clifford learned that he had bombed on a teacher evaluation, a so-called value-added model, similar to the one that led to Sarah Wysocki's firing. Clifford's score was an abysmal 6 out of 100.

He was devastated. "I didn't see how it was possible that I could have worked so hard and gotten such poor results," he later told me. "To be honest, when I first learned my low score, I felt ashamed and didn't tell anyone for a day or so. However, I learned that there were actually two other teachers who scored below me in my school. That emboldened me to share my results, because I wanted those teachers to know it wasn't only them."

If Clifford hadn't had tenure, he could have been dismissed that year, he said. "Even with tenure," he said, "scoring low in consecutive years is bound to put a target on a teacher's back to some degree." What's more, when tenured teachers register low scores, it emboldens school reformers, who make the case that job security protects incompetent educators. Clifford approached the following year with trepidation.

The value-added model had given him a failing grade but no advice on how to improve it. So Clifford went on teaching the way he always had and hoped for the best. The following year, his score was a 96.

"You'd think I'd have been elated, but I wasn't," he said. "I knew that my low score was bogus, so I could hardly rejoice at getting a high score using the same flawed formula. The 90 percent difference in scores only made me realize how ridiculous the entire value-added model is when it comes to education."

Bogus is the word for it. In fact, misinterpreted statistics run through the history of teacher evaluation. The problem started with a momentous statistical boo-boo in the analysis of the original *Nation at Risk* report. It turned out that the very researchers who were decrying a national catastrophe were basing their judgment on a fundamental error, something an undergrad should have caught. In fact, if they wanted to serve up an example of America's educational shortcomings, their own misreading of statistics could serve as exhibit A.

Seven years after *A Nation at Risk* was published with such fanfare, researchers at Sandia National Laboratories took a second look at the data gathered for the report. These people were no amateurs when it came to statistics—they build and maintain nuclear weapons—and they quickly found the error. Yes, it was true that SAT scores had gone down on average. However, the number of students taking the test had ballooned over the course of those seventeen years. Universities were opening their doors to more poor students and minorities. Opportunities were expanding. This signaled social success. But naturally, this influx of newcomers dragged down the average scores. However, when statisticians broke down the population into income groups, scores for every single group were rising, from the poor to the rich.

In statistics, this phenomenon is known as Simpson's Paradox: when a whole body of data displays one trend, yet when broken into subgroups, the opposite trend comes into view for each of those subgroups. The damning conclusion in the *Nation at Risk* report, the one that spurred the entire teacher evaluation movement, was drawn from a grievous misinterpretation of the data.

Tim Clifford's diverging scores are the result of yet another case of botched statistics, this one all too common. The teacher scores derived from the tests measured *nothing*. This may sound like hyperbole. After all, kids took tests, and those scores contributed to Clifford's. That much is true. But Clifford's scores, both his humiliating 6 and his chest-thumping 96, were based almost entirely on approximations that were so weak they were essentially random.

The problem was that the administrators lost track of accuracy in their quest to be fair. They understood that it wasn't right for teachers in rich schools to get too much credit when the sons and daughters of doctors and lawyers marched off toward elite universities. Nor should teachers in poor districts be held to the same standards of achievement. We cannot expect them to perform miracles.

So instead of measuring teachers on an absolute scale, they tried to adjust for social inequalities in the model. Instead of comparing Tim Clifford's students to others in different neighborhoods, they would compare them with forecast models of *themselves*. The students each had a predicted score. If they surpassed this prediction, the teacher got the credit. If they came up short, the teacher got the blame. If that sounds primitive to you, believe me, it is.

Statistically speaking, in these attempts to free the tests from class and color, the administrators moved from a primary to a secondary model. Instead of basing scores on direct measurement of the students, they based them on the so-called error term—the gap between results and expectations. Mathematically, this is a much sketchier proposition. Since the expectations themselves are derived from statistics, these amount to guesses on top of guesses. The result is a model with loads of random results, what statisticians call "noise."

Now, you might think that large numbers would bring the scores into focus. After all, New York City, with its 1.1 million public school students, should provide a big enough data set to create meaningful predictions. If eighty thousand eighth graders take the test, wouldn't it be feasible to establish reliable averages for struggling, middling, and thriving schools?

Yes. And if Tim Clifford were teaching a large sampling of students, say ten thousand, then it might be reasonable to measure that cohort against the previous year's average and draw some conclusions from it. Large numbers balance out the exceptions and outliers. Trends, theoretically, would come into focus. But it's almost impossible for a class of twenty-five or thirty students to match up with the larger population. So if a class has certain types of students, they will tend to rise faster than the average. Others will rise more slowly. Clifford was given virtually no information about the opaque WMD that gave him such wildly divergent scores, but he assumed this variation in his classes had something to do with it. The year he scored poorly, Clifford said, "I taught many special education students as well as many top performers. And I think serving either the neediest or the top students—or both—creates problems. Needy students' scores are hard to move because they have learning problems, and top students' scores are hard to move because they have already scored high so there's little room for improvement."

The following year, he had a different mix of students, with more of them falling between the extremes. And the results made it look as though Clifford had progressed from being a failing teacher to being a spectacular one. Such results were all too common. An analysis by a blogger and educator named Gary Rubinstein found that of teachers who taught the same subject in consecutive years, one in four registered a 40-point difference. That suggests that the evaluation data is practically random. It wasn't the teachers' performance that was bouncing all over the place. It was the scoring generated by a bogus WMD.

While its scores are meaningless, the impact of value-added modeling is pervasive and nefarious. "I've seen some great teachers convince themselves that they were mediocre at best based on those scores," Clifford said. "It moved them away from the great lessons they used to teach, toward increasing test prep. To a young teacher, a poor value-added score is punishing, and a good one may lead to a false sense of accomplishment that has not been earned."

As in the case of so many WMDs, the existence of value-added modeling stems from good intentions. The Obama administration realized early on that school districts punished under the 2001 No Child Left Behind reforms, which mandated high-stakes standardized testing, tended to be poor and disadvantaged. So it offered waivers to districts that could demonstrate the effectiveness of their teachers, ensuring that these schools would not be punished even if their students were lagging.*

The use of value-added models stems in large part from this regulatory change. But in late 2015 the teacher testing craze took what may be an even more dramatic turn. First, Congress and the White House agreed to revoke No Child Left Behind and replace it with a law that gives states more latitude to develop their own approaches for turning around underperforming school districts. It also gives them a broader range of criteria to consider, including student and teacher engagement, access to advanced coursework, school climate, and safety. In other words, education officials can attempt to study what's happening at each individual school—and

---

* No Child Left Behind sanctions include offering students in failing schools the option of attending another, more successful school. In dire cases, the law calls for a failing school to be closed and replaced by a charter school.

pay less attention to WMDs like value-added models. Or better yet, jettison them entirely.

At around the same time, New York governor Andrew Cuomo's education task force called for a four-year moratorium on the use of exams to evaluate teachers. This change, while welcome, does not signal a clear rejection of the teacher evaluation WMDs, much less a recognition that they're unfair. The push, in fact, came from the parents, who complained that the testing regime was wearing out their kids and taking too much time in the school year. A boycott movement had kept 20 percent of third through eighth graders out of the tests in the spring of 2015, and it was growing. In bowing to the parents, the Cuomo administration delivered a blow to value-added modeling. After all, without a full complement of student tests, the state would lack the data to populate it.

Tim Clifford was cheered by this news but still wary. "The opt-out movement forced Cuomo's hand," he wrote in an e-mail. "He feared losing the support of wealthier voters in top school districts, who were the very people who most staunchly supported him. To get ahead of the issue, he's placed this moratorium on using test scores." Clifford fears that the tests will be back.

Maybe so. And, given that value-added modeling has become a proven tool against teachers' unions, I don't expect it to disappear anytime soon. It's well entrenched, with forty states and the District of Columbia using or developing one form of it or another. That's all the more reason to spread the word about these and other WMDs. Once people recognize them and understand their statistical flaws, they'll demand evaluations that are fairer for both students and teachers. However, if the goal of the testing is to find someone to blame, and to intimidate workers, then, as we've seen, a WMD that spews out meaningless scores gets an A-plus.

8

COLLATERAL DAMAGE

Landing Credit

Local bankers used to stand tall in a town. They controlled the money. If you wanted a new car or a mortgage, you'd put on your Sunday best and pay a visit. And as a member of your community, this banker would probably know the following details about your life. He'd know about your churchgoing habits, or lack of them. He'd know all the stories about your older brother's run-ins with the law. He'd know what your boss (and his golfing buddy) said about you as a worker. Naturally, he'd know your race and ethnic group, and he'd also glance at the numbers on your application form.

The first four factors often worked their way, consciously or not, into the banker's judgment. And there's a good chance he was more likely to trust people from his own circles. This was only human. But it meant that for millions of Americans the predigital status quo was just as awful as some of the WMDs I've been describing. Outsiders, including minorities and women, were routinely locked out. They had to put together an impressive financial portfolio—and then hunt for open-minded bankers.

It just wasn't fair. And then along came an algorithm, and things improved. A mathematician named Earl Isaac and his engineer friend, Bill Fair, devised a model they called FICO to evaluate the risk that an individual would default on a loan. This FICO score was fed by a formula that looked only at a borrower's finances—mostly her debt load and bill-paying record. The score was color blind. And it turned out to be great for the banking industry, because it predicted risk far more accurately while opening the door to millions of new customers. FICO scores, of course, are still around. They're used by the credit agencies, including Experian, Transunion, and Equifax, which each contribute different sources of information to the FICO model to come up with their own scores. These scores have lots of commendable and non-WMD attributes. First, they have a clear feedback loop. Credit companies can see which borrowers default on their loans, and they can match those numbers against their scores. If borrowers with high scores seem to be defaulting on loans more frequently than the model would predict, FICO and the credit agencies can tweak those models to make them more accurate. This is a sound use of statistics.

The credit scores are also relatively transparent. FICO's website, for example, offers simple instructions on how to improve your score. (Reduce debt, pay bills on time, and stop ordering new credit cards.) Equally important, the credit-scoring industry is regulated. If you have questions about your score, you have the legal right to ask for your credit report, which includes all the information that goes into the score, including your record of mortgage and utility payments, your total debt, and the percentage of available credit you're using. Though the process can be slow to the point of torturous, if you find mistakes, you can have them fixed.

Since Fair and Isaac's pioneering days, the use of scoring has of course proliferated wildly. Today we're added up in every conceivable way as statisticians and mathematicians patch together a mishmash of data, from our zip codes and Internet surfing patterns to our recent purchases. Many of their pseudoscientific models attempt to predict our creditworthiness, giving each of us so-called e-scores. These numbers, which we rarely see, open doors for some of us, while slamming them in the face of others. Unlike the FICO scores they resemble, e-scores are arbitrary, unaccountable, unregulated, and often unfair—in short, they're WMDs.

A Virginia company called Neustar offers a prime example. Neustar provides customer targeting services for companies, including one that helps manage call center traffic. In a flash, this technology races through available data on callers and places them in a hierarchy. Those at the top are deemed to be more profitable prospects and are quickly funneled to a human operator. Those at the bottom either wait much longer or are dispatched into an outsourced overflow center, where they are handled largely by machines.

Credit card companies such as Capital One carry out similar rapid-fire calculations as soon as someone shows up on their website. They can often access data on web browsing and purchasing patterns, which provide loads of insights about the potential customer. Chances are, the person clicking for new Jaguars is richer than the one checking out a 2003 Taurus on Carfax.com. Most scoring systems also pick up the location of the visitor's computer. When this is matched with real estate data, they can draw inferences about wealth. A person using a computer on San Francisco's Balboa Terrace is a far better prospect than the one across the bay in East Oakland.

The existence of these e-scores shouldn't be surprising. We've seen models feeding on similar data when targeting us for predatory loans or weighing the odds that we might steal a car. For better or worse, they've guided us to school (or jail) and toward a job, and then they've optimized us inside the workplace. Now that it might be time to buy a house or car, it's only natural that financial models would mine the same trove of data to size us up.

But consider the nasty feedback loop that e-scores create. There's a very high chance that the e-scoring system will give the borrower from the rough section of East Oakland a low score. A lot of people default there. So the credit card offer popping up on her screen will be targeted to a riskier demographic. That means less available credit and higher interest rates for those who are already struggling.

Much of the predatory advertising we've been discussing, including the ads for payday loans and for-profit colleges, is generated through such e-scores. They're stand-ins for credit scores. But since companies are legally prohibited from using credit scores for marketing purposes, they make do with this sloppy substitute.

There's a certain logic to that prohibition. After all, our credit history includes highly personal data, and it makes sense that we should have control over who sees it. But the consequence is that companies end up diving into largely unregulated pools of data, such as clickstreams and geo-tags, in order to create a parallel data marketplace. In the process, they can largely avoid government oversight. They then measure success by gains in efficiency, cash flow, and profits. With few exceptions, concepts like justice and transparency don't fit into their algorithms.

Let's compare that for a moment to the 1950s-era banker. Consciously or not, that banker was weighing various data points that had little or nothing to do with his would-be borrower's ability to shoulder a mortgage. He looked across his desk and saw his customer's race, and drew conclusions from that. Her father's criminal record may have counted against her, while her regular church attendance may have been seen favorably.

All of these data points were proxies. In his search for financial responsibility, the banker could have dispassionately studied the numbers (as some exemplary bankers no doubt did). But instead he drew correlations to race, religion, and family connections. In doing so, he avoided scrutinizing the borrower as an individual and instead placed him in a group of people—what statisticians today would call a "bucket." "People like you," he decided, could or could not be trusted.

Fair and Isaac's great advance was to ditch the proxies in favor of the relevant financial data, like past behavior with respect to paying bills. They focused their analysis on the individual in question—and not on other people with similar attributes. E-scores, by contrast, march us back in time. They analyze the individual through a veritable blizzard of proxies. In a few milliseconds, they carry out thousands of "people like you" calculations. And if enough of these "similar" people turn out to be deadbeats or, worse, criminals, that individual will be treated accordingly.

From time to time, people ask me how to teach ethics to a class of data scientists. I usually begin with a discussion of how to build an e-score model and ask them whether it makes sense to use "race" as an input in the model. They inevitably respond that such a question would be unfair and probably illegal. The next question is whether to use "zip code." This seems fair enough, at first. But it doesn't take long for the students to see that they are codifying past injustices into their model. When they include an attribute such as "zip code," they are expressing the opinion that the history of human behavior in that patch of real estate should determine, at least in part, what kind of loan a person who lives there should get.

In other words, the modelers for e-scores have to make do with trying to answer the question "How have people like you behaved in the past?" when ideally they would ask, "How have *you* behaved in the past?"

The difference between these two questions is vast. Imagine if a highly motivated and responsible person with modest immigrant beginnings is trying to start a business and needs to rely on such a system for early investment. Who would take a chance on such a person? Probably not a model trained on such demographic and behavioral data.

I should note that in the statistical universe proxies inhabit, they often work. More times than not, birds of a feather *do* fly together. Rich people buy cruises and BMWs. All too often, poor people need a payday loan. And since these statistical models appear to work much of the time, efficiency rises and profits surge. Investors double down on scientific systems that can place thousands of people into what appear to be the correct buckets. It's the triumph of Big Data.

And what about the person who is misunderstood and placed in the wrong bucket? That happens. And there's no feedback to set the system straight. A statistics-crunching engine has no way to learn that it dispatched a valuable potential customer to call center hell. Worse, losers in the unregulated e-score universe have little recourse to complain, much less correct the system's error. In the realm of WMDs, they're collateral damage. And since the whole murky system grinds away in distant server farms, they rarely find out about it. Most of them probably conclude, with reason, that life is simply unfair.

. . .

In the world I've described so far, e-scores nourished by millions of proxies exist in the shadows, while our credit reports, packed with pertinent and relevant data, operate under rule of law. But sadly, it's not quite that simple. All too often, credit reports serve as proxies, too.

It should come as little surprise that many institutions in our society, from big companies to the government, are on the hunt for people who are trustworthy and reliable. In the chapter on getting a job, we saw them sorting through résumés and red-lighting candidates whose psychological tests pointed to undesirable personal attributes. Another all-too-common approach is to consider the applicant's credit score. If people pay their bills on time and avoid debt, employers ask, wouldn't that signal trustworthiness and dependability? It's not *exactly* the same thing, they know. But wouldn't there be a significant overlap?

That's how the credit reports have expanded far beyond their original turf. Creditworthiness has become an all-too-easy stand-in for other virtues. Conversely, bad credit has grown to signal a host of sins and shortcomings that have nothing to do with paying bills. As we'll see, all sorts of companies turn credit reports into their own versions of credit scores and use them as proxies. This practice is both toxic and ubiquitous.

For certain applications, such a proxy might appear harmless. Some online dating services, for example, match people on the basis of credit scores. One of them, CreditScoreDating, proclaims that "good credit scores are sexy." We can debate the wisdom of linking financial behavior to love. But at least the customers of

CreditScoreDating know what they're getting into and why. It's up to them.

But if you're looking for a job, there's an excellent chance that a missed credit card payment or late fees on student loans could be working against you. According to a survey by the Society for Human Resource Management, nearly half of America's employers screen potential hires by looking at their credit reports. Some of them check the credit status of current employees as well, especially when they're up for a promotion.

Before companies carry out these checks, they must first ask for permission. But that's usually little more than a formality; at many companies, those refusing to surrender their credit data won't even be considered for jobs. And if their credit record is poor, there's a good chance they'll be passed over. A 2012 survey on credit card debt in low- and middle-income families made this point all too clear. One in ten participants reported hearing from employers that blemished credit histories had sunk their chances, and it's anybody's guess how many were disqualified by their credit reports but left in the dark. While the law stipulates that employers must alert job seekers when credit issues disqualify them, it's hardly a stretch to believe that some of them simply tell candidates that they weren't a good fit or that others were more qualified.

The practice of using credit scores in hirings and promotions creates a dangerous poverty cycle. After all, if you can't get a job because of your credit record, that record will likely get worse, making it even harder to land work. It's not unlike the problem young people face when they look for their first job—and are disqualified for lack of experience. Or the plight of the longtime unemployed, who find that few will hire them because they've been without a job for too long. It's a spiraling and defeating feedback loop for the unlucky people caught up in it.

Employers, naturally, have little sympathy for this argument.

Good credit, they argue, is an attribute of a responsible person, the kind they want to hire. But framing debt as a moral issue is a mistake. Plenty of hardworking and trustworthy people lose jobs every day as companies fail, cut costs, or move jobs offshore. These numbers climb during recessions. And many of the newly unemployed find themselves without health insurance. At that point, all it takes is an accident or an illness for them to miss a payment on a loan. Even with the Affordable Care Act, which reduced the ranks of the uninsured, medical expenses remain the single biggest cause of bankruptcies in America.

People with savings, of course, can keep their credit intact during tough times. Those living from paycheck to paycheck are far more vulnerable. Consequently, a sterling credit rating is not just a proxy for responsibility and smart decisions. It is also a proxy for wealth. And wealth is highly correlated with race.

Consider this. As of 2015, white households held on average roughly ten times as much money and property as black and Hispanic households. And while only 15 percent of whites had zero or negative net worth, more than a third of blacks and Hispanic households found themselves with no cushion. This wealth gap increases with age. By their sixties, whites are eleven times richer than African Americans. Given these numbers, it is not hard to argue that the poverty trap created by employer credit checks affects society unequally and along racial lines. As I write this, ten states have passed legislation to outlaw the use of credit scores in hiring. In banning them, the New York City government declared that using credit checks "disproportionately affects low-income applicants and applicants of color." Still, the practice remains legal in forty states.

This is not to say that personnel departments across America are intentionally building a poverty trap, much less a racist one. They no doubt believe that credit reports hold relevant facts that help them make important decisions. After all, "The more data, the better" is the guiding principle of the Information Age. Yet in the name of fairness, some of this data should remain uncrunched.

• • •

Imagine for a moment that you're a recent graduate of Stanford University's law school and are interviewing for a job at a prestigious law firm in San Francisco. The senior partner looks at his computer-generated file and breaks into a laugh. "It says here that you've been arrested for running a meth lab in Rhode Island!" He shakes his head. Yours is a common name, and computers sure make silly mistakes. The interview proceeds.

At the high end of the economy, human beings tend to make the important decisions, while relying on computers as useful tools. But in the mainstream and, especially, in the lower echelons of the economy, much of the work, as we've seen, is automated. When mistakes appear in a dossier—and they often do—even the best-designed algorithms will make the wrong decision. As data hounds have long said: garbage in, garbage out.

A person at the receiving end of this automated process can suffer the consequences for years. Computer-generated terrorism no-fly lists, for example, are famously rife with errors. An innocent person whose name resembles that of a suspected terrorist faces a hellish ordeal every time he has to get on a plane. (Wealthy travelers, by contrast, are often able to pay to acquire "trusted traveler" status, which permits them to waltz through security. In effect, they're spending money to shield themselves from a WMD.)

Mistakes like this pop up everywhere. The Federal Trade Commission reported in 2013 that 5 percent of consumers—or an estimated ten million people—had an error on one of their credit reports serious enough to result in higher borrowing costs. That's troublesome, but at least credit reports exist in the regulated side of the data economy. Consumers can (and should) request to see them once a year and amend potentially costly errors.*

Still, the unregulated side of the data economy is even more hazardous. Scores of companies, from giants like Acxiom Corp. to a host of fly-by-night operations, buy information from retailers, advertisers, smartphone app makers, and companies that run sweepstakes or operate social networks in order to assemble a cornucopia of facts on every consumer in the country. They might note, for example, whether a consumer has diabetes, lives in a house with a smoker, drives an SUV, or owns a pair of collies (who may live on in the dossier long after their earthly departure). These companies also scrape all kinds of publicly available government data, including voting and arrest records and housing sales. All of this goes into a consumer profile, which they sell.

Some data brokers, no doubt, are more dependable than others. But any operation that attempts to profile hundreds of millions of people from thousands of different sources is going to get a lot of the facts wrong. Take the case of a Philadelphian named Helen Stokes. She wanted to move into a local senior living center but kept getting rejected because of arrests on her background record. It was true that she had been arrested twice during altercations with her former husband. But she had not been convicted and had managed to have the records expunged from government databases. Yet the arrest records remained in files assembled by a company called RealPage, Inc., which provides background checks on tenants.

For RealPage and other companies like it, creating and selling reports brings in revenue. People like Helen Stokes are not

---

* Even so, I should add, fixing them can be a nightmare. A Mississippi resident named Patricia Armour tried for two years to get Experian to expunge from her file a $40,000 debt she no longer owed. It took a call to Mississippi's attorney general, she told the *New York Times*, before Experian corrected her record.

customers. They're the product. Responding to their complaints takes time and costs money. After all, while Stokes might say that the arrests have been expunged, verifying that fact eats up time and money. An expensive human being might have to spend a few minutes on the Internet or even—heaven forbid—make a phone call or two. Little surprise, then, that Stokes didn't get her record cleared until she sued. And even after RealPage responded, how many other data brokers might still be selling files with the same poisonous misinformation? It's anybody's guess.

Some data brokers do offer consumers access to their data. But these reports are heavily curated. They include the facts but not always the conclusions data brokers' algorithms have drawn from them. Someone who takes the trouble to see her file at one of the many brokerages, for example, might see the home mortgage, a Verizon bill, and a $459 repair on the garage door. But she won't see that she's in a bucket of people designated as "Rural and Barely Making It," or perhaps "Retiring on Empty." Fortunately for the data brokers, few of us get a chance to see these details. If we did, and the FTC is pushing for more accountability, the brokers would likely find themselves besieged by consumer complaints— millions of them. It could very well disrupt their business model. For now, consumers learn about their faulty files only when word slips out, often by chance.

An Arkansas resident named Catherine Taylor, for example, missed out on a job at the local Red Cross several years ago. Those things happen. But Taylor's rejection letter arrived with a valuable nugget of information. Her background report included a criminal charge for the intent to manufacture and sell metham- phetamines. This wasn't the kind of candidate the Red Cross was looking to hire.

Taylor looked into it and discovered that the criminal charges belonged to another Catherine Taylor, who happened to be born on the same day. She later found that at least ten other companies were tarring her with inaccurate reports—one of them connected to her application for federal housing assistance, which had been denied. Was the housing rejection due to a mistaken identity?

In an automatic process, it no doubt could have been. But a human being intervened. When applying for federal housing assistance, Taylor and her husband met with an employee of the housing authority to complete a background check. This employee, Wanda Taylor—no relation—was using information provided by Tenant Tracker, the data broker. It was riddled with errors and blended identities. It linked Taylor, for example, with the possible alias of Chantel Taylor, a convicted felon who happened to be born on the same day. It also connected her to the other Catherine Taylor she had heard about, who had been convicted in Illinois of theft, forgery, and possession of a controlled substance.

The dossier, in short, was a toxic mess. But Wanda Taylor had experience with such things. She began to dig through it. She promptly drew a line through the possible alias, Chantel, which seemed improbable to her. She read in the file that the Illinois thief had a tattoo on her ankle with the name Troy. After checking Catherine Taylor's ankle, she drew a line through that felon's name as well. By the end of the meeting, one conscientious human being had cleared up the confusion generated by webcrawling data-gathering programs. The housing authority knew which Catherine Taylor it was dealing with.

The question we're left with is this: How many Wanda Taylors are out there clearing up false identities and other errors in our data? The answer: not nearly enough. Humans in the data economy are outliers and throwbacks. The systems are built to run automatically as much as possible. That's the efficient way; that's where the profits are. Errors are inevitable, as in any statistical program, but the quickest way to reduce them is to fine-tune the algorithms running the machines. Humans on the ground only gum up the works.

This trend toward automation is leaping ahead as computers make sense of more and more of our written language, in some cases processing thousands of written documents in a second. But they still misunderstand all sorts of things. IBM's *Jeopardy!*-playing supercomputer Watson, for all its brilliance, was flummoxed by language or context about 10 percent of the time. It was heard saying that a butterfly's diet was "Kosher," and it once confused Oliver Twist, the Charles Dickens character, with the 1980s techno-pop band the Pet Shop Boys.

Such errors are sure to pile up in our consumer profiles, confusing and misdirecting the algorithms that manage more and more of our lives. These errors, which result from automated data collection, poison predictive models, fueling WMDs. And this collection will only grow. Computers are already busy expanding beyond the written word. They're harvesting spoken language and images and using them to capture more information about everything in the universe—including us. These new technologies will mine new troves for our profiles, while expanding the risk for errors.

Recently, Google processed images of a trio of happy young African Americans and its automatic photo-tagging service labeled them as gorillas. The company apologized profusely, but in systems like Google's, errors are inevitable. It was most likely faulty machine learning (and probably not a racist running loose in the Googleplex) that led the computer to confuse *Homo sapiens* with our close cousin, the gorilla. The software itself had flipped through billions of images of primates and had made its own distinctions. It focused on everything from shades of color to the distance between eyes and the shape of the ear. Apparently, though, it wasn't thoroughly tested before being released.

Such mistakes are learning opportunities—as long as the system receives feedback on the error. In this case, it did. But injustice persists. When automatic systems sift through our data to size us up for an e-score, they naturally project the past into the future. As we saw in recidivism sentencing models and predatory loan algorithms, the poor are expected to remain poor forever and are treated accordingly—denied opportunities, jailed more often, and gouged for services and loans. It's inexorable, often hidden and beyond appeal, and unfair.

Yet we can't count on automatic systems to address the issue. For all of their startling power, machines cannot yet make adjustments for fairness, at least not by themselves. Sifting through data and judging what is fair is utterly foreign to them and enormously complicated. Only human beings can impose that constraint.

There's a paradox here. If we return one last time to that '50s-era banker, we see that his mind was occupied with human distortions—desires, prejudice, distrust of outsiders. To carry out the job more fairly and efficiently, he and the rest of his industry handed the work over to an algorithm.

Sixty years later, the world is dominated by automatic systems chomping away on our error-ridden dossiers. They urgently require the context, common sense, and fairness that only humans can provide. However, if we leave this issue to the marketplace, which prizes efficiency, growth, and cash flow (while tolerating a certain degree of errors), meddling humans will be instructed to stand clear of the machinery.

• • •

This will be a challenge, because even as the problems with our old credit models become apparent, powerful newcomers are storming in. Facebook, for example, has patented a new type of credit rating, one based on our social networks. The goal, on its face, is reasonable. Consider a college graduate who goes on a religious mission for five years, helping to bring potable water to impoverished villages in Africa. He comes home with no credit rating and has trouble getting a loan. But his classmates on Facebook are investment bankers, PhDs, and software designers. Birds-of-a-feather analysis would indicate that he's a good bet. But that same analysis likely works against a hardworking housecleaner in East St. Louis, who might have numerous unemployed friends and a few in jail.

Meanwhile, the formal banking industry is frantically raking through personal data in its attempts to boost business. But licensed banks are subject to federal regulation and disclosure requirements, which means that customer profiling carries reputational and legal risk. American Express learned this the hard way in 2009, just as the Great Recession was gearing up. No doubt looking to reduce risk on its own balance sheet, Amex cut the spending limits of some customers. Unlike the informal players in the e-score economy, though, the credit card giant had to send them a letter explaining why.

This is when Amex delivered a low blow. Cardholders who shopped at certain establishments, the company wrote, were more likely to fall behind on payments. It was a matter of statistics, plain and simple, a clear correlation between shopping patterns and default rates. It was up to the unhappy Amex customers to guess which establishment had poisoned their credit. Was it the weekly shop at Walmart or perhaps the brake job at Grease Monkey that placed them in the bucket of potential deadbeats?

Whatever the cause, it left them careening into a nasty recession with less credit. Worse, the lowered spending limit would appear within days on their credit reports. In fact, it was probably there even before the letters arrived. This would lower their scores and drive up their borrowing costs. Many of these cardholders, it's safe to say, frequented "stores associated with poor repayments" because they weren't swimming in money. And wouldn't you know it? An algorithm took notice and made them poorer.

Cardholders' anger attracted the attention of the mainstream press, including the *New York Times*, and Amex promptly announced that it would not correlate stores to risk. (Amex later insisted that it had chosen the wrong words in its message and that it had scrutinized only broader consumer patterns, not specific merchants.)

It was a headache and an embarrassment for American Express. If they had indeed found a strong correlation between shopping at a certain store and credit risk, they certainly couldn't use it now. Compared to most of the Internet economy, they're boxed in, regulated, in a certain sense handicapped. (Not that they should complain. Over the decades, lobbyists for the incumbents have crafted many of the regulations with an eye to defending the entrenched powers—and keeping pesky upstarts locked out.)

So is it any surprise that newcomers to the finance industry would choose the freer and unregulated route? Innovation, after all, hinges on the freedom to experiment. And with petabytes of behavioral data at their fingertips and virtually no oversight, opportunities for the creation of new business models are vast.

Multiple companies, for example, are working to replace payday lenders. These banks of last resort cater to the working poor, tiding them over from one paycheck to the next and charging exorbitant interest rates. After twenty-two weeks, a $500 loan could cost $1,500. So if an efficient newcomer could find new ways to rate risk, then pluck creditworthy candidates from this desperate pool of people, it could charge them slightly lower interest and still make a mountain of money.

That was Douglas Merrill's idea. A former chief operating officer at Google, Merrill believed that he could use Big Data to calculate risk and offer payday loans at a discount. In 2009, he founded a start-up called ZestFinance. On the company web page, Merrill proclaims that "all data is credit data." In other words, anything goes.

ZestFinance buys data that shows whether applicants have kept up with their cell phone bills, along with plenty of other publicly available or purchased data. As Merrill promised, the company's rates are lower than those charged by most payday lenders. A typical $500 loan at ZestFinance costs $900 after twenty-two weeks—60 percent lower than the industry standard.

It's an improvement, but is it fair? The company's algorithms process up to ten thousand data points per applicant, including unusual observations, such as whether applicants use proper spelling and capitalization on their application form, how long it takes them to read it, and whether they bother to look at the terms and conditions. "Rule followers," the company argues, are better credit risks.

That may be true. But punctuation and spelling mistakes also point to low education, which is highly correlated with class and race. So when poor people and immigrants qualify for a loan, their substandard language skills might drive up their fees. If they then have trouble paying those fees, this might validate that they were a high risk to begin with and might further lower their credit scores. It's a vicious feedback loop, and paying bills on time plays only a bit part.

When new ventures are built on WMDs, troubles are bound to follow, even when the players have the best intentions. Take the case of the "peer-to-peer" lending industry. It started out in the last decade with the vision of borrowers and lenders finding each other on matchmaking platforms. This would represent the democratization of banking. More people would get loans, and at the same time millions of everyday people would become small-time bankers and make a nice return. Both sides would bypass the big greedy banks.

One of the first peer-to-peer exchanges, Lending Club, launched as an application on Facebook in 2006 and received funding a year later to become a new type of bank. To calculate the borrower's risk, Lending Club blended the traditional credit report with data gathered from around the web. Their algorithm, in a word, generated e-scores, which they claimed were more accurate than credit scores.

Lending Club and its chief rival, Prosper, are still tiny. They've generated less than $10 billion in loans, which is but a speck in the $3 trillion consumer lending market. Yet they're attracting loads of attention. Executives from Citigroup and Morgan Stanley serve as directors of peer-to-peer players, and Wells Fargo's investment fund is the largest investor in Lending Club. Lending Club's stock offering in December of 2014 was the biggest tech IPO of the year. It raised $870 million and reached a valuation of $9 billion, making it the fifteenth most valuable bank in America.

The fuss has little to do with democratizing capital or cutting out the middleman. According to a report in *Forbes*, institutional money now accounts for more than 80 percent of all the activity on peer-to-peer platforms. For big banks, the new platforms provide a convenient alternative to the tightly regulated banking economy. Working through peer-to-peer systems, a lender can analyze nearly any data it chooses and develop its own e-scores. It can develop risk correlations for neighborhoods, zip codes, and the stores customers shop at—all without having to send them embarrassing letters explaining why.

And what does that mean for us? With the relentless growth of e-scores, we're batched and bucketed according to secret formulas, some of them fed by portfolios loaded with errors. We're viewed not as individuals but as members of tribes, and we're stuck with that designation. As e-scores pollute the sphere of finance, opportunities dim for the have-nots. In fact, compared to the slew of WMDs running amok, the prejudiced loan officer of yesteryear doesn't look all that bad. At the very least, a borrower could attempt to read his eyes and appeal to his humanity.

9

NO SAFE ZONE

Getting Insurance

Late in the nineteenth century, a renowned statistician named Frederick Hoffman created a potent WMD. It's very likely that Hoffman, a German who worked for the Prudential Life Insurance Company, meant no harm. Later in his life, his research contributed mightily to public health. He did valuable work on malaria and was among the first to associate cancer with tobacco. Yet on a spring day in 1896, Hoffman published a 330-page report that set back the cause of racial equality in the United States and reinforced the status of millions as second-class citizens. His report used exhaustive statistics to make the case that the lives of black Americans were so precarious that the entire race was uninsurable.

Hoffman's analysis, like many of the WMDs we've been discussing, was statistically flawed. He confused causation with correlation, so that the voluminous data he gathered served only to
confirm his thesis: that race was a powerful predictor of life expec-
tancy. Racism was so ingrained in his thinking that he apparently
never stopped to consider whether poverty and injustice might
have something to do with the death rate of African Americans,
whether the lack of decent schools, modern plumbing, safe work-
places, and access to health care might kill them at a younger age.

Hoffman also made a fundamental statistical error. Like the
presidential commission that issued the 1983 *Nation at Risk* report, Hoffman neglected to stratify his results. He saw blacks
only as a large and homogeneous group. So he failed to separate
them into different geographical, social, or economic cohorts.
For him, a black schoolteacher leading an orderly life in Boston
or New York was indistinguishable from a sharecropper laboring
twelve hours a day barefoot in the Mississippi Delta. Hoffman was
blinded by race.

And so was his industry. With time, of course, insurers advanced a bit in their thinking and sold policies to African American families. After all, there was money to be made. But they
clung for decades to Hoffman's idea that entire groups of people
were riskier than others—and some of them too risky. Insurance
companies as well as bankers delineated neighborhoods where
they would not invest. This cruel practice, known as redlining,
has been outlawed by various pieces of legislation, including the
Fair Housing Act of 1968.

Nearly a half century later, however, redlining is still with us,
though in far more subtle forms. It's coded into the latest generation of WMDs. Like Hoffman, the creators of these new models
confuse correlation with causation. They punish the poor, and
especially racial and ethnic minorities. And they back up their

analysis with reams of statistics, which give them the studied air of evenhanded science.

On this algorithmic voyage through life, we've clawed our way through education and we've landed a job (even if it is one that runs us on a chaotic schedule). We've taken out loans and seen how our creditworthiness is a stand-in for other virtues or vices. Now it's time to protect our most treasured assets—our home and car and our family's health—and make arrangements for those we one day leave behind.

Insurance grew out of actuarial science, a discipline whose roots reach back to the seventeenth century. This was a period in which Europe's growing bourgeoisie was acquiring great wealth. It allowed many the luxury, for the first time, to think ahead to future generations.

While advances in math were providing the tools necessary to make predictions, an early generation of data hounds was looking for new things to count. One was a draper in London named John Graunt. He went through birth and death records and in 1682 came up with the first study of the mortality rates of an entire community of people. He calculated, for example, that children in London faced a 6 percent death risk in each of the first six years of their lives. (And with statistics, he was able to dispel the myth that the plague swept through every year a new monarch came into power.) For the first time, mathematicians could calculate the most probable arc of a person's life. These numbers didn't work for individuals, of course. But with big enough numbers, the average and range were predictable.

Mathematicians didn't pretend to foresee the fate of each individual. That was unknowable. But they could predict the prevalence of accidents, fires, and deaths within large groups of people. Over the following three centuries, a vast insurance industry grew around these predictions. The new industry gave people, for the first time, the chance to pool their collective risk, protecting individuals when misfortune struck.

Now, with the evolution of data science and networked computers, insurance is facing fundamental change. With ever more information available—including the data from our genomes, the patterns of our sleep, exercise, and diet, and the proficiency of our driving—insurers will increasingly calculate risk for the individual and free themselves from the generalities of the larger pool. For many, this is a welcome change. A health enthusiast today can demonstrate, with data, that she sleeps eight hours a night, walks ten miles a day, and eats little but green vegetables, nuts, and fish oil. Why shouldn't she get a break on her health insurance?

The move toward the individual, as we'll see, is embryonic. But already insurers are using data to divide us into smaller tribes, to offer us different products and services at varying prices. Some might call this customized service. The trouble is, it's not individual. The models place us into groups we cannot see, whose behavior appears to resemble ours. Regardless of the quality of the analysis, its opacity can lead to gouging.

Take auto insurance. In 2015, researchers at Consumer Reports conducted an extensive nationwide study looking for disparities in pricing. They analyzed more than two billion price quotes from all the major insurers for hypothetical customers from every one of the 33,419 zip codes in the country. What they found was wildly unfair, and rooted—as we saw in the last chapter—in credit scores.

Insurers draw these scores from credit reports, and then, using the insurer's proprietary algorithm, create their own ratings, or e-scores. These are proxies for responsible driving. But Consumer Reports found that the e-scores, which include all sorts of demographic data, often count for more than the driver's record. In other words, how you manage money can matter more than how you drive a car. In New York State, for example, a dip in a driver's credit rating from "excellent" to merely "good" could jack up the annual cost of insurance by $255. And in Florida, adults with clean driving records and poor credit scores paid an average of $1,552 more than the same drivers with excellent credit and a *drunk driving conviction.*

We've already discussed how the growing reliance on credit scores across the economy works against the poor. This is yet another example of that trend, and an egregious one—especially since auto insurance is mandatory for anyone who drives. What's different here is the focus on the proxy when far more relevant data is available. I cannot imagine a more meaningful piece of data for auto insurers than a drunk driving record. It is evidence of risk in precisely the domain they're attempting to predict. It's far better than other proxies they consider, such as a high school student's grade point average. Yet it can count far less in their formula than a score drawn from financial data thrown together on a credit report (which, as we've seen, is sometimes erroneous).

So why would their models zero in on credit scores? Well, like other WMDs, automatic systems can plow through credit scores with great efficiency and at enormous scale. But I would argue that the chief reason has to do with profits. If an insurer has a system that can pull in an extra $1,552 a year from a driver with a clean record, why change it? The victims of their WMD, as we've seen elsewhere, are more likely to be poor and less educated, a good number of them immigrants. They're less likely to know that they're being ripped off. And in neighborhoods with more payday loan offices than insurance brokers, it's harder to shop for lower rates. In short, while an e-score might not correlate with safe driving, it does create a lucrative pool of vulnerable drivers. Many of them are desperate to drive—their jobs depend on it. Overcharging them is good for the bottom line.

From the auto insurer's perspective, it's a win-win. A good driver with a bad credit score is low risk and superhigh reward. What's more, the company can use some of the proceeds from that policy to address the inefficiencies in the model. Those might include the drivers with pristine credit reports who pay low premiums and crash their cars while drunk.

That may sound a tad cynical. But consider the price optimization algorithm at Allstate, the insurer self-branded as "the Good Hands People." According to a watchdog group, the Consumer Federation of America, Allstate analyzes consumer and demographic data to determine the likelihood that customers will shop for lower prices. If they aren't likely to, it makes sense to charge them more. And that's just what Allstate does.

It gets worse. In a filing to the Wisconsin Department of Insurance, the CFA listed one hundred thousand microsegments in Allstate's pricing schemes. These pricing tiers are based on how much each group can be expected to pay. Consequently, some receive discounts of up to 90 percent off the average rate, while others face an increase of 800 percent. "Allstate's insurance pricing has become untethered from the rules of risk-based premiums and from the rule of law," said J. Robert Hunter, CFA's director of insurance and the former Texas insurance commissioner. Allstate responded that the CFA's charges were inaccurate. The company did concede, however, that "marketplace considerations, consistent with industry practices, have been appropriate in developing insurance prices." In other words, its models study a host of proxies to calculate how much to charge customers. And the rest of the industry does, too.

The resulting pricing is unfair. This abuse could not occur if insurance pricing were transparent and customers could easily comparison-shop. But like other WMDs, it is opaque. Every person gets a different experience, and the models are optimized to draw as much money as they can from the desperate and the ignorant. The result—another feedback loop—is that poor drivers who can least afford outrageous premiums are squeezed for every penny they have. The model is fine-tuned to draw as much money as possible from this subgroup. Some of them, inevitably, fall too far, defaulting on their auto loans, credit cards, or rent. That further punishes their credit scores, which no doubt drops them into an even more forlorn microsegment.

· · ·

When Consumer Reports issued its damning report on the auto insurers, it also launched a campaign directed at the National Association of Insurance Commissioners (NAIC), complete with its own Twitter campaign: @NAIC_News to Insurance Commissioners: Price me by how I drive, not by who you think I am! #FixCarInsurance.

The underlying idea was that drivers should be judged by their records—their number of speeding tickets, or whether they've been in an accident—and not by their consumer patterns or those of their friends or neighbors. Yet in the age of Big Data, urging insurers to judge us by how we drive means something entirely new.

Insurance companies now have manifold ways to study drivers' behavior in exquisite detail. For a preview, look no further than the trucking industry.

These days, many trucks carry an electronic logging device that registers every turn, every acceleration, every time they touch the brakes. And in 2015, Swift Transportation, the nation's largest trucking company, started to install cameras pointed in two directions, one toward the road ahead, the other at the driver's face.

The stated goal of this surveillance is to reduce accidents. About seven hundred truckers die on American roads every year. And their crashes also claim the lives of many in other vehicles. In addition to the personal tragedy, this costs lots of money. The average cost of a fatal crash, according to the Federal Motor Carrier Safety Administration, is $3.5 million.

But with such an immense laboratory for analytics at their fingertips, trucking companies aren't stopping at safety. If you combine geoposition, onboard tracking technology, and cameras, truck drivers deliver a rich and constant stream of behavioral data. Trucking companies can now analyze different routes, assess fuel management, and compare results at different times of the day and night. They can even calculate ideal speeds for different road surfaces. And they use this data to figure out which patterns provide the most revenue at the lowest cost.

They can also compare individual drivers. Analytics dashboards give each driver a scorecard. With a click or two, a manager can identify the best and worst performers across a broad range of metrics. Naturally, this surveillance data can also calculate the risk for each driver.

This promise is not lost on the insurance industry. Leading insurers including Progressive, State Farm, and Travelers are already offering drivers a discount on their rates if they agree to share their driving data. A small telemetric unit in the car, a simple version of the black boxes in airplanes, logs the speed of the car and how the driver brakes and accelerates. A GPS monitor tracks the car's movements.

In theory, this meets the ideal of the Consumer Reports campaign. The individual driver comes into focus. Consider eighteen-year-olds. Traditionally they pay sky-high rates because their age group, statistically, indulges in more than its share of recklessness. But now, a high school senior who avoids jackrabbit starts, drives at a consistent pace under the speed limit, and eases to a stop at red lights might get a discounted rate. Insurance companies have long given an edge to young motorists who finish driver's ed or make the honor roll. Those are proxies for responsible driving. But driving data is the real thing. That's better, right?

There are a couple of problems. First, if the system attributes risk to geography, poor drivers lose out. They are more likely to drive in what insurers deem risky neighborhoods. Many also have long and irregular commutes, which translates into higher risk.

Fine, you might say. If poor neighborhoods are riskier, especially for auto theft, why should insurance companies ignore that information? And if longer commutes increase the chance of accidents, that's something the insurers are entitled to consider. The judgment is still based on the driver's behavior, not on extraneous details like her credit rating or the driving records of people her age. Many would consider that an improvement.

To a degree, it is. But consider a hypothetical driver who lives in a rough section of Newark, New Jersey, and must commute thirteen miles to a barista job at a Starbucks in the wealthy suburb of Montclair. Her schedule is chaotic and includes occasional clopenings. So she shuts the shop at 11, drives back to Newark, and returns before 5 a.m. To save ten minutes and $1.50 each way on the Garden State Parkway, she takes a shortcut, which leads her down a road lined with bars and strip joints.

A data-savvy insurer will note that cars traveling along that route in the wee hours have an increased risk of accidents. There are more than a few drunks on the road. And to be fair, our barista is adding a bit of risk by taking the shortcut and sharing the road with the people spilling out of the bars. One of them might hit her. But as far as the insurance company's geo-tracker is concerned, not only is she mingling with drunks, she may *be* one.

In this way, even the models that track our personal behavior gain many of their insights, and assess risk, by comparing us to others. This time, instead of bucketing people who speak Arabic or Urdu, live in the same zip codes, or earn similar salaries, they assemble groups of us who act in similar ways. The prediction is that those who act alike will take on similar levels of risk. If you haven't noticed, this is birds of a feather all over again, with many of the same injustices.

When I talk to most people about black boxes in cars, it's not the analysis they object to as much as the surveillance itself. People insist to me that they won't give in to monitors. They don't want to be tracked or have their information sold to advertisers or handed over to the National Security Agency. Some of these people might succeed in resisting this surveillance. But privacy, increasingly, will come at a cost.

In these early days, the auto insurers' tracking systems are opt-in. Only those willing to be tracked have to turn on their black boxes. They get rewarded with a discount of between 5 and 50 percent and the promise of more down the road. (And the rest of us subsidize those discounts with higher rates.) But as insurers gain more information, they'll be able to create more powerful predictions. That's the nature of the data economy. Those who squeeze out the most intelligence from this information, turning it into profits, will come out on top. They'll predict group risk with greater accuracy (though individuals will always confound them). And the more they benefit from the data, the harder they'll push for more of it.

At some point, the trackers will likely become the norm. And consumers who want to handle insurance the old-fashioned way, withholding all but the essential from their insurers, will have to pay a premium, and probably a steep one. In the world of WMDs, privacy is increasingly a luxury that only the wealthy can afford.

At the same time, surveillance will change the very nature of insurance. Insurance is an industry, traditionally, that draws on the majority of the community to respond to the needs of an unfortunate minority. In the villages we lived in centuries ago, families, religious groups, and neighbors helped look after each other when fire, accident, or illness struck. In the market economy, we outsource this care to insurance companies, which keep a portion of the money for themselves and call it profit.

As insurance companies learn more about us, they'll be able to pinpoint those who appear to be the riskiest customers and then either drive their rates to the stratosphere or, where legal, deny them coverage. This is a far cry from insurance's original purpose, which is to help society balance its risk. In a targeted world, we no longer pay the average. Instead, we're saddled with anticipated costs. Instead of smoothing out life's bumps, insurance companies will demand payment for those bumps in advance. This undermines the point of insurance, and the hits will fall especially hard on those who can least afford them.

・・・

As insurance companies scrutinize the patterns of our lives and our bodies, they will sort us into new types of tribes. But these won't be based on traditional metrics, such as age, gender, net worth, or zip code. Instead, they'll be behavioral tribes, generated almost entirely by machines.

For a look at how such sorting will proliferate, consider a New York City data company called Sense Networks. A decade ago, researchers at Sense began to analyze cell phone data showing where people went. This data, provided by phone companies in Europe and America, was anonymous: just dots moving on maps. (Of course, it wouldn't have taken much sleuthing to associate one of those dots with the address it returned to every night of the week. But Sense was not about individuals; it was about tribes.)

The team fed this mobile data on New York cell phone users to

its machine-learning system but provided scant additional guidance. They didn't instruct the program to isolate suburbanites or
millennials or to create different buckets of shoppers. The software would find similarities on its own. Many of them would be
daft—people who spend more than 50 percent of their days on
streets starting with the letter J, or those who take most of their
lunch breaks outside. But if the system explored millions of these
data points, patterns would start to emerge. Correlations would
emerge, presumably including many that humans would never
consider.

As the days passed and Sense's computer digested its massive trove of data, the dots started to take on different colors. Some
turned toward red, others toward yellow, blue, and green. The
tribes were emerging.

What did these tribes represent? Only the machine knew, and
it wasn't talking. "We wouldn't necessarily recognize what these
people have in common," said Sense's cofounder and former
CEO Greg Skibiski. "They don't fit into the traditional buckets
that we'd come up with." As the tribes took on their colors, the
Sense team could track their movements through New York. By
day, certain neighborhoods would be dominated by blue, then
turn red in the evening, with a sprinkling of yellows. One tribe,
recalled Skibiski, seemed to frequent a certain spot late at night.
Was it a dance club? A crack house? When the Sense team looked
up the address, they saw it was a hospital. People in that tribe appear to be getting hurt more often, or sick. Or maybe they were
doctors, nurses, and emergency medical workers.

Sense was sold in 2014 to YP, a mobile advertising company
spun off from AT&T. So for the time being, its sorting will be
used to target different tribes for ads. But you can imagine how
machine-learning systems fed by different streams of behavioral
data will be soon placing us not just into one tribe but into hun-

dreds of them, even thousands. Certain tribes will respond to similar ads. Others may resemble each other politically or land in jail more frequently. Some might love fast food.

My point is that oceans of behavioral data, in coming years, will feed straight into artificial intelligence systems. And these will remain, to human eyes, black boxes. Throughout this process, we will rarely learn about the tribes we "belong" to or why we belong there. In the era of machine intelligence, most of the variables will remain a mystery. Many of those tribes will mutate hour by hour, even minute by minute, as the systems shuttle people from one group to another. After all, the same person acts very differently at 8 a.m. and 8 p.m.

These automatic programs will increasingly determine how we are treated by the other machines, the ones that choose the ads we see, set prices for us, line us up for a dermatologist appointment, or map our routes. They will be highly efficient, seemingly arbitrary, and utterly unaccountable. No one will understand their logic or be able to explain it.

If we don't wrest back a measure of control, these future WMDs will feel mysterious and powerful. They'll have their way with us, and we'll barely know it's happening.

• • •

In 1943, at the height of World War II, when the American armies and industries needed every troop or worker they could find, the Internal Revenue Service tweaked the tax code, granting tax-free status to employer-based health insurance. This didn't seem to be a big deal, certainly nothing to rival the headlines about the German surrender in Stalingrad or Allied landings on Sicily. At the time, only about 9 percent of American workers received private health coverage as a job benefit. But with the new tax-free status, businesses set about attracting scarce workers by offering health insurance. Within ten years, 65 percent of Americans would come under their employers' systems. Companies already exerted great control over our finances. But in that one decade, they gained a measure of control—whether they wanted it or not—over our bodies.

Seventy-five years later, health care costs have metastasized and now consume $3 trillion per year. Nearly one dollar of every five we earn feeds the vast health care industry.

Employers, which have long been nickel and diming workers to lower their costs, now have a new tactic to combat these growing costs. They call it "wellness." It involves growing surveillance, including lots of data pouring in from the Internet of Things—the Fitbits, Apple Watches, and other sensors that relay updates on how our bodies are functioning.

The idea, as we've seen so many times, springs from good intentions. In fact, it is encouraged by the government. The Affordable Care Act, or Obamacare, invites companies to engage workers in wellness programs, and even to "incentivize" health. By law, employers can now offer rewards and assess penalties reaching as high as 50 percent of the cost of coverage. Now, according to a study by the Rand Corporation, more than half of all organizations employing fifty people or more have wellness programs up and running, and more are joining the trend every week.

There's plenty of justification for wellness programs. If they work—and, as we'll see, that's a big "if"—the biggest beneficiary is the worker and his or her family. Yet if wellness programs help workers avoid heart disease or diabetes, employers gain as well. The fewer emergency room trips made by a company's employees, the less risky the entire pool of workers looks to the insurance company, which in turn brings premiums down. So if we can just look past the intrusions, wellness may appear to be win-win.

Trouble is, the intrusions cannot be ignored or wished away.

Nor can the coercion. Take the case of Aaron Abrams. He's a math professor at Washington and Lee University in Virginia. He is covered by Anthem Insurance, which administers a wellness program. To comply with the program, he must accrue 3,250 "HealthPoints." He gets one point for each "daily log-in" and 1,000 points each for an annual doctor's visit and an on-campus health screening. He also gets points for filling out a "Health Survey" in which he assigns himself monthly goals, getting more points if he achieves them. If he chooses not to participate in the program, Abrams must pay an extra $50 per month toward his premium.

Abrams was hired to teach math. And now, like millions of other Americans, part of his job is follow a host of health dictates and to share that data not only with his employer but also with the third-party company that administers the program. He resents it, and he foresees the day when the college will be able to extend its surveillance. "It is beyond creepy," he says, "to think of anyone reconstructing my daily movements based on my own 'self-tracking' of my walking."

My fear goes a step further. Once companies amass troves of data on employees' health, what will stop them from developing health scores and wielding them to sift through job candidates? Much of the proxy data collected, whether step counts or sleeping patterns, is not protected by law, so it would theoretically be perfectly legal. And it would make sense. As we've seen, they routinely reject applicants on the basis of credit scores and personality tests. Health scores represent a natural—and frightening—next step.

Already, companies are establishing ambitious health standards for workers and penalizing them if they come up short. Michelin, the tire company, sets its employees goals for metrics ranging from blood pressure to glucose, cholesterol, triglycerides, and waist size. Those who don't reach the targets in three categories have to pay an extra $1,000 a year toward their health insurance. The national drugstore chain CVS announced in 2013 that it would require employees to report their levels of body fat, blood sugar, blood pressure, and cholesterol—or pay $600 a year.

The CVS move prompted this angry response from Alissa Fleck, a columnist at Bitch Media: "Attention everyone, everywhere. If you've been struggling for years to get in shape, whatever that means to you, you can just quit whatever it is you're doing right now because CVS has got it all figured out. It turns out whatever silliness you were attempting, you just didn't have the proper incentive. Except, as it happens, this regimen already exists and it's called humiliation and fat-shaming. Have someone tell you you're overweight, or pay a major fine."

At the center of the weight issue is a discredited statistic, the body mass index. This is based on a formula devised two centuries ago by a Belgian mathematician, Lambert Adolphe Jacques Quetelet, who knew next to nothing about health or the human body. He simply wanted an easy formula to gauge obesity in a large population. He based it on what he called the "average man."

"That's a useful concept," writes Keith Devlin, the mathematician and science author. "But if you try to apply it to any one person, you come up with the absurdity of a person with 2.4 children. Averages measure entire populations and often don't apply to individuals." Devlin adds that the BMI, with numerical scores, gives "mathematical snake oil" the air of scientific authority.

The BMI is a person's weight in kilograms divided by their height in centimeters. It's a crude numerical proxy for physical fitness. It's more likely to conclude that women are overweight. (After all, we're not "average" men.) What's more, because fat weighs less than muscle, chiseled athletes often have sky-high BMIs. In the alternate BMI universe, LeBron James qualifies as overweight. When economic "sticks and carrots" are tied to BMI, large groups of workers are penalized for the kind of body they have. This comes down especially hard on black women, who often have high BMIs.

But isn't it a good thing, wellness advocates will ask, to help people deal with their weight and other health issues? The key question is whether this help is an offer or a command. If companies set up free and voluntary wellness programs, few would have reason to object. (And workers who opt in to such programs do, in fact, register gains, though they might well have done so without them.) But tying a flawed statistic like BMI to compensation, and compelling workers to mold their bodies to the corporation's ideal, infringes on freedom. It gives companies an excuse to punish people they don't like to look at—and to remove money from their pockets at the same time.

All of this is done in the name of health. Meanwhile, the $6 billion wellness industry trumpets its successes loudly—and often without offering evidence. "Here are the facts," writes Joshua Love, president of Kinema Fitness, a corporate wellness company. "Healthier people work harder, are happier, help others and are more efficient. Unhealthy workers are generally sluggish, overtired and unhappy, as the work is a symptom of their way of life."

Naturally, Love didn't offer a citation for these broad assertions. And yet even if they were true, there's scant evidence that mandatory wellness programs actually make workers healthier. A research report from the California Health Benefits Review Program concludes that corporate wellness programs fail to lower the average blood pressure, blood sugar, or cholesterol of those who participate in them. Even when people succeed in losing weight on one of these programs, they tend to gain it back. (The one area where wellness programs do show positive results is in quitting smoking.)

It also turns out that wellness programs, despite well-publicized individual successes, often don't lead to lower health care spending. A 2013 study headed by Jill Horwitz, a law professor at UCLA, rips away the movement's economic underpinning. Randomized studies, according to the report, "raise doubts" that smokers and obese workers chalk up higher medical bills than others. While it is true that they are more likely to suffer from health problems, these tend to come later in life, when they're off the corporate health plan and on Medicare. In fact, the greatest savings from wellness programs come from the penalties assessed on the workers. In other words, like scheduling algorithms, they provide corporations with yet another tool to raid their employees' paychecks.

Despite my problems with wellness programs, they don't (yet) rank as full WMDs. They're certainly widespread, they intrude on the lives of millions of employees, and they inflict economic pain. But they are not opaque, and, except for the specious BMI score, they're not based on mathematical algorithms. They're a simple and widespread case of wage theft, one wrapped up in flowery health rhetoric.

Employers are already overdosing on our data. They're busy using it, as we've seen, to score us as potential employees and as workers. They're trying to map our thoughts and our friendships and predict our productivity. Since they're already deeply involved in insurance, with workforce health care a major expense, it's only natural that they would extend surveillance on a large scale to workers' health. And if companies cooked up their own health and productivity models, this could grow into a full-fledged WMD.

10

THE TARGETED CITIZEN

Civic Life

As you know by now, I am outraged by all sorts of WMDs. So let's imagine that I decide to launch a campaign for tougher regulations on them, and I post a petition on my Facebook page. Which of my friends will see it on their news feed?

I have no idea. As soon as I hit send, that petition belongs to Facebook, and the social network's algorithm makes a judgment about how to best use it. It calculates the odds that it will appeal to each of my friends. Some of them, it knows, often sign petitions, and perhaps share them with their own networks. Others tend to scroll right past. At the same time, a number of my friends pay more attention to me and tend to click the articles I post. The

Facebook algorithm takes all of this into account as it decides who will see my petition. For many of my friends, it will be buried so low on their news feed that they'll never see it.

This is what happens when the immensely powerful network we share with 1.5 billion users is also a publicly traded corporation. While Facebook may feel like a modern town square, the company determines, according to its own interests, what we see and learn on its social network. As I write this, about two-thirds of American adults have a profile on Facebook. They spend thirty-nine minutes a day on the site, only four minutes less than they dedicate to face-to-face socializing. Nearly half of them, according to a Pew Research Center report, count on Facebook to deliver at least some of their news, which leads to the question: By tweaking its algorithm and molding the news we see, can Facebook game the political system?

The company's own researchers have been looking into this. During the 2010 and 2012 elections, Facebook conducted experiments to hone a tool they called the "voter megaphone." The idea was to encourage people to spread word that they had voted. This seemed reasonable enough. By sprinkling people's news feeds with "I voted" updates, Facebook was encouraging Americans— more than sixty-one million of them—to carry out their civic duty and make their voices heard. What's more, by posting about people's voting behavior, the site was stoking peer pressure to vote. Studies have shown that the quiet satisfaction of carrying out a civic duty is less likely to move people than the possible judgment of friends and neighbors.

At the same time, Facebook researchers were studying how different types of updates influenced people's voting behavior. No researcher had ever worked in a human laboratory of this scale. Within hours, Facebook could harvest information from tens of millions of people, or more, measuring the impact that their words and shared links had on each other. And it could use that knowledge to influence people's actions, which in this case happened to be voting.

That's a significant amount of power. And Facebook is not the only company to wield it. Other publicly held corporations, including Google, Apple, Microsoft, Amazon, and cell phone providers like Verizon and AT&T, have vast information on much of humanity—and the means to steer us in any way they choose.

Usually, as we've seen, they're focused on making money. However, their profits are tightly linked to government policies. The government regulates them, or chooses not to, approves or blocks their mergers and acquisitions, and sets their tax policies (often turning a blind eye to the billions parked in offshore tax havens). This is why tech companies, like the rest of corporate America, inundate Washington with lobbyists and quietly pour hundreds of millions of dollars in contributions into the political system. Now they're gaining the wherewithal to fine-tune our political behavior—and with it the shape of American government—just by tweaking their algorithms.

The Facebook campaign started out with a constructive and seemingly innocent goal: to encourage people to vote. And it succeeded. After comparing voting records, researchers estimated that their campaign had increased turnout by 340,000 people. That's a big enough crowd to swing entire states, and even national elections. George W. Bush, after all, won in 2000 by a margin of 537 votes in Florida. The activity of a single Facebook algorithm on Election Day, it's clear, could not only change the balance of Congress but also decide the presidency.

Facebook's potency comes not only from its reach but also from its ability to use its own customers to influence their friends. The vast majority of the sixty-one million people in the experiment received a message on their news feed encouraging them to vote.

The message included a display of photos: six of the user's Facebook friends, randomly selected, who had clicked the "I Voted" button. The researchers also studied two control groups, each numbering around six hundred thousand. One group saw the "I Voted" campaign, but without the pictures of friends. The other received nothing at all.

By sprinkling its messages through the network, Facebook was studying the impact of friends' behavior on our own. Would people encourage their friends to vote, and would this affect their behavior? According to the researchers' calculations, seeing that friends were participating made all the difference. People paid much more attention when the "I Voted" updates came from friends, and they were more likely to share those updates. About 20 percent of the people who saw that their friends had voted also clicked on the "I Voted" button. Among those who didn't get the button from friends, only 18 percent did. We can't be sure that all the people who clicked the button actually voted, or that those who didn't click it stayed home. Still, with sixty-one million potential voters on the network, a possible difference of two points can be huge.

Two years later, Facebook took a step further. For three months leading up to the election between President Obama and Mitt Romney, a researcher at the company, Solomon Messing, altered the news feed algorithm for about two million people, all of them politically engaged. These people got a higher proportion of hard news, as opposed to the usual cat videos, graduation announcements, or photos from Disney World. If their friends shared a news story, it showed up high on their feed.

Messing wanted to see if getting more news from friends changed people's political behavior. Following the election, Messing sent out surveys. The self-reported results indicated that the voter participation in this group inched up from 64 to 67 percent.

"When your friends deliver the newspaper," said Lada Adamic, a computational social scientist at Facebook, "interesting things happen." Of course, it wasn't really the friends delivering the newspaper, but Facebook itself. You might argue that newspapers have exerted similar power for eons. Editors pick the front-page news and decide how to characterize it. They choose whether to feature bombed Palestinians or mourning Israelis, a policeman rescuing a baby or battering a protester. These choices can no doubt influence both public opinion and elections. The same goes for television news. But when the *New York Times* or CNN covers a story, everyone sees it. Their editorial decision is clear, on the record. It is not opaque. And people later debate (often on Facebook) whether that decision was the right one.

Facebook is more like the Wizard of Oz: we do not see the human beings involved. When we visit the site, we scroll through updates from our friends. The machine appears to be only a neutral go-between. Many people still believe it is. In 2013, when a University of Illinois researcher named Karrie Karahalios carried out a survey on Facebook's algorithm, she found that 62 percent of the people were unaware that the company tinkered with the news feed. They believed that the system instantly shared everything they posted with all of their friends.

The potential for Facebook to hold sway over our politics extends beyond its placement of news and its Get Out the Vote campaigns. In 2012, researchers experimented on 680,000 Facebook users to see if the updates in their news feeds could affect their mood. It was already clear from laboratory experiments that moods are contagious. Being around a grump is likely to turn you into one, if only briefly. But would such contagions spread online?

Using linguistic software, Facebook sorted positive (stoked!) and negative (bummed!) updates. They then reduced the volume of downbeat postings in half of the news feeds, while reducing the cheerful quotient in the others. When they studied the users' sub-sequent posting behavior, they found evidence that the doctored new feeds had indeed altered their moods. Those who had seen fewer cheerful updates produced more negative posts. A similar pattern emerged on the positive side.

Their conclusion: "Emotional states can be transferred to others . . . , leading people to experience the same emotions without their awareness." In other words, Facebook's algorithms can affect how millions of people feel, and those people won't know that it's happening. What would occur if they played with people's emotions on Election Day?

I have no reason to believe that the social scientists at Facebook are actively gaming the political system. Most of them are serious academics carrying out research on a platform that they could only have dreamed about two decades ago. But what they have demonstrated is Facebook's enormous power to affect what we learn, how we feel, and whether we vote. Its platform is massive, powerful, and opaque. The algorithms are hidden from us, and we see only the results of the experiments researchers choose to publish.

Much the same is true of Google. Its search algorithm appears to be focused on raising revenue. But search results, if Google so chose, could have a dramatic effect on what people learn and how they vote. Two researchers, Robert Epstein and Ronald E. Robertson, recently asked undecided voters in both the United States and India to use a search engine to learn about upcoming elections. The engines they used were programmed to skew the search results, favoring one party over another. Those results, they said, shifted voting preferences by 20 percent.

This effect was powerful, in part, because people widely trust search engines. Some 73 percent of Americans, according to a Pew Research report, believe that search results are both accurate and impartial. So companies like Google would be risking their own reputation, and inviting a regulatory crackdown, if they doctored results to favor one political outcome over another.

Then again, how would anyone know? What we learn about these Internet giants comes mostly from the tiny proportion of their research that they share. Their algorithms represent vital trade secrets. They carry out their business in the dark.

I wouldn't yet call Facebook or Google's algorithms political WMDs, because I have no evidence that the companies are using their networks to cause harm. Still, the potential for abuse is vast. The drama occurs in code and behind imposing firewalls. And as we'll see, these technologies can place each of us into our own cozy political nook.

• • •

By late spring of 2012, the former governor of Massachusetts, Mitt Romney, had the Republican nomination sewn up. The next step was to build up his war chest for the general election showdown with President Obama. And so on May 17, he traveled to Boca Raton, Florida, for a fund-raiser at the palatial home of Marc Leder, a private equity investor. Leder had already poured $225,000 into the pro-Romney Super PAC Restore Our Future and had given another $63,330 to the Romney Victory PAC. He had gathered a host of rich friends, most of them in finance and real estate, to meet the candidate. Naturally, the affair would be catered.

Romney could safely assume that he was walking into a closed setting with a group of people who thought much like Marc Leder. If this had been a televised speech, Romney would have taken great care not to ruffle potential Republican voters. Those ranged from Evangelical Christians and Wall Street financiers to Cuban Americans and suburban soccer moms. Trying to please everyone is one reason most political speeches are boring (and Romney's, even his supporters groused, were especially so). But at an intimate gathering at Marc Leder's house, a small and influential group might get closer to the real Mitt Romney and hear what the candidate really believed, unfiltered. They had already given him large donations. A frank chat was the least they could expect for their investment.

Basking in the company of people he believed to be supportive and like-minded, Romney let loose with his observation that 47 percent of the population were "takers," living off the largesse of big government. These people would never vote for him, the governor said—which made it especially important to reach out to the other 53 percent. But Romney's targeting, it turned out, was inexact. The caterers circulating among the donors, serving drinks and canapés, were outsiders. And like nearly everyone in the developed world, they carried phones equipped with video cameras. Romney's dismissive remarks, captured by a bartender, went viral. The gaffe very likely cost Romney any chance he had of winning the White House.

Success for Romney at that Boca Raton gathering required both accurate targeting and secrecy. He wanted to be the ideal candidate for Marc Leder and friends. And he trusted that Leder's house represented a safe zone in which to be that candidate. In a dream world, politicians would navigate countless such targeted safe zones so that they could tailor their pitch for every subgroup—without letting the others see it. One candidate could be many candidates, with each part of the electorate seeing only the parts they liked.

This duplicity, or "multiplicity," is nothing new in politics. Politicians have long tried to be many things to many people, whether they're eating kielbasa in Milwaukee, quoting the Torah in Brooklyn, or pledging allegiance to corn-based ethanol in Iowa. But as Romney discovered, video cameras can now bust them if they overdo their contortions.

Modern consumer marketing, however, provides politicians with new pathways to specific voters so that they can tell them what they know they want to hear. Once they do, those voters are likely to accept the information at face value because it confirms their previous beliefs, a phenomenon psychologists call confirmation bias. It is one reason that none of the invited donors at the Romney event questioned his assertion that nearly half of voters were hungry for government handouts. It only bolstered their existing beliefs.

This merging of politics and consumer marketing has been developing for the last half century, as the tribal rituals of American politics, with their ward bosses and long phone lists, have given way to marketing science. In *The Selling of the President*, which followed Richard Nixon's 1968 campaign, the journalist Joe McGinniss introduced readers to the political operatives working to market the presidential candidate like a consumer good. By using focus groups, Nixon's campaign was able to hone his pitch for different regions and demographics.

But as time went on, politicians wanted a more detailed approach, one that would ideally reach each voter with a personalized come-on. This desire gave birth to direct-mail campaigns. Borrowing tactics from the credit card industry, political operatives built up huge databases of customers—voters, in this case—and placed them into various subgroups, reflecting their values and their demographics. For the first time, it was possible for next-door neighbors to receive different letters or brochures from the same politician, one vowing to protect wilderness and the other stressing law and order.

Direct mail was microtargeting on training wheels. The convergence of Big Data and consumer marketing now provides politicians with far more powerful tools. They can target microgroups of citizens for both votes and money and appeal to each of them with a meticulously honed message, one that no one else is likely to see. It might be a banner on Facebook or a fund-raising email. But each one allows candidates to quietly sell multiple versions of themselves—and it's anyone's guess which version will show up for work after inauguration.

...

In July of 2011, more than a year before President Obama would run for reelection, a data scientist named Rayid Ghani posted an update on LinkedIn:

> *Hiring analytics experts who want to make a difference. The Obama re-election campaign is growing the analytics team to work on high-impact large-scale data mining problems.*
>
> *We have several positions available at all levels of experience. Looking for experts in statistics, machine learning, data mining, text analytics, and predictive analytics to work with large amounts of data and help guide election strategy.*

Ghani, a computer scientist educated at Carnegie Mellon, would be heading up the data team for Obama's campaign. In his previous position, at Accenture Labs in Chicago, Ghani had developed consumer applications for Big Data, and he trusted that he could apply his skills to politics. The goal for the Obama campaign was to create tribes of like-minded voters, people as uniform in their values and priorities as the guests at Marc Leder's reception—but without the caterers. Then they could target them with the messaging most likely to move them toward specific objectives, including voting, organizing, and fund-raising.

One of Ghani's projects at Accenture involved modeling supermarket shoppers. A major grocer had provided the Accenture team with a massive database of anonymized consumer purchases. The idea was to dig into this data to study each consumer's buying habits and then to place the shoppers into hundreds of different consumer buckets. There would be the impulse shoppers who bought candy at the checkout counter and the health nuts who were willing to pay triple for organic kale. Those were the obvious categories. But others were more surprising. Ghani and his team, for example, could spot people who stuck close to a brand and others who would switch for even a tiny discount. There were buckets for these "persuadables," too. The end goal was to come up with a different plan for each shopper and to guide them through the store, leading them to all the foods they were most likely to want and buy.

Unfortunately for Accenture's clients, this ultimate vision hinged upon the advent of computerized shopping carts, which haven't yet caught on in a big way and maybe never will. But despite the disappointment in supermarkets, Ghani's science translated perfectly into politics. Those fickle shoppers who switched brands to save a few cents, for example, behaved very much like swing voters. In the supermarket, it was possible to estimate how much it would cost to turn each shopper from one brand of ketchup or coffee to another more profitable brand. The supermarket could then pick out, say, the 15 percent most likely to switch and provide them with coupons. Smart targeting was essential. They certainly didn't want to give coupons to shoppers who were ready to pay full price. That was like burning money.*

Would similar calculations work for swing voters? Armed with massive troves of consumer, demographic, and voting data, Ghani

---

* Similarly, consumer websites are much more likely to offer discounts to people who are not already logged in. This is another reason to clear your cookies regularly.

and his team set out to investigate. However, they faced one crucial difference. In the supermarket project, all of the available data related precisely to the shopping domain. They studied shopping patterns to predict (and influence) what people would buy. But in politics there was very little relevant data available. Data teams for both campaigns needed proxies, and this required research.

They started out by interviewing several thousand people in great depth. These folks fell into different groups. Some cared about education or gay rights, others worried about Social Security or the impact of fracking on freshwater aquifers. Some supported the president unconditionally. Others sat on the fence. A good number liked him but didn't usually get around to voting. Some of them—and this was vital—were ready to contribute money to Obama's campaign.

Once Ghani's data team understood this small group of voters, their desires, their fears, and what it took to change their behavior, the next challenge was to find millions of other voters (and donors) who resembled them. This involved plowing through the consumer data and demographics of the voters they had interviewed and building mathematical profiles of them. Then it was just a matter of scouring national databases, finding people with similar profiles, and placing them into the same buckets.

The campaign could then target each group with advertisements, perhaps on Facebook or the media sites they visited, to see if they responded as expected. They carried out the same kind of A/B testing that Google uses to see which shade of blue garners more clicks on a button. Trying different approaches, they found, for example, that e-mail subject lines reading only "Hey!" bugged people but also led to more engagement and sometimes more donations. Through thousands of tests and tweaks, the campaign finally sized up its audience—including an all-important contingent of fifteen million swing voters.

Throughout this process, each campaign developed profiles of American voters. Each profile contained numerous scores, which not only gauged their value as a potential voter, volunteer, and donor but also reflected their stances on different issues. One voter might have a high score on environmental issues but a low one on national security or international trade. These political profiles are very similar to those that Internet companies, like Amazon and Netflix, use to manage their tens of millions of customers. Those companies' analytics engines churn out nearly constant cost/benefit analyses to maximize their revenue per customer.

Four years later, Hillary Clinton's campaign built upon the methodology established by Obama's team. It contracted a micro-targeting start-up, the Groundwork, financed by Google chairman Eric Schmidt and run by Michael Slaby, the chief technology officer of Obama's 2012 campaign. The goal, according to a report in Quartz, was to build a data system that would create a political version of systems that companies like Salesforce.com develop to manage their millions of customers.

The appetite for fresh and relevant data, as you might imagine, is intense. And some of the methods used to gather it are unsavory, not to mention intrusive. In late 2015, the *Guardian* reported that a political data firm, Cambridge Analytica, had paid academics in the United Kingdom to amass Facebook profiles of US voters, with demographic details and records of each user's "likes." They used this information to develop psychographic analyses of more than forty million voters, ranking each on the scale of the "big five" personality traits: openness, conscientiousness, extroversion, agreeableness, and neuroticism. Groups working with the Ted Cruz presidential campaign then used these studies to develop television commercials targeted for different types of voters, placing them in programming they'd be most likely to watch. When the Republican Jewish Coalition was meeting at the Venetian

in Las Vegas in May 2015, for instance, the Cruz campaign un-
leashed a series of web-based advertisements visible only inside
the hotel complex that emphasized Cruz's devotion to Israel and
its security.

I should mention here that not all of these targeting campaigns have proven to be effective. Some, no doubt, are selling
little more than snake oil. The microtargeters, after all, are themselves marketing to campaigns and political action groups with
millions of dollars to spend. They sell them grand promises of
priceless databases and pinpoint targeting, many of which are
bound to be exaggerated. So in this sense the politicians not only
purvey questionable promises but also consume them (at exorbitant expense). That said, as the Obama team demonstrated, some
of these methods are fruitful. And so the industry—serious data
scientists and hucksters alike—zeros in on voters.

Political microtargeters, however, face unique constraints,
which make their work far more complex. The value of each voter,
for example, rises or falls depending on the probability that his or
her state will be in play. A swing voter in a swing state, like Florida, Ohio, or Nevada, is highly valuable. But if polls show the state
tilting decisively to either blue or red, that voter's value plummets,
and the marketing budget is quickly shifted toward other voters
whose value is climbing.

In this sense, we can think of the voting public very much as we
think of financial markets. With the flow of information, values
rise and fall, as do investments. In these new political markets,
each one of us represents a stock with its own fluctuating price.
And each campaign must decide if and how to invest in us. If we
merit the investment, then they decide not only what information
to feed us but also how much and how to deliver it.

Similar calculations, on a macro scale, have been going on for
decades, as campaigns plot their TV spending. As polling num-

bers change, they might cut ads in Pittsburgh and move those dollars to Tampa or Las Vegas. But with microtargeting, the focus shifts from the region to the individual. More important, that individual alone sees the customized version of the politician.

The campaigns use similar analysis to identify potential donors and to optimize each one. Here it gets complicated, because many of the donors themselves are carrying out their own calculations. They want the biggest bang for their buck. They know that if they immediately hand over the maximum contribution the campaign will view them as "fully tapped" and therefore irrelevant. But refusing to give any money will also render them irrelevant. So many give a drip-feed of money based on whether the messages they hear are ones they agree with. For them, managing a politician is like training a dog with treats. This training effect is all the more powerful for contributors to Super PACS, which do not limit political contributions.

The campaigns, of course, are well aware of this tactic. With microtargeting, they can send each of those donors the information most likely to pry more dollars from their bank accounts. And these messages will vary from one donor to the next.

• • •

These tactics aren't limited to campaigns. They infect our civic life, with lobbyists and interest groups now using these targeting methods to carry out their dirty work. In 2015, the Center for Medical Progress, an antiabortion group, posted videos featuring what they claimed was an aborted fetus at a Planned Parenthood clinic. The videos asserted that Planned Parenthood doctors were selling baby parts for research, and they spurred a wave of protest, and a Republican push to eliminate the organization's funding.

Research later showed that the video had been doctored: the so-called fetus was actually a photo of a stillborn baby born to a woman in rural Pennsylvania. And Planned Parenthood does not sell fetal tissue. The Center for Medical Progress admitted that the video contained misinformation. That weakened its appeal for a mass market. But with microtargeting, antiabortion activists could continue to build an audience for the video, despite the flawed premise, and use it to raise funds to fight Planned Parenthood.

While that campaign launched into public view, hundreds of others continue to hover below the surface, addressing individual voters. These quieter campaigns are equally deceptive and even less accountable. And they deliver ideological bombs that politicians will only hint at on the record. According to Zeynep Tufekci, a techno-sociologist and professor at the University of North Carolina, these groups pinpoint vulnerable voters and then target them with fear-mongering campaigns, scaring them about their children's safety or the rise of illegal immigration. At the same time, they can keep those ads from the eyes of voters likely to be turned off (or even disgusted) by such messaging.

Successful microtargeting, in part, explains why in 2015 more than 43 percent of Republicans, according to a survey, still believed the lie that President Obama is a Muslim. And 20 percent of Americans believed he was born outside the United States and, consequently, an illegitimate president. (Democrats may well spread their own disinformation in microtargeting, but nothing that has surfaced matches the scale of the anti-Obama campaigns.)

Even with the growth of microtargeting, political campaigns are still directing 75 percent of their media buy, on average, to television. You might think that this would have an equalizing effect, and it does. Television delivers the broader, and accountable, messaging, while microtargeting does its work in the shadows. But even television is moving toward personalized advertising. New advertising companies like Simulmedia, in New York, assemble

TV viewers into behavioral buckets, so that advertisers can target audiences of like-minded people, whether hunters, pacifists, or buyers of tank-sized SUVs. As television and the rest of the media move toward profiling their viewers, the potential for political microtargeting grows.

As this happens, it will become harder to access the political messages our neighbors are seeing—and as a result, to understand why they believe what they do, often passionately. Even a nosy journalist will struggle to track down the messaging. It is not enough simply to visit the candidate's web page, because they, too, automatically profile and target each visitor, weighing everything from their zip codes to the links they click on the page, even the photos they appear to look at. It's also fruitless to create dozens of "fake" profiles, because the systems associate each real voter with deep accumulated knowledge, including purchasing records, addresses, phone numbers, voting records, and even social security numbers and Facebook profiles. To convince the system it's real, each fake would have to come with its own load of data. Fabricating one would require far too much work for a research project (and in the worst-case scenario it might get the investigator tangled up in fraud).

The result of these subterranean campaigns is a dangerous imbalance. The political marketers maintain deep dossiers on us, feed us a trickle of information, and measure how we respond to it. But we're kept in the dark about what our neighbors are being fed. This resembles a common tactic used by business negotiators. They deal with different parties separately so that none of them knows what the other is hearing. This asymmetry of information prevents the various parties from joining forces—which is precisely the point of a democratic government.

This growing science of microtargeting, with its profiles and predictions, fits all too neatly into our dark collection of WMDs.

It is vast, opaque, and unaccountable. It provides cover to politicians, encouraging them to be many things to many people.

The scoring of individual voters also undermines democracy, making a minority of voters important and the rest little more than a supporting cast. Indeed, looking at the models used in presidential elections, we seem to inhabit a shrunken country. As I write this, the entire voting population that *matters* lives in a handful of counties in Florida, Ohio, Nevada, and a few other swing states. Within those counties is a small number of voters whose opinions weigh in the balance. I might point out here that while many of the WMDs we've been looking at, from predatory ads to policing models, deliver most of their punishment to the struggling classes, political microtargeting harms voters of every economic class. From Manhattan to San Francisco, rich and poor alike find themselves disenfranchised (though the truly affluent, of course, can more than compensate for this with campaign contributions).

In any case, the entire political system—the money, the attention, the fawning—turns to targeted voters like a flower following the sun. The rest of us are virtually ignored (except for fund-raising come-ons). The programs have already predicted our voting behavior, and any attempt to change it is not worth the investment.*

This creates a nefarious feedback loop. The disregarded voters are more likely to grow disenchanted. The winners know how to play the game. They get the inside story, while the vast majority of consumers receive only market-tested scraps.

---

* At the federal level, this problem could be greatly alleviated by abolishing the Electoral College system. It's the winner-take-all mathematics from state to state that delivers so much power to a relative handful of voters. It's as if in politics, as in economics, we have a privileged 1 percent. And the money from the financial 1 percent underwrites the microtargeting to secure the votes of the political 1 percent. Without the Electoral College, by contrast, every vote would be worth exactly the same. That would be a step toward democracy.

Indeed, there is an added asymmetry. People who are expected to be voters but who, for one reason or another, skip an election find themselves lavished with attention the next time round. They still seem to brim with high voting potential. But those expected not to vote are largely ignored. The systems are searching for the cheapest votes to convert, with the highest return for each dollar spent. And nonvoters often look expensive. This dynamic prods a certain class of people to stay active and lets the rest lie fallow forever.

As is often the case with WMDs, the very same models that inflict damage could be used to humanity's benefit. Instead of targeting people in order to manipulate them, it could line them up for help. In a mayoral race, for example, a microtargeting campaign might tag certain voters for angry messages about un-affordable rents. But if the candidate knows these voters are angry about rent, how about using the same technology to identify the ones who will most benefit from affordable housing and then help them find it?

With political messaging, as with most WMDs, the heart of the problem is almost always the objective. Change that objec-tive from leeching off people to helping them, and a WMD is disarmed—and can even become a force for good.

CONCLUSION

In this march through a virtual lifetime, we've visited school and college, the courts and the workplace, even the voting booth. Along the way, we've witnessed the destruction caused by WMDs. Promising efficiency and fairness, they distort higher education, drive up debt, spur mass incarceration, pummel the poor at nearly every juncture, and undermine democracy. It might seem like the logical response is to disarm these weapons, one by one.

The problem is that they're feeding on each other. Poor people are more likely to have bad credit and live in high-crime neighborhoods, surrounded by other poor people. Once the dark universe of WMDs digests that data, it showers them with predatory ads for subprime loans or for-profit schools. It sends more police to arrest them, and when they're convicted it sentences them to longer terms. This data feeds into other WMDs, which score the same people as high risks or easy targets and proceed to block them from jobs, while jacking up their rates for mortgages, car loans, and every kind of insurance imaginable. This drives their credit rating down further, creating nothing less than a death spiral of modeling. Being poor in a world of WMDs is getting more and more dangerous and expensive.

The same WMDs that abuse the poor also place the comfortable classes of society in their own marketing silos. They jet them off to vacations in Aruba and wait-list them at Wharton. For many of them, it can feel as though the world is getting smarter and easier. Models highlight bargains on prosciutto and chianti, recommend a great movie on Amazon Prime, or lead them, turn by turn, to a café in what used to be a "sketchy" neighborhood. The quiet and personal nature of this targeting keeps society's winners from seeing how the very same models are destroying lives, sometimes just a few blocks away.

Our national motto, E Pluribus Unum, means "Out of Many, One." But WMDs reverse the equation. Working in darkness, they carve one into many, while hiding us from the harms they inflict upon our neighbors near and far. And those harms are legion. They unfold when a single mother can't arrange child care fast enough to adapt to her work schedule, or when a struggling young person is red-lighted for an hourly job by a workplace personality test. We see them when a poor minority teenager gets stopped, roughed up, and put on warning by the local police, or when a gas station attendant who lives in a poor zip code gets hit with a higher insurance bill. It's a silent war that hits the poor hardest but also hammers the middle class. Its victims, for the most part, lack economic power, access to lawyers, or well-funded political organizations to fight their battles. The result is widespread damage that all too often passes for inevitability.

We cannot count on the free market itself to right these wrongs. To understand why, let's compare WMDs to another scourge our society has been grappling with, homophobia.

In September of 1996, two months before his reelection, President Bill Clinton signed the Defense of Marriage Act. This law, defining marriage as between one man and one woman, promised to firm up support for the president in conservative patches of battleground states, including Ohio and Florida.

Only a week later, the tech giant IBM announced that it would provide medical benefits to the same-sex partners of its employees. You might wonder why Big Blue, a pillar of the corporate establishment, would open this door and invite controversy when a putatively progressive American president was moving in the opposite direction.

The answer has to do with the bottom line. In 1996, the Internet gold rush was just taking off, and IBM was battling for brainpower with Oracle, Microsoft, Hewlett-Packard, and a host of start-ups, including Amazon and Yahoo. Most of those other companies were already providing benefits to same-sex partners and attracting gay and lesbian talent. IBM could not afford to miss out. "In terms of business competitiveness, it made sense for us," an IBM spokesperson told *BusinessWeek* at the time.

If we think about human resources policies at IBM and other companies as algorithms, they codified discrimination for decades. The move to equalize benefits nudged them toward fairness. Since then, gays and lesbians have registered impressive progress in many domains. This progress is uneven, of course. Many gay, lesbian, and transgender Americans are still victims of prejudice, violence, and WMDs. This is especially true among poor and minority populations. Still, as I write this, a gay man, Tim Cook, is the chief executive of Apple, the most valuable company on earth. And if he so chooses, he has the constitutional right to marry a man.

Now that we've seen how corporations can move decisively to right a wrong in their hiring algorithms, why can't they make similar adjustments to the mathematical models wreaking havoc on our society, the WMDs?

Unfortunately, there's a glaring difference. Gay rights benefited in many ways from market forces. There was a highly educated and increasingly vocal gay and lesbian talent pool that companies were eager to engage. So they optimized their models to attract them. But they did this with the focus on the bottom line. Fairness, in most cases, was a by-product. At the same time, businesses across the country were starting to zero in on wealthy LGBT consumers, offering cruises, happy hours, and gay-themed TV shows. While inclusiveness no doubt caused grumbling in some pockets of intolerance, it also paid rich dividends.

Dismantling a WMD doesn't always offer such obvious payoff. While more fairness and justice would of course benefit society as a whole, individual companies are not positioned to reap the rewards. For most of them, in fact, WMDs appear to be highly effective. Entire business models, such as for-profit universities and payday loans, are built upon them. And when a software program successfully targets people desperate enough to pay 18 percent a month, those raking in the profits think it's working just fine.

The victims, of course, feel differently. But the greatest number of them—the hourly workers and unemployed, the people dragging low credit scores through life—are poor. Prisoners are powerless. And in our society, where money buys influence, these WMD victims are nearly voiceless. Most are disenfranchised politically. Indeed, all too often the poor are blamed for their poverty, their bad schools, and the crime that afflicts their neighborhoods. That's why few politicians even bother with antipoverty strategies. In the common view, the ills of poverty are more like a disease, and the effort—or at least the rhetoric—is to quarantine it and keep it from spreading to the middle class. We need to think about how we assign blame in modern life and how models exacerbate this cycle.

But the poor are hardly the only victims of WMDs. Far from it. We've already seen how malevolent models can blacklist qualified job applicants and dock the pay of workers who don't fit a corporation's picture of ideal health. These WMDs hit the middle class as hard as anyone. Even the rich find themselves microtargeted by political models. And they scurry about as frantically as the rest of us to satisfy the remorseless WMD that rules college admissions and pollutes higher education.

It's also important to note that these are the early days. Naturally, payday lenders and their ilk start off by targeting the poor and the immigrants. Those are the easiest targets, the low-hanging fruit. They have less access to information, and more of them are desperate. But WMDs generating fabulous profit margins are not likely to remain cloistered for long in the lower ranks. That's not the way markets work. They'll evolve and spread, looking for new opportunities. We already see this happening as mainstream banks invest in peer-to-peer loan operations like Lending Club. In short, WMDs are targeting us all. And they'll continue to multiply, sowing injustice, until we take steps to stop them.

Injustice, whether based in greed or prejudice, has been with us forever. And you could argue that WMDs are no worse than the human nastiness of the recent past. In many cases, after all, a loan officer or hiring manager would routinely exclude entire races, not to mention an entire gender, from being considered for a mortgage or a job offer. Even the worst mathematical models, many would argue, aren't nearly that bad.

But human decision making, while often flawed, has one chief virtue. It can evolve. As human beings learn and adapt, we change, and so do our processes. Automated systems, by contrast, stay stuck in time until engineers dive in to change them. If a Big Data college application model had established itself in the early 1960s, we still wouldn't have many women going to college, because it would have been trained largely on successful men. If museums at the same time had codified the prevalent ideas of great art, we would still be looking almost entirely at work by white men, the people paid by rich patrons to create art. The University of Alabama's football team, needless to say, would still be lily white.

Big Data processes codify the past. They do not invent the future. Doing that requires moral imagination, and that's something only humans can provide. We have to explicitly embed better values into our algorithms, creating Big Data models that follow our ethical lead. Sometimes that will mean putting fairness ahead of profit.

In a sense, our society is struggling with a new industrial revolution. And we can draw some lessons from the last one. The turn of the twentieth century was a time of great progress. People could light their houses with electricity and heat them with coal. Modern railroads brought in meat, vegetables, and canned goods from a continent away. For many, the good life was getting better.

Yet this progress had a gruesome underside. It was powered by horribly exploited workers, many of them children. In the absence of health or safety regulations, coal mines were death traps. In 1907 alone, 3,242 miners died. Meatpackers worked twelve to fifteen hours a day in filthy conditions and often shipped toxic products. Armour and Co. dispatched cans of rotten beef by the ton to US Army troops, using a layer of boric acid to mask the stench. Meanwhile, rapacious monopolists dominated the railroads, energy companies, and utilities and jacked up customers' rates, which amounted to a tax on the national economy.

Clearly, the free market could not control its excesses. So after journalists like Ida Tarbell and Upton Sinclair exposed these and other problems, the government stepped in. It established safety protocols and health inspections for food, and it outlawed child labor. With the rise of unions, and the passage of laws safeguarding them, our society moved toward eight-hour workdays and weekends off. These new standards protected companies that didn't want to exploit workers or sell tainted foods, because their competitors had to follow the same rules. And while they no doubt raised the costs of doing business, they also benefited society as a whole. Few of us would want to return to a time before they existed.

...

How do we start to regulate the mathematical models that run more and more of our lives? I would suggest that the process begin with the modelers themselves. Like doctors, data scientists should pledge a Hippocratic Oath, one that focuses on the possible misuses and misinterpretations of their models. Following the market crash of 2008, two financial engineers, Emanuel Derman and Paul Wilmott, drew up such an oath. It reads:

~ I will remember that I didn't make the world, and it doesn't satisfy my equations.

~ Though I will use models boldly to estimate value, I will not be overly impressed by mathematics.

~ I will never sacrifice reality for elegance without explaining why I have done so.

~ Nor will I give the people who use my model false comfort about its accuracy. Instead, I will make explicit its assumptions and oversights.

~ I understand that my work may have enormous effects
on society and the economy, many of them beyond my
comprehension.

That's a good philosophical grounding. But solid values and self-
regulation rein in only the scrupulous. What's more, the Hippocratic Oath ignores the on-the-ground pressure that data scientists
often confront when bosses push for specific answers. To eliminate WMDs, we must advance beyond establishing best practices
in our data guild. Our laws need to change, too. And to make that
happen we must reevaluate our metric of success.

Today, the success of a model is often measured in terms of
profit, efficiency, or default rates. It's almost always something
that can be counted. What should we be counting, though? Consider this example. When people look for information about food
stamps on a search engine, they are often confronted with ads for
go-betweens, like FindFamilyResources, of Tempe, Arizona. Such
sites look official and provide links to real government forms. But
they also gather names and e-mail addresses for predatory advertisers, including for-profit colleges. They rake in lead generation
fees by providing a superfluous service to people, many of whom
are soon targeted for services they can ill afford.

Is the transaction successful? It depends on what you count.
For Google, the click on the ad brings in a quarter, fifty cents, or
even a dollar or two. That's a success. Naturally, the lead generator
also makes money. And so it looks as though the system is functioning efficiently. The wheels of commerce are turning.

Yet from society's perspective, a simple hunt for government
services puts a big target on the back of poor people, leading a
certain number of them toward false promises and high-interest
loans. Even considered strictly from an economic point of view,

it's a drain on the system. The fact that people need food stamps in the first place represents a failing of the market economy. The government, using tax dollars, attempts to compensate for it, with the hope that food stamp recipients will eventually be able to fully support themselves. But the lead aggregators push them toward needless transactions, leaving a good number of them with larger deficits, and even more dependent on public assistance. The WMD, while producing revenue for search engines, lead aggregators, and marketers, is a leech on the economy as a whole.

A regulatory system for WMDs would have to measure such hidden costs, while also incorporating a host of non-numerical values. This is already the case for other types of regulation. Though economists may attempt to calculate costs for smog or agricultural runoff, or the extinction of the spotted owl, numbers can never express their value. And the same is often true of fairness and the common good in mathematical models. They're concepts that reside only in the human mind, and they resist quantification. And since humans are in charge of making the models, they rarely go the extra mile or two to even try. It's just considered too difficult. But we need to impose human values on these systems, even at the cost of efficiency. For example, a model might be programmed to make sure that various ethnicities or income levels are represented within groups of voters or consumers. Or it could highlight cases in which people in certain zip codes pay twice the average for certain services. These approximations may be crude, especially at first, but they're essential. Mathematical models should be our tools, not our masters.

The achievement gap, mass incarceration, and voter apathy are big, nationwide problems that no free market nor mathematical algorithm will fix. So the first step is to get a grip on our techno-utopia, that unbounded and unwarranted hope in what algorithms and technology can accomplish. Before asking them to do better, we have to admit they can't do everything.

To disarm WMDs, we also need to measure their impact and conduct algorithmic audits. The first step, before digging into the software code, is to carry out research. We'd begin by treating the WMD as a black box that takes in data and spits out conclusions. This person has a medium risk of committing another crime, this one has a 73 percent chance of voting Republican, this teacher ranks in the lowest decile. By studying these outputs, we could piece together the assumptions behind the model and score them for fairness.

Sometimes, it is all too clear from the get-go that certain WMDs are only primitive tools, which hammer complexity into simplicity, making it easier for managers to fire groups of people or to offer discounts to others. The value-added model used in New York public schools, for example, the one that rated Tim Clifford a disastrous 6 one year and then a high-flying 96 a year later, is a statistical farce. If you plot year-to-year scores on a chart, the dots are nearly as randomly placed as hydrogen atoms in a room. Many of the math students in those very schools could study those statistics for fifteen minutes and conclude, with confidence, that the scores measure nothing. Good teachers, after all, tend to be good one year after the next. Unlike, say, relief pitchers in baseball, they rarely have great seasons followed by disasters. (And also unlike relief pitchers, their performance resists quantitative analysis.)

There's no fixing a backward model like the value-added model. The only solution in such a case is to ditch the unfair system. Forget, at least for the next decade or two, about building tools to measure the effectiveness of a teacher. It's too complex to model, and the only available data are crude proxies. The model is simply not good enough yet to inform important decisions about the people we trust to teach our children. That's a job that requires subtlety and context. Even in the age of Big Data, it remains a problem for humans to solve.

Of course, the human analysts, whether the principal or administrators, should consider lots of data, including the students' test scores. They should incorporate positive feedback loops. These are the angelic cousins of the pernicious feedback loops we've come to know so well. A positive loop simply provides information to the data scientist (or to the automatic system) so that the model can be improved. In this case, it's simply a matter of asking teachers and students alike if the evaluations make sense for them, if they understand and accept the premises behind them. If not, how could they be enhanced? Only when we have an ecosystem with positive feedback loops can we expect to improve teaching using data. Until then it's just punitive.

It is true, as data boosters are quick to point out, that the human brain runs internal models of its own, and they're often tinged with prejudice or self-interest. So its outputs—in this case, teacher evaluations—must also be audited for fairness. And these audits have to be carefully designed and tested by human beings, and afterward automated. In the meantime, mathematicians can get to work on devising models to help teachers measure their own effectiveness and improve.

Other audits are far more complicated. Take the criminal recidivism models that judges in many states consult before sentencing prisoners. In these cases, since the technology is fairly new, we have a before and an after. Have judges' sentencing patterns changed since they started receiving risk analysis from the WMD? We'll see, no doubt, that a number of the judges ran similarly troubling models in their heads long before the software arrived, punishing poor prisoners and minorities more severely than others. In some of those cases, conceivably, the software might temper their judgments. In others, not. But with enough data, patterns will become clear, allowing us to evaluate the strength and the tilt of the WMD.

If we find (as studies have already shown) that the recidivism models codify prejudice and penalize the poor, then it's time to take a look at the inputs. In this case, they include loads of birds-of-a-feather connections. They predict an individual's behavior on the basis of the people he knows, his job, and his credit rating—details that would be inadmissible in court. The fairness fix is to throw out that data.

But wait, many would say. Are we going to sacrifice the accuracy of the model for fairness? Do we have to dumb down our algorithms?

In some cases, yes. If we're going to be equal before the law, or be treated equally as voters, we cannot stand for systems that drop us into different castes and treat us differently.* Companies like Amazon and Netflix can plunk their paying customers into little buckets and optimize them all they want. But the same algorithm cannot deliver justice or democracy.

Movements toward auditing algorithms are already afoot. At Princeton, for example, researchers have launched the Web Transparency and Accountability Project. They create software robots that masquerade online as people of all stripes—rich, poor, male, female, or suffering from mental health issues. By study-

---

* You might think that an evenhanded audit would push to eliminate variables such as race from the analysis. But if we're going to measure the impact of a WMD, we need that data. Currently, most of the WMDs avoid directly tracking race. In many cases, it's against the law. It is easier, however, to expose racial discrimination in mortgage lending than in auto loans, because mortgage lenders are required to ask for the race of the applicant, while auto lenders are not. If we include race in the analysis, as the computer scientist Cynthia Dwork has noted, we can quantify racial injustice where we find it. Then we can publicize it, debate the ethics, and propose remedies. Having said that, race is a social construct and as such is difficult to pin down even when you intend to, as any person of mixed race can tell you.

ing the treatment these robots receive, the academics can detect biases in automated systems from search engines to job placement sites. Similar initiatives are taking root at universities like Carnegie Mellon and MIT.

Academic support for these initiatives is crucial. After all, to police the WMDs we need people with the skills to build them. Their research tools can replicate the immense scale of the WMDs and retrieve data sets large enough to reveal the imbalances and injustice embedded in the models. They can also build crowdsourcing campaigns, so that people across society can provide details on the messaging they're receiving from advertisers or politicians. This could illuminate the practices and strategies of microtargeting campaigns.

Not all of them would turn out to be nefarious. Following the 2012 presidential election, for example, ProPublica built what it called a Message Machine, which used crowdsourcing to reverse-engineer the model for the Obama campaign's targeted political ads. Different groups, as it turned out, heard glowing remarks about the president from different celebrities, each one presumably targeted for a specific audience. This was no smoking gun. But by providing information and eliminating the mystery behind the model, the Message Machine reduced (if only by a tad) grounds for dark rumors and suspicion. That's a good thing.

If you consider mathematical models as the engines of the digital economy—and in many ways they are—these auditors are opening the hoods, showing us how they work. This is a vital step, so that we can equip these powerful engines with steering wheels—and brakes.

Auditors face resistance, however, often from the web giants, which are the closest thing we have to information utilities. Google, for example, has prohibited researchers from creating scores of fake profiles in order to map the biases of the search engine.* If the company does in fact carry out bias audits, its preference is to keep them internal. That way they shield the algorithm's inner workings, and its prejudices, from outsiders. But insiders, suffering as we all do from confirmation bias, are more likely to see what they expect to find. They might not ask the most probing questions. And if they find injustices that appear to boost Google's bottom line . . . well, that could lead to uncomfortable discussions, ones they'd certainly want to keep out of the public light. So there are powerful business arguments for secrecy. But as the public learns more about WMDs, and demands more accountability from these utilities, Google, I'm hoping, will have little choice but to let outsiders in.

Facebook, too. The social network's rigorous policy to tie users to their real names severely limits the research outsiders can carry out there. The real-name policy is admirable in many ways, not least because it pushes users to be accountable for the messages they post. But Facebook also must be accountable to all of us—which means opening its platform to more data auditors.

The government, of course, has a powerful regulatory role to play, just as it did when confronted with the excesses and tragedies of the first industrial revolution. It can start by adapting and then enforcing the laws that are already on the books.

As we discussed in the chapter on credit scores, the civil rights laws referred to as the Fair Credit Reporting Act (FCRA) and the Equal Credit Opportunity Act (ECOA) were meant to ensure fairness in credit scoring. The FCRA guarantees that a consumer can see the data going into their score and correct any errors, and the ECOA prohibits linking race or gender to a person's score.

---

* Google has expressed interest in working to eliminate bias from its algorithm, and some Google employees briefly talked to me about this. One of the first things I tell them is to open the platform to more outside researchers.

These regulations are not perfect, and they desperately need updating. Consumer complaints are often ignored, and there's nothing explicitly keeping credit-scoring companies from using zip codes as proxies for race. Still, they offer a good starting point. First, we need to demand transparency. Each of us should have the right to receive an alert when a credit score is being used to judge or vet us. And each of us should have access to the information being used to compute that score. If it is incorrect, we should have the right to challenge and correct it.

Next, the regulations should expand to cover new types of credit companies, like Lending Club, which use newfangled e-scores to predict the risk that we'll default on loans. They should not be allowed to operate in the shadows.

The Americans with Disabilities Act (ADA), which protects people with medical issues from being discriminated against at work, also needs an update. The bill currently prohibits medical exams as part of an employment screening. But we need to update it to take into account Big Data personality tests, health scores, and reputation scores. They all sneak around the law, and they shouldn't be able to. One possibility already under discussion would extend protection of the ADA to include "predicted" health outcomes down the road. In other words, if a genome analysis shows that a person has a high risk for breast cancer, or for Alzheimer's, that person should not be denied job opportunities.

We must also expand the Health Insurance Portability and Accountability Act (HIPAA), which protects our medical information, in order to cover the medical data currently being collected by employers, health apps, and other Big Data companies. Any health-related data collected by brokers, such as Google searches for medical treatments, must also be protected.

If we want to bring out the big guns, we might consider moving toward the European model, which stipulates that any data collected must be approved by the user, as an opt-in. It also prohibits the reuse of data for other purposes. The opt-in condition is all too often bypassed by having a user click on an inscrutable legal box. But the "not reusable" clause is very strong: it makes it illegal to sell user data. This keeps it from the data brokers whose dossiers feed toxic e-scores and microtargeting campaigns. Thanks to this "not reusable" clause, the data brokers in Europe are much more restricted, assuming they follow the law.

Finally, models that have a significant impact on our lives, including credit scores and e-scores, should be open and available to the public. Ideally, we could navigate them at the level of an app on our phones. In a tight month, for example, a consumer could use such an app to compare the impact of unpaid phone and electricity bills on her credit score and see how much a lower score would affect her plans to buy a car. The technology already exists. It's only the will we're lacking.

. . .

On a summer day in 2013, I took the subway to the southern tip of Manhattan and walked to a large administrative building across from New York's City Hall. I was interested in building mathematical models to help society—the opposite of WMDs. So I'd signed on as an unpaid intern in a data analysis group within the city's Housing and Human Services Departments. The number of homeless people in the city had grown to sixty-four thousand, including twenty-two thousand children. My job was to help create a model that would predict how long a homeless family would stay in the shelter system and to pair each family with the appropriate services. The idea was to give people what they needed to take care of themselves and their families and to find a permanent home.

My job, in many ways, was to help come up with a recidivism

model. Much like the analysts building the LSI–R model, I was interested in the forces that pushed people back to shelters and also those that led them to stable housing. Unlike the sentencing WMD, though, our small group was concentrating on using these findings to help the victims and to reduce homelessness and despair. The goal was to create a model for the common good.

On a separate but related project, one of the other researchers had found an extremely strong correlation, one that pointed to a solution. A certain group of homeless families tended to disappear from shelters and never return. These were the ones who had been granted vouchers under a federal affordable housing program called Section 8. This shouldn't have been too surprising. If you provide homeless families with affordable housing, not too many of them will opt for the streets or squalid shelters.

Yet that conclusion might have been embarrassing to then-mayor Michael Bloomberg and his administration. With much fanfare, the city government had moved to wean families from Section 8. It instituted a new system called Advantage, which limited subsidies to three years. The idea was that the looming expiration of their benefits would push poor people to make more money and pay their own way. This proved optimistic, as the data made clear. Meanwhile, New York's booming real estate market was driving up rents, making the transition even more daunting. Families without Section 8 vouchers streamed back into the shelters.

The researcher's finding was not welcome. For a meeting with important public officials, our group prepared a PowerPoint presentation about homelessness in New York. After the slide with statistics about recidivism and the effectiveness of Section 8 was put up, an extremely awkward and brief conversation took place. Someone demanded the slide be taken down. The party line prevailed.

While Big Data, when managed wisely, can provide important insights, many of them will be disruptive. After all, it aims to find patterns that are invisible to human eyes. The challenge for data scientists is to understand the ecosystems they are wading into and to present not just the problems but also their possible solutions. A simple workflow data analysis might highlight five workers who appear to be superfluous. But if the data team brings in an expert, they might help discover a more constructive version of the model. It might suggest jobs those people could fill in an optimized system and might identify the training they'd need to fill those positions. Sometimes the job of a data scientist is to know when you don't know enough.

As I survey the data economy, I see loads of emerging mathematical models that might be used for good and an equal number that have the potential to be great—if they're not abused. Consider the work of Mira Bernstein, a slavery sleuth. A Harvard PhD in math, she created a model to scan vast industrial supply chains, like the ones that put together cell phones, sneakers, or SUVs, to find signs of forced labor. She built her slavery model for a non-profit company called Made in a Free World. Its goal is to use the model to help companies root out the slave-built components in their products. The idea is that companies will be eager to free themselves from this scourge, presumably because they oppose slavery, but also because association with it could devastate their brand.

Bernstein collected data from a number of sources, including trade data from the United Nations, statistics about the regions where slavery was most prevalent, and detailed information about the components going into thousands of industrial products, and incorporated it all into a model that could score a given product from a certain region for the likelihood that it was made using slave labor. "The idea is that the user would contact his supplier and say, 'Tell me more about where you're getting the following parts of your computers,'" Bernstein told *Wired* magazine. Like many responsible models, the slavery detector does not overreach. It merely points to suspicious places and leaves the last part of the hunt to human beings. Some of the companies find, no doubt, that the suspected supplier is legit. (Every model produces false positives.) That information comes back to Made in a Free World, where Bernstein can study the feedback.

Another model for the common good has emerged in the field of social work. It's a predictive model that pinpoints households where children are most likely to suffer abuse. The model, developed by Eckerd, a child and family services nonprofit in the southeastern United States, launched in 2013 in Florida's Hillsborough County, an area encompassing Tampa. In the previous two years, nine children in the area had died from abuse, including a baby who was thrown out a car window. The modelers included 1,500 child abuse cases in their database, including the fatalities. They found a number of markers for abuse, including a boyfriend in the home, a record of drug use or domestic violence, and a parent who had been in foster care as a child.

If this were a program to target potential criminals, you can see right away how unfair it could be. Having lived in a foster home or having an unmarried partner in the house should not be grounds for suspicion. What's more, the model is much more likely to target the poor—and to give a pass to potential abuse in wealthy neighborhoods.

Yet if the goal is not to punish the parents, but instead to provide help to children who might need it, a potential WMD turns benign. It funnels resources to families at risk. And in the two years following implementation of the model, according to the *Boston Globe*, Hillsborough County suffered no fatalities from child abuse.

Models like this will abound in coming years, assessing our risk of osteoporosis or strokes, swooping in to help struggling students with calculus II, even predicting the people most likely to suffer life-altering falls. Many of these models, like some of the WMDs we've discussed, will arrive with the best intentions. But they must also deliver transparency, disclosing the input data they're using as well as the results of their targeting. And they must be open to audits. These are powerful engines, after all. We must keep our eyes on them.

Data is not going away. Nor are computers—much less mathematics. Predictive models are, increasingly, the tools we will be relying on to run our institutions, deploy our resources, and manage our lives. But as I've tried to show throughout this book, these models are constructed not just from data but from the choices we make about which data to pay attention to—and which to leave out. Those choices are not just about logistics, profits, and efficiency. They are fundamentally moral.

If we back away from them and treat mathematical models as a neutral and inevitable force, like the weather or the tides, we abdicate our responsibility. And the result, as we've seen, is WMDs that treat us like machine parts in the workplace, that blackball employees and feast on inequities. We must come together to police these WMDs, to tame and disarm them. My hope is that they'll be remembered, like the deadly coal mines of a century ago, as relics of the early days of this new revolution, before we learned how to bring fairness and accountability to the age of data. Math deserves much better than WMDs, and democracy does too.

NOTES

INTRODUCTION

3   *one out of every two:* Robert Stillwell, *Public School Graduates and Dropouts from the Common Core of Data: School Year 2006–07,* NCES 2010-313 (Washington, DC: National Center for Education Statistics, Institute of Education Sciences, US Department of Education, 2009), 5, http://nces.ed.gov/pubsearch/pubsinfo.asp ?pubid=2010313.

3   8 *percent of eighth graders:* Jihyun Lee, Wendy S. Grigg, and Gloria S. Dion, *The Nation's Report Card Mathematics 2007,* NCES 2007-494 (Washington, DC: National Center for Education Statistics, Institute of Education Sciences, US Department of Education, 2007), 32, https://nces.ed.gov/nationsreportcard/pdf/ main2007/2007494.pdf.

4   *Rhee developed a teacher assessment tool:* Bill Turque, "Rhee Dismisses 241 D.C. Teachers; Union Vows to Contest Firings," *Washington Post,* July 24, 2010, www.washingtonpost.com/wp-dyn/ content/article/2010/07/23/AR2010072303093.html.

4   *the district fired all the teachers:* Steven Sawchuck, "Rhee to Dismiss Hundreds of Teachers for Poor Performance," *Education Week Blog,* July 23, 2010, http://blogs.edweek.org/edweek/teacher beat/2010/07/_states_and_districts_across.html.

4   *another 5 percent, or 205 teachers:* Bill Turque, "206 Low-Performing D.C. Teachers Fired," *Washington Post,* July 15, 2011, www.washingtonpost.com/local/education/206-low-performing-dc -teachers-fired/2011/07/15/gIQANEj5GI_story.html.

4   *Sarah Wysocki, a fifth-grade teacher:* Bill Turque, " 'Creative . . . Motivating' and Fired," *Washington Post,* March 6, 2012, www

.washingtonpost.com/local/education/creative—motivating-and
-fired/2012/02/04/gIQAwzZpvR_story.html.

4   *One evaluation praised her:* Ibid.

4   *Wysocki received a miserable score:* Ibid.

4   *represented half of her overall evaluation:* Ibid.

5   *The district had hired a consultancy:* Ibid.

6   *"There are so many factors":* Sarah Wysocki, e-mail interview by
     author, August 6, 2015.

8   *a math teacher named Sarah Bax:* Guy Brandenburg, "DCPS
     Administrators Won't or Can't Give a DCPS Teacher the IMPACT
     Value-Added Algorithm," *GFBrandenburg's Blog,* February 27, 2011,
     https://gfbrandenburg.wordpress.com/2011/02/27/dcps-administrators
     -wont-or-cant-give-a-dcps-teacher-the-impact-value-added
     -algorithm/.

9   *29 percent of the students:* Turque, "'Creative . . . Motivating' and
     Fired."

9   **USA Today** *revealed a high level:* Jack Gillum and Marisol Bello,
     "When Standardized Test Scores Soared in D.C., Were the Gains
     Real?," *USA Today,* March 30, 2011, http://usatoday30.usatoday.com/
     news/education/2011-03-28-1Aschooltesting28_CV_N.htm.

9   *bonuses of up to $8,000:* Ibid.

10   *the erasures were "suggestive":* Turque, "'Creative . . . Motivating'
     and Fired."

11   *Sarah Wysocki was out of a job:* Ibid.

CHAPTER 1

16   *Boudreau, perhaps out of desperation:* David Waldstein, "Who's on
     Third? In Baseball's Shifting Defenses, Maybe Nobody," *New York
     Times,* May 12, 2014, www.nytimes.com/2014/05/13/sports/baseball/
     whos-on-third-in-baseballs-shifting-defenses-maybe-nobody.html?
     _r=0.

17   **Moneyball:** Michael Lewis, *Moneyball: The Art of Winning an Unfair Game* (New York: W. W. Norton, 2003).

23   *In 1997, a convicted murderer:* Manny Fernandez, "Texas Execution Stayed Based on Race Testimony," *New York Times*, September 16, 2011, www.nytimes.com/2011/09/17/us/experts -testimony-on-race-led -to-stay-of-execution-in-texas.html?page wanted =all.

23   *made a reference to Buck's race:* Ibid.

24   *"It is inappropriate to allow race":* Alan Berlow, "See No Racism, Hear No Racism: Despite Evidence, Perry About to Execute Another Texas Man," *National Memo*, September 15, 2011, www .nationalmemo.com/perry-might-let-another-man-die/.

24   *Buck never got a new hearing:* NAACP Legal Defense Fund, "Texas Fifth Circuit Rejects Appeal in Case of Duane Buck," NAACP LDF website, August 21, 2015, www.naacpldf.org/update/ texas-fifth-circuit-rejects-appeal-case-duane-buck.

24   *prosecutors were three times more likely:* OpenFile, "TX: Study Finds Harris County Prosecutors Sought Death Penalty 3-4 Times More Often Against Defendants of Color," *Open File, Prosecutorial Misconduct and Accountability*, March 15, 2013, www.prosecutorial accountability.com/2013/03/15/tx-study-finds-harris-county -prosecutors-sought-death-penalty-3-4-times-more-often-against -defendants-of-color/.

24   *sentences imposed on black men:* American Civil Liberties Union, *Racial Disparities in Sentencing, Hearing on Reports of Racism in the Justice System of the United States*, submitted to the Inter- American Commission on Human Rights, 153rd Session, October 27, 2014, www.aclu.org/sites/default/files/assets/141027_iachr_racial _disparities_aclu_submission_0.pdf.

24   *blacks fill up 40 percent of America's prison cells:* Federal Bureau of Prisons, Statistics web page, accessed January 8, 2016, www.bop .gov/about/statistics/statistics_inmate_race.jsp.

24   *courts in twenty-four states:* Sonja Starr, "Sentencing, by the Numbers," *New York Times*, August 10, 2014, www.nytimes.com/ 2014/08/11/opinion/sentencing-by-the-numbers.html.

25 *average of* $31,000 *a year:* Christian Henrichson and Ruth Delaney, *The Price of Prisons: What Incarceration Costs Taxpayers* (New York: VERA Institute of Justice, 2012), www.vera.org/sites/default/files/ resources/downloads/price-of-prisons-updated-version-021914.pdf.

25 **A 2013 *study by the New York Civil Liberties Union:*** New York Civil Liberties Union, "Stop-and-Frisk 2011," NYCLU Briefing, May 9, 2012, www.nyclu.org/files/publications/NYCLU_2011_Stop-and -Frisk_Report.pdf.

26 ***such as Rhode Island:*** Rhode Island Department of Corrections, Planning and Research Unit, "Level of Service Inventory–Revised: A Portrait of RIDOC Offenders," April 2011, accessed January 8, 2016, www.doc.ri.gov/administration/planning/docs/LSINewsletterFINAL .pdf.

26 ***including Idaho:*** Center for Sentencing Initiatives, Research Division, National Center for State Courts, "Use of Risk and Needs Assessment Information at Sentencing: 7th Judicial District, Idaho," December 2013, accessed January 8, 2016, www.ncsc.org/~/media/ Microsites/Files/CSI/RNA%20Brief%20-%207th%20Judicial%20 District%20ID%20csi.ashx.

26 ***and Colorado:*** Ibid.

30 ***at least twenty-four of them:*** LSI–R is used in the following twenty-four states, according to these documents (mostly published by the corresponding departments of corrections); all links accessed January 13, 2016.

    Alaska, www.correct.state.ak.us/pnp/pdf/902.03.pdf

    Colorado, www.doc.state.co.us/sites/default/files/phase_ii.pdf

    Connecticut, www.ct.gov/opm/lib/opm/cjppd/cjabout/mainnav/ risk_assessment_strategy.pdf

    Delaware, https://ltgov.delaware.gov/taskforces/djrtf/DJRTFVOP AppendixBFINAL.pdf

    Hawaii, http://ag.hawaii.gov/cpja/files/2013/01/AH-UH-Mainland -Prison-Study-2011.pdf

    Idaho, http://sentencing.isc.idaho.gov/

Illinois, www.illinoiscourts.gov/supremecourt/annualreport/2012/adminsumm/administrative.pdf

Indiana, www.in.gov/idoc/files/CEBP_long_report(1).pdf and http://indianacourts.us/times/2011/04/risk-assessment/

Iowa, http://publications.iowa.gov/13104/

Kansas, www.doc.ks.gov/kdoc-policies/AdultIMPP/chapter-14/14-111a/view

Maine, www.bja.gov/Funding/14SmartSup-MDOCapp.pdf

Maryland, www.justicepolicy.org/images/upload/09-03_rpt_mdparole_ac-md-ps-rd.pdf

Minnesota, www.doc.state.mn.us/DocPolicy2/html/DPW_Display_TOC.asp?Opt=203.015.htm

Nebraska, www.uc.edu/content/dam/uc/ccjr/docs/vitas/VITA10_PVV.pdf

Nevada, www.leg.state.nv.us/74th/Exhibits/Assembly/JUD/AJUD77H.pdf

New Hampshire, www.nh.gov/nhdoc/policies/documents/6-33.pdf

North Carolina, www.ncids.org/Reports%20&%20Data/Latest%20Releases/SentencingServicesContReview3-1-10.pdf

North Dakota, www.nd.gov/docr/adult/docs/DOCR%20Programs%20Reference%20Guide%20(Rev.%204-14).pdf

Oklahoma, www.ok.gov/doc/documents/LSI-R%20White%20Paper.pdf

Pennsylvania, http://pacrimestats.info/PCCDReports/Related Publications/Publications/Publications/Pennsylvania%20Board%20of%20Probation%20and%20Parole/Ctr%20for%20Effective%20Public%20Policy.pdf

Rhode Island, www.doc.ri.gov/administration/planning/docs/LSINewsletterFINAL.pdf

South Dakota, https://doc.sd.gov/documents/about/policies/LSI-R%20Assessment%20and%20Case%20Planning.pdf

Utah, http://ucjc.utah.edu/wp-content/uploads/LSI
-Implementation-Report-final.pdf

Washington, http://static.nicic.gov/Library/019033.pdf

CHAPTER 2

40   *Alberto Ramirez, who made $14,000 a year:* Carol Lloyd,
     "Impossible Loan Turns Dream Home into Nightmare," *SFGate*,
     April 15, 2007, www.sfgate.com/business/article/Impossible-loan
     -turns-dream-home-into-nightmare-2601880.php.

40   *Baltimore officials charged Wells Fargo:* Michael Powell, "Bank
     Accused of Pushing Mortgage Deals on Blacks," *New York Times*,
     June 6, 2009, www.nytimes.com/2009/06/07/us/07baltimore.html.

40   *a former bank loan officer, Beth Jacobson:* Ibid.

40   *71 percent of them were in largely African American
     neighborhoods:* Ibid.

40   *Wells Fargo settled the suit:* Luke Broadwater, "Wells Fargo Agrees
     to Pay $175M Settlement in Pricing Discrimination Suit," *Baltimore
     Sun*, July 12, 2012, http://articles.baltimoresun.com/2012-07-12/news/
     bs-md-ci-wells-fargo-20120712_1_mike-heid-wells-fargo-home
     -mortgage -subprime-mortgages.

CHAPTER 3

51   *the staff at* U.S. News: Robert Morse, "The Birth of the College
     Rankings," *U.S. News*, May 16, 2008, www.usnews.com/news/
     national/articles/2008/05/16/the-birth-of-the-college-rankings.

53   *In the other quarter:* Julie Rawe, "A Better Way to Rank Colleges?"
     Time, June 20, 2007, http://content.time.com/time/nation/article/
     0,8599,1635326,00.html.

54   *Baylor University paid the fee:* Sara Rimer, "Baylor Rewards
     Freshmen Who Retake SAT," *New York Times*, October 14, 2008,
     www.nytimes.com/2008/10/15/education/15baylor.html.

54   *including Bucknell University*: Nick Anderson, "Five Colleges
     Misreported Data to U.S. News, Raising Concerns About Rankings,
     Reputation," *Washington Post*, February 6, 2013, www .washington
     post.com/local/education/five-colleges-misreported-data -to-us-news
     -raising-concerns-about-rankings-reputation/2013/02/06/cb437876
     -6b17-11e2-af53-7b2b2a7510a8_story.html.

54   *And Iona College*: Robert Morse, "Iona College Admits to Inflating
     Rankings Data for 9 Years," *U.S. News*, December 1, 2011, www
     .usnews.com/education/blogs/college-rankings-blog/2011/12/01/iona
     -college-admits-to-inflating-rankings-data-for-9-years.

56   *was tumbling in the U.S. News ranking*: Logan Wilson, "University
     Drops in Ranking for the Third Time in a Row," *TCU 360*,
     September 4, 2008, www.tcu360.com/story/university-drops-in
     -ranking-for-third-time-in-a-row-12287643/.

56   *Raymond Brown, the dean*: Ibid.

56   *TCU launched a $250 million fund-raising drive*: TCUleads, "U.S.
     News & World Report Rankings Show Improvement for TCU,"
     Texas Christian University, September 9, 2014, accessed January 9,
     2016, http://newsevents.tcu.edu/stories/u-s-news-world-report
     -rankings-show-improvement-for-tcu/.

57   *applications to BC*: Sean Silverthorne, "The Flutie Effect: How
     Athletic Success Boosts College Applications," *Forbes*, April 29, 2013,
     www.forbes.com/sites/hbsworkingknowledge/2013/04/29/the-flutie
     -effect-how-athletic-success-boosts-college-applications/.

58   *Its rank in the U.S. News list climbed*: TCUleads, "U.S. News &
     World Report Rankings."

60   *the cost of higher education rose*: Michelle Jamrisko and Ilan Kolet,
     "College Costs Surge 500% in U.S. Since 1985: Chart of the Day,"
     Bloomberg Business, August 26, 2013, www.bloomberg.com/news/
     articles/2013-08-26/college-costs-surge-500-in-u-s-since-1985-chart-of
     -the-day.

61   *"any other characteristic you desire"*: Ruffalo Noel Levitz,
     "ForecastPlus for Student Recruitment™," accessed January 9,
     2016, www.ruffalonl.com/enrollment-management/enrollment
     -marketing-services-to-target-and-recruit-students/recruitment

-technologies/forecast-plus-student-recruitment-predictive
-modeling.

62   *mathematics department at Saudi Arabia's King Abdulaziz
     University:* Megan Messerly, "Citations for Sale," *Daily Californian*,
     December 5, 2014, www.dailycal.org/2014/12/05/citations-sale/.

63   *authorities began to suspect:* Malcolm Moore, "Riot after Chinese
     Teachers Try to Stop Pupils Cheating," *Telegraph*, June 20, 2013,
     www.telegraph.co.uk/news/worldnews/asia/china/10132391/Riot-after
     -Chinese-teachers-try-to-stop-pupils-cheating.html.

64   *a company called Top Tier Admissions:* Application Boot Camp,
     accessed January 9, 2016, www.toptieradmissions.com/boot-camp/
     application-boot-camp/.

64   *Ma, founder of ThinkTank Learning:* Peter Waldman, "How to Get
     into an Ivy League College—Guaranteed," *Bloomberg BusinessWeek*,
     September 4, 2014, www.bloomberg.com/news/articles/2014-09-04/
     how-to-get-into-an-ivy-league-college-guaranteed.

65   *President Obama suggested:* Li Zhou, "Obama's New College
     Scorecard Flips the Focus of Rankings," *Atlantic Monthly*, September
     15, 2015, www.theatlantic.com/education/archive/2015/09/obamas
     -new-college-scorecard-flips-the-focus-of-rankings/405379/.

67   A New York Times *report in* 2011: David Segal, "Is Law School a
     Losing Game?," *New York Times*, January 8, 2011, www.nytimes
     .com/2011/01/09/business/09law.html.

CHAPTER 4

70   *$50 million on Google ads:* Meghan Kelly, "96 Percent of Google's
     Revenue Is Advertising, Who Buys It?," *Venture Beat*, January 29,
     2012, http://venturebeat.com/2012/01/29/google-advertising/.

70   *Between 2004 and 2014, for-profit enrollment tripled:* David
     Deming, Claudia Goldin, and Lawrence Katz, "For-Profit Colleges,"
     Postsecondary Education in the United States 23 (Spring 2013):
     137–63, http://futureofchildren.org/futureofchildren/publications/
     journals/article/index.xml?journalid=79&articleid=584.

70 *the industry now accounts for 11 percent:* Emily Jane Fox, "White House Crackdown on For-Profit Colleges Begins Today," CNN, July 1, 2015, http://money.cnn.com/2015/07/01/pf/college/for-profit -colleges-debt/.

71 *had more than eighty thousand students:* Melody Peterson, "State Sues Corinthian Colleges, Citing 'Predatory' Tactics," *Orange County Register,* October 10, 2013, www.ocregister.com/articles/ company-530539-students-corinthian.html.

71 *The complaint pointed out:* Corinthian Colleges Inc., "California Attorney General Complaint Allegations vs. Facts," accessed January 9, 2016, http://hles.shareholder.com/downloads/COCO/3283532602x 0x709108/11BC55FD-B86F-45DB-B082-5C6AEB6D8D30/CCi _Response_to_California_Attorney_General_Lawsuit.pdf.

71 *the Obama administration put a hold:* Review & Outlook, "Obama's Corinthian Kill, Review and Outlook," *Wall Street Journal,* July 15 2014, www.wsj.com/articles/obamas-corinthian -kill-1406327662.

71 *In mid-2015:* Shahien Nasiripour, "Corinthian Colleges Files for Bankruptcy," *Huffington Post,* May 4, 2015, www.huffingtonpost .com/2015/05/04/corinthian-colleges-bankruptcy_n_7205344.html.

71 *"unlawful, unfair, and fraudulent":* Megan Woolhouse, "For-Profit Colleges Get Harsh Grades by Former Students," *Boston Globe,* October 20, 2014, www.bostonglobe.com/business/2014/10/19/high -debt-unfulfilled-dreams/KuDKIWiyRO5E5HDpRpSLRO/story .html.

71 A 2012 *Senate committee report:* Sheryl Harris, "For-Profit Colleges Provide Lesson in Strong-Arm Sales: Plain Dealing," *cleveland .com,* August 4, 2012, www.cleveland.com/consumeraffairs/index .ssf/2012/08/for-profit_colleges_provide_le.html.

73 *"We deal with people that live in the moment":* David Halperin, "What College Was Michael Brown About to Attend?," *Huffington Post,* August 26, 2014, www.huffingtonpost.com/davidhalperin/what -college-was-michael_b_5719731.html.

73 *recruiting team at the ITT Technical Institute:* Committee on Health, Education, Labor, and Pensions, "For-Profit Higher

Education: The Failure to Safeguard the Federal Investment and Ensure Student Success," *Senate Committee Print*, S. Prt. 112-37, vol. 1, July 30, 2012, p. 60, www.gpo.gov/fdsys/granule/CPRT-112SPRT74931/CPRT-112SPRT74931/content-detail.html.

73 *spent $120 million annually:* Screenshot by author from a LinkedIn advertisement for a position in online marketing.

77 *"Obama Asks Moms":* Sharona Coutts, "Bogus 'Obama Mom' Grants Lure Students," *ProPublica*, July 23, 2010, www.propublica .org/article/bogus-obama-mom-grants-lure-students.

78 *colleges will pay as much as $150 each:* Jenna Leventoff, "For-Profit Colleges Under Scrutiny for Targeting Vulnerable Students," *Equal Future*, May 6, 2015, www.equalfuture.us/2015/05/06/for-profit -colleges-targeting-vulnerable-students/.

78 *Salt Lake City–based Neutron Interactive:* David Halperin, "More Scam Websites to Lure the Poor to For-Profit Colleges," *Huffington Post*, November 13, 2014, www.huffingtonpost.com/davidhalperin/ more-scam-websites-to-lur_b_6151650.html.

78 *Each one was worth as much as $85:* Coutts, "Bogus 'Obama Mom.'"

78 *US Government Accountability Office report:* US Government Accountability Office, "For-Profit Colleges: Undercover Testing Finds Colleges Encouraged Fraud and Engaged in Deceptive and Questionable Marketing Practices," GAO-10-948T, August 4, 2010, www.gao.gov/products/GAO-10-948T.

78 *According to Mara Tucker:* Mara Tucker, in-person interview by author, June 15, 2015.

78 *Cassie Magesis, another readiness counselor:* Cassie Magesis, phone interview by author, June 16, 2015.

79 *spent more than a billion dollars:* Howard Hotson, "Short Cuts," *London Review of Books*, June 2, 2011, www.lrb.co.uk/v33/n11/howard -hotson/short-cuts.

79 *Portland Community College:* Mike Dang, "For-Profit Colleges Still Terrible," *Billfold*, August 1, 2012, https://thebillfold.com/for -profit-colleges-still-terrible-7e3b5bd3442b#.4ti2e2y8o.

79 *the so-called 90-10 rule:* Rebecca Schuman, "'This Is Your Money' Why For-Profit Colleges Are the Real Welfare Queens," *Slate,* June 4, 2015, www.slate.com/articles/life/education/2015/06/for_profit _colleges_and_federal_aid_they_get_more_than_90_percent_of _their.html.

80 *Corinthian Colleges amounted to $3.5 billion:* Tamar Lewin, "Government to Forgive Student Loans at Corinthian Colleges," *New York Times,* June 8, 2015, www.nytimes.com/2015/06/09/ education/us-to-forgive-federal-loans-of-corinthian-college-students .html.

80 *investigators at CALDER/American Institutes:* Rajeev Darolia, Cory Koedel, Paco Martorell, Katie Wilson, and Francisco Perez-Arce, "Do Employers Prefer Workers Who Attend For-Profit Colleges? Evidence from a Field Experiment," RAND Corporation, Santa Monica, CA, 2014, accessed January 9, 2016, www.rand.org/ pubs/working_papers/WR1054.html.

80 *The top 20 percent of the population:* William Domhoff, "Wealth, Income, and Power," *Who Rules America?,* first posted September 2005, updated February 2013, accessed January 9, 2016, http:// whorulesamerica.net/power/wealth.html.

81 *Gregory W. Cappelli:* Josh Harkinson, "The Nation's 10 Most Overpaid CEOs," *Mother Jones,* July 12, 2012, www.motherjones .com/politics/2012/07/executive-pay-america-top-10-overpaid-ceo.

82 *interest rates that average 574 percent:* Gwen Ifill and Andrew Schmertz, "Fighting the Debt Trap of Triple-Digit Interest Rate Payday Loads," *PBS Newshour,* January 6, 2016, www.pbs.org/ newshour/bb/fighting-the-debt-trap-of-triple-digit-interest-rate -payday-loans/.

82 *In 2015, the Federal Trade Commission:* Lindsay Wise, "Feds Charge Data Broker with Selling Consumer Info to Scammers," *McClatchyDC,* August 12, 2015, www.mcclatchydc.com/news/nation -world/national/article30862680.html.

CHAPTER 5

84   *The small city of Reading:* Rob Engle, "The Guilded [*sic*] Age in Reading Pennsylvania," *Historical Review of Berks County,* Summer 2005, www.berkshistory.org/multimedia/articles/the-guilded-age-in -reading-pennsylvania/.

84   *the highest poverty rate:* Sabrina Tavernise, "Reading, Pa., Knew It Was Poor. Now It Knows Just How Poor," *New York Times,* September 26, 2011, www.nytimes.com/2011/09/27/us/reading-pa -tops-list-poverty-list-census-shows.html.

85   *crime prediction software made by PredPol:* Steven Henshaw, "Homicides in Reading Rise, Other Crimes Down, Police Say," *Reading Eagle,* August 30, 2015, www.readingeagle.com/news/ article/homicides-in-reading-rise-other-crimes-down-police-say.

85   *Philadelphia police are using a local product:* Juliana Reyes, "Philly Police Will Be First Big City Cops to Use Azavea's Crime Predicting Software," *Technically Philly,* November 7, 2013, http:// technical.ly/philly/2013/11/07/azavea-philly-police-crime-prediction -software/.

85   *based on seismic software:* Nate Berg, "Predicting Crime, LAPD-Style," *Guardian,* June 25, 2014, www.theguardian.com/cities/2014/ jun/25/predicting-crime-lapd-los-angeles-police-data-analysis -algorithm-minority-report.

86   *Jeffrey Brantingham, the UCLA anthropology professor:* Jeff Brantingham, PredPol's chief of research and development, phone interview by author, February 3, 2015.

87   *criminologist named George Kelling:* George Kelling and James Wilson, "Broken Windows: The Police and Neighborhood Safety," *Atlantic Monthly,* March 1982, www.theatlantic.com/magazine/ archive/1982/03/broken-windows/304465/.

87   *zero-tolerance campaigns:* Judith Greene, "Zero Tolerance: A Case Study of Police Policies and Practices in New York City," *Crime and Delinquency* 45 (April 1999): 171–87, doi:10.1177/0011128799045 002001.

88   **Freakonomics:** Steven Levitt and Stephen Dubner, *Freakonomics: A Rogue Economist Explores the Hidden Side of Everything* (New York: William Morrow, 2005).

89   *police in the British city of Kent:* Berg, "Predicting Crime, LAPD-Style."

89   *PredPol squares were ten times as efficient:* Kent Police, "PredPol Operational Review," 2014, www.statewatch.org/docbin/uk-2014-kent -police-predpol-op-review.pdf.

92   *the practice had drastically increased:* Jeffrey Bellin, "The Inverse Relationship between the Constitutionality and Effectiveness of New York City 'Stop and Frisk,'" *Boston University Law Review* 94 (May 6, 2014): 1495, William and Mary Law School Research Paper No. 09-274, http://ssrn.com/abstract=2413935.

92   *the number of stops had risen by 600 percent:* Ryan Devereaux, "Scrutiny Mounts as NYPD 'Stop-and-Frisk' Searches Hit Record High," *Guardian*, February 14, 2012, www.theguardian.com/world/ 2012/feb/14/nypd-stop-frisk-record-high.

92   *Homicides, which had reached 2,245 in 1990:* David Goodman and Al Baker, "Murders in New York Drop to a Record Low, but Officers Aren't Celebrating," *New York Times*, December 31, 2014, www .nytimes.com/2015/01/01/nyregion/new-york-city-murders-fall-but -the-police-arent-celebrating.html.

92   *an overwhelming majority of these encounters—about 85 percent:* Jason Oberholtzer, "Stop-and-Frisk by the Numbers," *Forbes*, July 17, 2012, www.forbes.com/sites/jasonoberholtzer/2012/07/17/stop-and -frisk-by-the-numbers/.

92   *Only 0.1 percent, or one of one thousand stopped:* Eric T. Schneiderman, "A Report on Arrests Arising from the New York City Police Department's Stop-and-Frisk Practices," New York State Office of the Attorney General, Civil Rights Bureau, November 2013, www.ag.ny.gov/pdfs/OAG_REPORT_ON_SQF_PRACTICES _NOV_2013.pdf.

93   *The NYCLU sued the Bloomberg administration:* "The Bronx Defenders Hails Today's 'Stop and Frisk' Decision by Federal Judge

Scheindlin," *Bronx Defenders*, August 12, 2013, www.bronxdefenders
.org/the-bronx-defenders-hails-todays-stop-and-frisk-decision-by
-federal-judge-scheindlin/.

94   *federal judge Shira A. Scheindlin ruled:* Ibid.

99   **Unfair: The New Science of Criminal Injustice:** Adam Benforado,
      Unfair: The New Science of Criminal Injustice (New York: Crown,
      2015).

99   *Privately run prisons:* Peter Kerwin, "Study Finds Private Prisons
      Keep Inmates Longer, Without Reducing Future Crime," *University
      of Wisconsin-Madison News*, June 10, 2015, http://news.wisc.edu/
      study-finds-private-prisons-keep-inmates-longer-without-reducing
      -future-crime/.

99   *private prisons make profits only when running at high
      capacity:* Julia Bowling, "Do Private Prison Contracts Fuel Mass
      Incarceration?," *Brennan Center for Justice Blog*, September 20, 2013,
      www.brennancenter.org/blog/do-private-prison-contracts-fuel-mass
      -incarceration.

100   *Michigan economics professor:* Allison Schrager, "In America,
      Mass Incarceration Has Caused More Crime Than It's Prevented,"
      Quartz, July 22, 2015, http://qz.com/458675/in-america-mass
      -incarceration-has-caused-more-crime-than-its-prevented/.

100   *San Diego police used this facial recognition program:* Timothy
      Williams, "Facial Recognition Software Moves from Overseas Wars
      to Local Police," *New York Times*, August 12, 2015, www.nytimes
      .com/2015/08/13/us/facial-recognition-software-moves-from-overseas
      -wars-to-local-police.html.

101   *Officials in Boston, for example:* Anthony Rivas, "Boston Police
      Used Facial Recognition Software on Concertgoers; Will It Really
      Stop Suspicious Activity or Just Encroach upon Our Rights?,"
      Medical Daily, August 18, 2014, www.medicaldaily.com/boston
      -police-used-facial-recognition-software-concertgoers-will-it-really
      -stop-suspicious-298540.

101   *In 2009, the Chicago Police Department:* Matt Stroud, "The
      Minority Report: Chicago's New Police Computer Predicts Crimes,
      but Is It Racist?," *Verge*, February 19, 2014, www.theverge

.com/2014/2/19/5419854/the-minority-report-this-computer-predicts
-crime-but-is-it-racist.

102   *the approximately four hundred people:* Ibid.

102   *a twenty-two-year-old high school dropout:* Ibid.

CHAPTER 6

105   *a young man named Kyle Behm:* Lauren Weber and Elizabeth
      Dwoskin, "Are Workplace Personality Tests Fair?," *Wall Street
      Journal,* September 29, 2014, www.wsj.com/articles/are-workplace
      -personality-tests-fair-1412044257.

106   *the "Five Factor Model" test:* Roland Behm, phone interview by
      author, April 1, 2015.

106   *Behm went on to send notices:* Weber and Dwoskin, "Are
      Workplace Personality Tests Fair?"

106   *considered a medical exam:* ADA National Network, "What
      Limitations Does the ADA Impose on Medical Examinations and
      Inquiries About Disability?," accessed January 9, 2016, https://adata
      .org/faq/what-limitations-does-ada-impose-medical-examinations
      -and-inquiries-about-disability.

107   *Founded in the* 1970s: "Kronos History: The Early Years," Kronos
      website, accessed January 9, 2016, www.kronos.com/about/history
      .aspx.

108   *Workforce Ready HR:* "Workforce Ready HR," Kronos website,
      accessed January 9, 2016, www.kronos.com/products/smb-solutions/
      workforce-ready/products/hr.aspx.

108   *$500 million annual business:* Weber and Dwoskin, "Are
      Workplace Personality Tests Fair?"

108   60 *to* 70 *percent of prospective workers:* Ibid.

108   **Griggs v. Duke Power Company:** NAACP Legal Defense Fund,
      "Case: Landmark: Griggs v. Duke Power Co.," NAACP LDF
      website, accessed January 9, 2016, www.naacpldf.org/case/griggs-v
      -duke-power-co.

108 **Frank Schmidt, a business professor:** Whitney Martin, "The Problem with Using Personality Tests for Hiring," *Harvard Business Review*, August 27, 2014, https://hbr.org/2014/08/the-problem-with -using-personality-tests-for-hiring.

109 **"The primary purpose of the test":** Roland Behm, phone interview by author, April 1, 2015.

109 **Regulators in Rhode Island:** Weber and Dwoskin, "Are Workplace Personality Tests Fair?"

110 **The** Wall Street Journal **asked:** Lauren Weber, "Better to Be Artistic or Responsible? Decoding Workplace Personality Tests," *Wall Street Journal*, September 29, 2014, http://blogs.wsj.com/ atwork/2014/09/29/better-to-be-artistic-or-responsible-decoding -workplace-personality-tests/.

113 **researchers from the University of Chicago:** Marianne Bertrand, "Racial Bias in Hiring: Are Emily and Brendan More Employable Than Lakisha and Jamal?," *Research Highlights from the Chicago Graduate School of Business* 4, no. 4 (2003), www.chicagobooth.edu/ capideas/spring03/racialbias.html.

113 **auditions with the musician hidden:** Curt Rice, "How Blind Auditions Help Orchestras to Eliminate Gender Bias," *Guardian*, October 14, 2013, www.theguardian.com/women-in-leadership/2013/ oct/14/blind-auditions-orchestras-gender-bias.

114 **72 percent of résumés are never seen:** Mona Abdel-Halim, "12 Ways to Optimize Your Resume for Applicant Tracking Systems," *Mashable*, May 27, 2012, http://mashable.com/2012/05/27/resume -tracking-systems/.

114 **words the specific job opening is looking for:** Ibid.

115 **St. George's Hospital Medical School:** Stella Lowry and Gordon MacPherson, "A Blot on the Profession," *British Medical Journal* 296 (March 5, 1988): 657–58.

118 **Replacing a worker earning $50,000 a year:** Heather Boushey and Sarah Jane Glynn, "There Are Significant Business Costs to Replacing Employees," *American Progress*, November 16, 2012, www .americanprogress.org/issues/labor/report/2012/11/16/44464/there-are -significant-business-costs-to-replacing-employees/.

118   *Evolv:* Jessica Leber, "The Machine-Readable Workforce:
       Companies Are Analyzing More Data to Guide How They Hire,
       Recruit, and Promote Their Employees," *MIT Technology Review,*
       May 27, 2013, www.technologyreview.com/news/514901/the-machine
       -readable-workforce/.

120   *A pioneer in this field is Gild:* Jeanne Meister, "2015: Social HR
       Becomes A Reality," *Forbes,* January 5, 2015, www.forbes.com/sites/
       jeannemeister/2015/01/05/2015-social-hr-becomes-a-reality/.

120   *Vivienne Ming, Gild's chief scientist:* Don Peck, "They're Watching
       You at Work," *Atlantic Monthly,* December 2013, www.theatlantic
       .com/magazine/archive/2013/12/theyre-watching-you-at-work/354681/.

CHAPTER 7

125   *the* **New York Times** *ran a story:* Jodi Kantor, "Working Anything
       but 9 to 5: Scheduling Technology Leaves Low-Income Parents with
       Hours of Chaos," *New York Times,* August 13, 2014, www.nytimes
       .com/interactive/2014/08/13/us/starbucks-workers-scheduling-hours
       .html?_r=0.

126   *Within weeks of the article's publication:* Jodi Kantor, "Starbucks to
       Revise Policies to End Irregular Schedules for Its 130,000 Baristas,"
       New York Times, August 14, 2014, www.nytimes.com/2014/08/15/us/
       starbucks-to-revise-work-scheduling-policies.html.

126   *Starbucks was failing to meet these targets:* Justine Hofherr,
       "Starbucks Employees Still Face 'Clopening,' Understaffing, and
       Irregular Workweeks," *Boston.com,* September 24, 2015, www
       .boston.com/jobs/news/2015/09/24/starbucks-employees
       -still-face-clopening-understaffing-and-irregular-workweeks/
       FgdhbalfQqC2p1WLaQm2SK/story.html.

127   *The Allies kept track:* William Ferguson Story, "A Short History
       of Operations Research in the United States Navy," master's thesis,
       Naval Postgraduate School, December 1968, https://archive.org/
       details/shorthistoryofopo0ostor.

127   *Following World War II:* US Congress, Offices of Technology
       Assessment, *A History of the Department of Defense Federally Funded*

Research and Development Centers, OTA-BP-ISS-157 (Washington, DC: US Government Printing Office, June 1995), www.princeton .edu/~ota/disk1/1995/9501/9501.PDF.

127 *In the 1960s, Japanese auto companies:* John Holusha, "'Just-In -Time' System Cuts Japan's Auto Costs," *New York Times,* March 25, 1983, www.nytimes.com/1983/03/25/business/just-in-time-system -cuts-japan-s-auto-costs.html.

129 *the Economic Policy Institute:* Leila Morsy and Richard Rothstein, "Parents' Non-standard Work Schedules Make Adequate Childrearing Difficult," Economic Policy Institute, August 6, 2015, www.epi.org/publication/parents-non-standard-work -schedules-make-adequate-childrearing-difficult-reforming-labor -market-practices-can-improve-childrens-cognitive-and-behavioral -outcomes/.

130 *The legislation died:* H.R. 5159—Schedules That Work Act, 113th Congress (2013–14), accessed January 10, 2016, www.congress.gov/ bill/113th-congress/house-bill/5159.

130 *a San Francisco company called Cataphora:* Stephen Baker, "Data Mining Moves to Human Resources," Bloomberg BusinessWeek, March 11, 2009, www.bloomberg.com/bw/stories/2009-03-11/data -mining-moves-to-human-resources.

131 *MIT researchers analyzed the behavior of call center employees:* Joshua Rothman, "Big Data Comes to the Office," *New Yorker,* June 3, 2014, www.newyorker.com/books/joshua-rothman/big-data-comes -to-the-office.

134 **A Nation at Risk:** National Commission on Excellence in Education, *A Nation at Risk: The Imperative for Educational Reform* (Washington, DC: National Commission on Excellence in Education, 1983), www2.ed.gov/pubs/NatAtRisk/index.html.

135 *case of Tim Clifford:* Tim Clifford, "Charting the Stages of Teacher Data Report Grief," WNYC-FM, March 9, 2012, www.wnyc.org/ story/302123-charting-the-stages-of-teacher-data-report-grief/.

135 *he later told me:* Tim Clifford, e-mail interview by the author, May 13, 2014.

136 *researchers at Sandia National Laboratories:* Tamim Ansary, "Education at Risk: Fallout from a Flawed Report," *Edutopia*, March 9, 2007, www.edutopia.org/landmark-education-report-nation-risk.

136 *Simpson's paradox:* Clifford Wagner, "Simpson's Paradox in Real Life," *American Statistician* 36, no. 1 (1982): 46–48.

138 *educator named Gary Rubinstein:* Gary Rubinstein, "Analyzing Released NYC Value-Added Data Part 2," *Gary Rubinstein's Blog*, February 28, 2012, https://garyrubinstein.wordpress.com/2012/02/28/ analyzing-released-nyc-value-added-data-part-2/.

139 *Congress and the White House agreed:* Julie Hirschfeld Davis, "President Obama Signs into Law a Rewrite of No Child Left Behind," *New York Times*, December 10, 2015, www.nytimes.com/ 2015/12/11/us/politics/president-obam-signs-into-law-a-rewrite-of-no -child-left-behind.html.

140 *Cuomo's education task force:* Yoav Gonen and Carl Campanile, "Cuomo Vacktracks on Common Core, Wants 4-Year Moratorium," *New York Post*, December 10, 2015, http://nypost.com/2015/12/10/ cuomo-backtracks-on-common-core-wants-4-year-moratorium/.

140 *boycott movement had kept 20 percent:* Elizabeth Harris, "20% of New York State Students Opted Out of Standardized Tests This Year," *New York Times*, August 12, 2015, www.nytimes .com/2015/08/13/nyregion/new-york-state-students-standardized-tests .html.

140 *Tim Clifford was cheered:* Tim Clifford, e-mail interview by author, December 15, 2015.

140 *a proven tool against teachers' unions:* Emma Brown, "Education Researchers Caution Against Using Students' Test Scores to Evaluate Teachers," *Washington Post*, November 12, 2015, www .washingtonpost.com/local/education/education-researchers-caution -against-using-value-added-models—ie-test-scores—to-evaluate -teachers/2015/11/12/72b6b45c-8950-11e5-be39-0034bb576eee_story .html.

CHAPTER 8

141 *this banker would probably know:* Dubravka Ritter, "Do We Still Need the Equal Credit Opportunity Act?," Discussion Paper, Payment Cards Center, Federal Reserve Bank of Philadelphia, September 2012, https://ideas.repec.org/p/fip/fedpdp/12-03.html.

142 *were routinely locked out:* Ibid.

142 *model they called FICO:* Martha Poon, "Scorecards as Devices for Consumer Credit: The Case of Fair, Isaac & Company Incorporated," *Sociological Review* 55 (October 2007): 284–306, doi: 10.1111/j.1467-954X.2007.00740.x.

142 *FICO's website:* FICO website, accessed January 10, 2016, www.myfico.com/CreditEducation/ImproveYourScore.aspx.

143 *you have the legal right to ask:* Free Credit Reports, Federal Trade Commission, Consumer Information, accessed January 10, 2016, www.consumer.ftc.gov/articles/0155-free-credit-reports.

143 *company called Neustar:* Natasha Singer, "Secret E-Scores Chart Consumers' Buying Power," *New York Times*, August 18, 2012, www.nytimes.com/2012/08/19/business/electronic-scores-rank-consumers-by-potential-value.html.

143 *Credit card companies such as Capital One:* Emily Steel and Julia Angwin, "On the Web's Cutting Edge, Anonymity in Name Only," *Wall Street Journal*, August 4, 2010, www.wsj.com/news/articles/SB10001424052748703294904575385532109190198.

147 *"good credit scores are sexy":* Website CreditScoreDating.com, accessed January 10, 2016, http://creditscoredating.com/.

148 *Society for Human Resource Management:* Gary Rivlin, "The Long Shadow of Bad Credit in a Job Search," *New York Times*, May 11, 2013, www.nytimes.com/2013/05/12/business/employers-pull-applicants-credit-reports.html.

148 *A 2012 survey on credit card debt:* Amy Traub, "Discredited: How Employment Credit Checks Keep Qualified Workers Out of a Job," *Demos*, February 2013, www.demos.org/sites/default/files/publications/Discredited-Demos.pdf.

149 *the single biggest cause of bankruptcies:* Christina LaMontagne, "NerdWallet Health Finds Medical Bankruptcy Accounts for Majority of Personal Bankruptcies," *NerdWallet*, March 26, 2014, www.nerdwallet.com/blog/health/medical-costs/medical -bankruptcy/.

149 *white households held on average:* Tami Luhby, "The Black-White Economic Divide in 5 Charts," *CNN Money*, November 25, 2015, http://money.cnn.com/2015/11/24/news/economy/blacks-whites -inequality/.

149 *only 15 percent of whites:* Rakesh Kochhar, Richard Fry, and Paul Taylor, "Wealth Gaps Rise to Record Highs Between Whites, Blacks, Hispanics: Twenty-to-One," Pew Research Center, July 26, 2011, www.pewsocialtrends.org/2011/07/26/wealth-gaps-rise-to-record -highs-between-whites-blacks-hispanics/.

149 *ten states have passed legislation:* National Conference of State Legislatures, "Use of Credit Information in Employment 2013 Legislation," NCSL website, updated September 29, 2014, www.ncsl .org/research/financial-services-and-commerce/use-of-credit-info-in -employ-2013-legis.aspx.

150 *The Federal Trade Commission reported:* Federal Trade Commission, "In FTC Study, Five Percent of Consumers Had Errors on Their Credit Reports That Could Result in Less Favorable Terms for Loans," FTC website, February 11, 2013, www.ftc.gov/ news-events/press-releases/2013/02/ftc-study-five-percent-consumers -had-errors-their-credit-reports.

151 *Mississippi's attorney general:* Gretchen Morgenson, "Held Captive by Flawed Credit Reports," *New York Times*, June 21, 2014, www .nytimes.com/2014/06/22/business/held-captive-by-flawed-credit -reports.html.

151 *a Philadelphian named Helen Stokes:* Joe Palazzolo and Gary Fields, "Fight Grows to Stop Expunged Criminal Records Living On in Background Checks," *Wall Street Journal*, May 7, 2015, www.wsj .com/articles/fight-grows-to-stop-expunged-criminal-records-living -on-in-background-checks-1430991002.

152 *in a bucket of people:* Office of Oversight and Investigations, "A Review of the Data Broker Industry: Collection, Use, and

Sale of Consumer Data for Marketing Purposes," Committee on Commerce, Science, and Transportation, December 18, 2013, http://educationnewyork.com/files/rockefeller_databroker.pdf.

152 **an Arkansas resident named Catherine Taylor:** Ylan Q. Mui, "Little-Known Firms Tracking Data Used in Credit Scores," *Washington Post,* July 16, 2011, www.washingtonpost.com/business/economy/little-known-firms-tracking-data-used-in-credit-scores/2011/05/24/gIQAXHcWII_story.html.

154 **a butterfly's diet was "Kosher":** Stephen Baker, "After 'Jeopardy,'" *Boston Globe,* February 15, 2011, www.boston.com/bostonglobe/editorial_opinion/oped/articles/2011/02/15/after_jeopardy/.

154 **labeled them as gorillas:** Alistair Barr, "Google Mistakenly Tags Black People as 'Gorillas,' Showing Limits of Algorithms," *Wall Street Journal,* July 1, 2015, http://blogs.wsj.com/digits/2015/07/01/google-mistakenly-tags-black-people-as-gorillas-showing-limits-of-algorithms/.

155 **Facebook, for example, has patented:** Robinson Meyer, "Could a Bank Deny Your Loan Based on Your Facebook Friends?," *Atlantic Monthly,* September 25, 2015, www.theatlantic.com/technology/archive/2015/09/facebooks-new-patent-and-digital-redlining/407287/.

156 **American Express learned this the hard way:** Ron Lieber, "American Express Kept a (Very) Watchful Eye on Charges," *New York Times,* January 30, 2009, www.nytimes.com/2009/01/31/your-money/credit-and-debit-cards/31money.html.

157 **Douglas Merrill's idea:** Steve Lohr, "Big Data Underwriting for Payday Loans," *New York Times,* January 19, 2015, http://bits.blogs.nytimes.com/2015/01/19/big-data-underwriting-for-payday-loans/.

158 **On the company web page:** Website ZestFinance.com, accessed January 9, 2016, www.zestfinance.com/.

158 **A typical $500 loan:** Lohr, "Big Data Underwriting."

158 **ten thousand data points:** Michael Carney, "Flush with $20M from Peter Thiel, ZestFinance Is Measuring Credit Risk Through Non-traditional Big Data," *Pando,* July 31, 2013, https://pando.com/2013/07/31/flush-with-20m-from-peter-thiel-zestfinance-is-measuring-credit-risk-through-non-traditional-big-data/.

159 *one of the first peer-to-peer exchanges, Lending Club*: Richard MacManus, "Facebook App, Lending Club, Passes Half a Million Dollars in Loans," *Readwrite*, July 29, 2007, http://readwrite .com/2007/07/29/facebook_app_lending_club_passes_half_a _million_in_loans.

159 *received funding a year later*: Lending Club, "Lending Club Completes $600 Million SEC Registration and Offers New Alternative for Consumer Credit," Lending Club, October 14, 2008, http://blog.lendingclub.com/lending-club-sec-registration/.

159 *less than $10 billion in loans*: Peter Renton, "Five Predictions for 2015," Lend Academy, January 5, 2015, www.lendacademy.com/five -predictions-2015/.

159 *Executives from Citigroup*: Nav Athwal, "The Disappearance of Peer-to-Peer Lending," *Forbes*, October 14, 2014, www.forbes.com/ sites/groupthink/2014/10/14/the-disappearance-of-peer-to-peer -lending/.

159 *Wells Fargo's investment fund*: Maureen Farrell, "Wells Fargo Is a Big Winner in Lending Club IPO," *Wall Street Journal*, December 12, 2014, http://blogs.wsj.com/moneybeat/2014/12/12/wells-fargo-is-a -big-winner-in-lending-club-ipo/.

159 *the biggest tech IPO*: Jeremy Quittner, "The 10 Biggest IPOs of 2014," *Inc.*, December 19, 2014, www.inc.com/jeremy-quittner/ biggest-ipos-of-2014.html.

159 *It raised $870 million*: Neha Dimri, "Update 1—Online Lender LendingClub Profit Beats Street as Fees Jump," *Reuters*, May 5, 2015, www.reuters.com/article/lendingclub-results -idUSL4N0XW4HO20150505.

159 *a report in* Forbes: Athwal, "Disappearance of Peer-To-Peer Lending."

CHAPTER 9

161 *Hoffman, a German*: Megan Wolff, "The Myth of the Actuary: Life Insurance and Frederick L. Hoffman's 'Race Traits and Tendencies of the American Negro,'" *Public Health Reports* 121, no. 1 (January/

February 2006): 84–91, www.ncbi.nlm.nih.gov/pmc/articles/
PMC1497788/.

162 *Insurance companies as well as bankers:* Gregory Squires,
"Insurance Redlining: Still Fact, Not Fiction," *Shelterforce* 79
(January/February 1995), www.nhi.org/online/issues/79/isurred
.html.

162 *the Fair Housing Act of 1968:* Fair Housing Laws and Presidential
Executive Orders, US Department of Housing and Urban
Development, accessed January 9, 2016, http://portal.hud.gov/
hudportal/HUD?src=/program_offices/fair_housing_equal_opp/
FHLaws.

163 *Insurance grew out of actuarial science:* Chris Lewin, "The
Creation of Actuarial Science," *Zentralblatt für Didaktik der
Mathematik* 33, no. 2 (April 2001): 61–66, http://link.springer.com/
article/10.1007%2FBF02652740.

163 *John Graunt:* Margaret De Valois, "Who Was Captain John
Graunt?," *Actuary,* September 2000, 38–39, www.theactuary.com/
archive/old-articles/part-3/who-was-captain-john-graunt-3F/.

163 *the first study of the mortality rates:* John Graunt, *Bills of Mortality*
(1662), www.neonatology.org/pdf/graunt.pdf.

163 *a 6 percent death risk:* De Valois, "Who Was Captain John
Graunt?"

164 *researchers at Consumer Reports:* "The Truth About Car
Insurance," *Consumer Reports,* Special Report, accessed January 10,
2016, www.consumerreports.org/cro/car-insurance/auto-insurance
-special-report/index.htm.

165 *And in Florida, adults with clean driving records:* Jeff Blyskal,
"Secrets of Car Insurance Prices," *Consumer Reports,* July 30, 2015,
www.consumerreports.org/cro/magazine/2015/07/car-insurance
-prices/index.htm.

166 *Consumer Federation of America:* Don Jergler, "Price Optimization
Allegations Challenged, NAIC Investigating Practice," *Insurance
Journal,* December 18, 2014, www.insurancejournal.com/news/
national/ 2014/12/18/350630.htm.

166 *Wisconsin Department of Insurance:* "CFA Rips Allstate's Auto Insurance Pricing," *Corporate Crime Reporter,* December 16, 2014, www.corporatecrimereporter.com/news/200/cfa-rips-allstates-auto -insurance-pricing-policy/.

166 *"Allstate's insurance pricing has become untethered":* Ellen Jean Hirst, "Allstate, Other Insurers Accused of Unfairly Pricing Premiums," *Chicago Tribune,* December 16, 2014, www .chicagotribune.com/business/ct-allstate-insurance-risk-premiums -1217-biz-20141216-story.html.

166 *"consistent with industry practices":* Mitch Lipka, "Watchdog: Allstate Auto Insurance Pricing Scheme Is Unfair," *Daily Finance,* December 16, 2014, www.dailyfinance.com/2014/12/16/allstate-auto -insurance-pricing-scheme-unfair/.

167 *its own Twitter campaign:* "Consumer Reports Digs into Car Insurance Quote Secrecy, Prices Are Rife with Inequities and Unfair Practices," *Clarksville Online,* August 6, 2015, www.clarksvilleonline .com/2015/08/06/consumer-reports-digs-into-car-insurance-quote -secrecy-prices-are-rife-with-inequities-and-unfair-practices/.

167 *Swift Transportation:* David Morris, "There's Pressure in the Industry to Monitor Truck Drivers—and Drivers Aren't Happy," *Fortune,* May 26, 2015, http://fortune.com/2015/05/26/driver-facing -truck-cameras/.

167 *About seven hundred truckers die:* Centers for Disease Control and Prevention, "Crashes Are the Leading Cause of on-the-Job Death for Truck Drivers in the US," press release, March 3, 2015, www.cdc.gov/ media/releases/2015/p0303-truck-driver-safety.html.

167 *The average cost of a fatal crash:* Morris, "There's Pressure."

168 *And they use this data:* Karen Levy, "To Fight Trucker Fatigue, Focus on Economics, Not Electronics," *Los Angeles Times,* July 15, 2014, www.latimes.com/opinion/op-ed/la-oe-levy-trucker-fatigue -20140716-story.html.

168 *Progressive, State Farm, and Travelers:* Mark Chalon Smith, "State Farm's In-Drive Discount: What's the Catch?," *CarInsurance,* June 12, 2015, www.carinsurance.com/Articles/state-farm-in-drive -discount.aspx.

170   *They get rewarded with a discount:* Ibid.

171   *data company called Sense Networks:* Stephen Baker, "Mapping a New, Mobile Internet," *Bloomberg,* February 25, 2009, www .bloomberg.com/bw/stories/2009-02-25/mapping-a-new-mobile -internet.

172   *"We wouldn't necessarily recognize":* Greg Skibiski and Tony Jebara, in-person interview by Stephen Baker, February, 2009.

172   *Sense was sold in 2014 to YP:* Anthony Ha, "In Its First Acquisition, YP Buys Mobile Ad Company Sense Networks," *TechCrunch,* January 6, 2014, http://techcrunch.com/2014/01/06/yp-acquires -sense-networks/.

173   *the Internal Revenue Service tweaked the tax code:* Congressional Budget Office, "The Tax Treatment of Employment-Based Health Insurance," March 1994, www.cbo.gov/sites/default/files/103rd -congress-1993-1994/reports/1994_03_taxtreatmentofinsurance.pdf.

173   *about 9 percent of American workers:* Alex Blumberg and Adam Davidson, "Accidents of History Created U.S. Health System," *NPR,* October 22, 2009, www.npr.org/templates/story/story .php?storyId=114045132.

174   *65 percent of Americans:* Ibid.

174   *$3 trillion per year:* Chad Terhune, "U.S. Health Spending Hits $3 Trillion as Obamacare and Rising Drug Costs Kick In," *Los Angeles Times,* December 2, 2015, www.latimes.com/business/healthcare/ la-fi-health-spending-increase-20151202-story.html.

174   *Nearly one dollar of every five:* Scott Thomas, "Nation's Total Personal Income Approaches $13 Trillion," *Business Journals,* December 4, 2012, www.bizjournals.com/bizjournals/on-numbers/ scott-thomas/2012/12/nations-total-personal-income.html.

174   *The Affordable Care Act, or Obamacare:* US Department of Labor, "The Affordable Care Act and Wellness Programs," fact sheet, accessed January 9, 2016, www.dol.gov/ebsa/newsroom/ fswellnessprogram.html.

174   *as high as 50 percent of the cost of coverage:* US Department of Labor, "Affordable Care Act."

174 *more than half of all organizations:* Soeren Mattke, Hangsheng Liu, John Caloyeras, Christina Huang, Kristin Van Busum, Dmitry Khodyakov, and Victoria Shier, "Workplace Wellness Programs Study," Rand Corporation Research Report, 2013, www.rand.org/content/dam/rand/pubs/research_reports/RR200/RR254/RAND_RR254.sum.pdf.

175 *the case of Aaron Abrams:* Aaron Abrams, e-mail interview by author, February 28, 2015.

175 *Anthem Insurance, which administers a wellness program:* Washington and Lee Wellness Program, accessed January 9, 2016, www.wlu.edu/human-resources/wellness/evolve-wellness-program.

175 *Michelin, the tire company:* Leslie Kwoh, "When Your Boss Makes You Pay for Being Fat," *Wall Street Journal,* April 5, 2013, www.wsj.com/articles/SB10001424127887324600704578402784123334550.

176 *CVS announced in* 2013: Ibid.

176 *"Attention everyone, everywhere":* Alissa Fleck, "CVS Drugstore Chain Unveils New Employee Diet Plan: Fat-Shaming and a $600 Fine," *Bitch Media,* March 21, 2013, https://bitchmedia.org/post/cvs-drugstore-chain-unveils-new-employee-diet-plan-fat-shaming-and-a-600-fine.

176 *Lambert Adolphe Jacques Quetelet:* Lily Dayton, "BMI May Not Be the Last Word on Health Risks, Some Experts Say," *Los Angeles Times,* December 19, 2014, www.latimes.com/health/la-he-bmi-20141220-story.html.

176 *Keith Devlin, the mathematician:* Keith Devlin, "Top 10 Reasons Why The BMI Is Bogus," *NPR,* July 4, 2009, www.npr.org/templates/story/story.php?storyId=106268439.

177 *the $6 billion wellness industry:* Rand Corporation, "Do Workplace Wellness Programs Save Employers Money?," Rand Corporation Research Brief, 2013, www.rand.org/content/dam/rand/pubs/research_briefs/RB9700/RB9744/RAND_RB9744.pdf.

177 *"Here are the facts":* Joshua Love, "4 Steps to Implement a Successful Employee Wellness Program," *Forbes,* November 28, 2012, www.forbes.com/sites/theyec/2012/11/28/4-steps-to-implement-a-successful-employee-wellness-program/.

177 *California Health Benefits Review Program:* California Health Benefits Review Program, "Analysis of Senate Bill 189: Health Care Coverage: Wellness Programs," report to the 2013–14 California Legislature, April 25, 2013, http://chbrp.ucop.edu/index .php?action=read&bill_id=149&doc_type=3.

178 **2013** *study headed by Jill Horwitz:* Jill Horwitz, Brenna Kelly, and John Dinardo, "Wellness Incentives in the Workplace: Cost Savings Through Cost Shifting to Unhealthy Workers," *Health Affairs* 32, no. 3 (March 2013): 468–76, doi: 10.1377/hlthaff.2012.0683.

CHAPTER 10

180 *two-thirds of American adults:* Andrew Perrin, "Social Media Usage: 2005–2015," Pew Research Center, October 8, 2015, www .pewinternet.org/2015/10/08/social-networking-usage-2005-2015/.

180 *thirty-nine minutes a day:* Victor Luckerson, "Here's How Facebook's News Feed Actually Works," *Time,* July 9, 2015, http:// time.com/3950525/facebook-news-feed-algorithm/.

180 *Nearly half of them:* Michael Barthel, Elisa Shearer, Jeffrey Gottfried, and Amy Mitchell, "The Evolving Role of News on Twitter and Facebook," Pew Research Center, July 14, 2015, www .journalism.org/2015/07/14/the-evolving-role-of-news-on-twitter-and -facebook/.

180 *Facebook conducted experiments:* Robert Bond, Christopher Fariss, Jason Jones, Adam Kramer, Cameron Marlow, Jaime Settle, and James Fowler, "A 61-Million-Person Experiment in Social Influence and Political Mobilization," *Nature* 489 (September 13, 2012): 295– 98, doi:10.1038/nature11421.

180 *the quiet satisfaction of carrying out a civic duty:* Alan Gerber, Donald Green, and Christopher Larimer, "Social Pressure and Voter Turnout: Evidence from a Large-Scale Field Experiment," *American Political Science Review* 102, no. 1 (February 2008): 33–48, doi:10.1017/S000305540808009X.

181 *inundate Washington with lobbyists:* Derek Willis and Claire Cain Miller, "Tech Firms and Lobbyists: Now Intertwined, but Not Eager

to Reveal It," *New York Times*, September 24, 2014, www.nytimes
.com/2014/09/25/upshot/tech-firms-and-lobbyists-now-intertwined
-but-not-eager-to-reveal-it.html?_r=0.

181   *their campaign had increased turnout by* 340,000: Bond et al.,
       "61-Million-Person Experiment."

181   *George W. Bush, after all, won in* 2000 *by a margin:* David Barstow
       and Don Van Natta Jr., "Examining the Vote; How Bush Took
       Florida: Mining the Overseas Absentee Vote," *New York Times*, July
       15, 2001, www.nytimes.com/2001/07/15/us/examining-the-vote-how
       -bush-took-florida-mining-the-overseas-absentee-vote.html.

182   *altered the news feed algorithm:* Eytan Bakshy, Solomon Messing,
       and Lada Adamic, "Exposure to Ideologically Diverse News and
       Opinion," *Science* 348, no. 6239 (May 7, 2015): 1130–32, doi:10.1126/
       science.aaa1160.

183   *Lada Adamic, a computational social scientist:* Lada Adamic,
       YouTube video from a talk titled "When Friends Deliver the
       Newspaper," originally given at O'Reilly's Foo Camp, November 25,
       2013, accessed January 10, 2016, www.youtube.com/watch?v=v2wv-oV
       C9sE&list=UUoXEyA50RIKnp7jkGrYw8ZQ–I.

183   *Karrie Karahalios:* Luckerson, "Here's How."

183   *researchers experimented on 680,000 Facebook users:* Adam
       Kramer, Jamie Guillory, and Jeffrey Hancock, "Experimental
       Evidence of Massive-Scale Emotional Contagion through Social
       Networks," *Proceedings of the National Academy of Sciences of the
       United States of America* 111, no. 24 (June 2, 2014): 8788–90, doi:
       10.1073/pnas.1320040111.

184   *Two researchers:* Robert Epstein and Ronald Robertson, "The
       Search Engine Manipulation Effect (SEME) and Its Possible Impact
       on the Outcomes of Elections," *Proceedings of the National Academy
       of Sciences of the United States of America* 112, no. 33 (August 18,
       2015): E4512–E4521, doi:10.1073/pnas.1419828112.

184   *Some 73 percent of Americans:* Kristin Purcell, Joanna Brenner,
       and Lee Rainie, "Search Engine Use 2012," *Pew Research Center*,
       March 9, 2012, www.pewinternet.org/2012/03/09/search-engine
       -use-2012/.

185   *he traveled to Boca Raton:* Dave Gilson, "Who Was at Romney's '47 Percent' Fundraiser?," *Mother Jones*, September 18, 2012, www.motherjones.com/mojo/2012/09/romney-47-percent-fundraiser-florida.

186   *captured by a bartender:* David Corn, "Meet Scott Prouty, the 47 Percent Video Source," *Mother Jones*, March 13, 2013, www.motherjones.com/politics/2013/03/scott-prouty-47-percent-video.

186   *very likely cost Romney any chance:* Henry Blodget, "Bloomberg: Mitt Romney Just Lost the Election," *Business Insider*, September 17, 2012, www.businessinsider.com/mitt-romney-just-lost-the-election-2012-9.

187   **The Selling of the President:** Joe McGinniss, *The Selling of the President* 1968 (New York: Trident Press, 1969).

188   *Rayid Ghani posted an update:* excerpted on Straight Dope Message Board, accessed January 9, 2016, http://boards.straightdope.com/sdmb/archive/index.php/t-617517.html.

188   *heading up the data team for Obama's campaign:* Alexis Madrigal, "What the Obama Campaign's Chief Data Scientist Is Up to Now," *Atlantic Monthly*, May 8, 2013, www.theatlantic.com/technology/archive/2013/05/what-the-obama-campaigns-chief-data-scientist-is-up-to-now/275676/.

188   *One of Ghani's projects at Accenture:* Chad Cumby, Andrew Fano, Rayid Ghani, and Marko Krema, "Predicting Customer Shopping Lists from Point-of-Sale Purchase Data," paper presented at the Proceedings of the Tenth ACM SIGKDD International Conference on Knowledge Discovery and Data Mining, Seattle, 2004, doi:10.1145/1014052.1014098.

191   *each campaign developed profiles of American voters:* Sasha Issenberg, "How President Obama's Campaign Used Big Data to Rally Individual Voters," *Technology Review*, December 19, 2012, www.technologyreview.com/featuredstory/509026/how-obamas-team-used-big-data-to-rally-voters/.

191   *Four years later:* Adam Pasick and Tim FernHolz, "The Stealthy, Eric Schmidt-Backed Startup That's Working to Put Hillary Clinton in the White House," *Quartz*, October 9, 2015, http://

qz.com/520652/groundwork-eric-schmidt-startup-working-for-hillary
-clinton-campaign/.

191 *In late 2015 the* Guardian *reported:* Harry Davies, "Ted Cruz Using
Firm That Harvested Data on Millions of Unwitting Facebook
Users," *Guardian,* December 11, 2015, www.theguardian.com/us
-news/2015/dec/11/senator-ted-cruz-president-campaign-facebook
-user-data.

191 ***When the Republican Jewish Coalition was meeting:*** Tom
Hamburger, "Cruz Campaign Credits Psychological Data and
Analytics for Its Rising Success," *Washington Post,* December 13,
2015, www.washingtonpost.com/politics/cruz
-campaign-credits-psychological-data-and-analytics-for-its-rising
-success/2015/12/13/4cb0baf8-9dc5-11e5-bce4-708fe33e3288_story
.html.

193 ***The Center for Medical Progress:*** Eugene Scott, "Anti-abortion
Group Releases Fifth Planned Parenthood Video," CNN, August 5,
2015, www.cnn.com/2015/08/04/politics/planned-parenthood-fifth
-video-houston/.

193 ***Research later showed:*** Jackie Calmes, "Planned Parenthood Videos
Were Altered, Analysis Finds," *New York Times,* August 27, 2015,
www.nytimes.com/2015/08/28/us/abortion-planned-parenthood
-videos.html. www.theguardian.com/us-news/2015/nov/29/suspect
-in-planned-parenthood-attack-said-no-more-baby-parts-after-arrest.

194 ***According to Zeynep Tufekci:*** Zeynep Tufekci, phone interview by
author, April 3, 2015.

194 ***more than 43 percent of Republicans:*** Peter Schroeder, "Poll:
43 Percent of Republicans Believe Obama Is a Muslim," *Hill,*
September 13, 2015, http://thehill.com/blogs/blog-briefing-room/
news/253515-poll-43-percent-of-republicans-believe-obama-is-a
-muslim.

194 ***still directing 75 percent of their media buy:*** Elizabeth Wilner,
"Romney and Republicans Outspent Obama, but Couldn't Out-
advertise Him," *Advertising Age,* November 9, 2012, http://adage
.com/article/campaign-trail/romney-outspent-obama
-advertise/238241/.

194   *Simulmedia, in New York:* Steven Perlberg, "Targeted Ads? TV Can
Do That Now Too," *Wall Street Journal,* November 20, 2014, www
.wsj.com/articles/targeted-ads-tv-can-do-that-now-too-1416506504.

CONCLUSION

201   *President Bill Clinton signed:* Richard Socarides, "Why Bill
Clinton Signed the Defense of Marriage Act," *New Yorker,* March 8,
2013, www.newyorker.com/news/news-desk/why-bill-clinton-signed
-the-defense-of-marriage-act.

201   *tech giant IBM announced:* Nick Gillespie, "What's Good for
IBM . . . ," *Chicago Tribune,* November 5, 1996, http://articles
.chicagotribune.com/1996-11-05/news/9611050018_1_gay-marriage
-defense-of-marriage-act-same-sex.

201   *"In terms of business competitiveness":* Businessweek Archives,
"Same Sex Benefits: Where IBM Goes, Others May Follow,"
Bloomberg Business, October 6, 1996, www.bloomberg.com/bw/
stories/1996-10-06/same-sex-benefits-where-ibm-goes-others-may
-follow.

201   *a gay man, Tim Cook:* Timothy Donald Cook, "Tim Cook Speaks
Up," *Bloomberg Business,* October 30, 2014, www.bloomberg.com/
news/articles/2014-10-30/tim-cook-speaks-up.

201   *Apple, the most valuable company:* Verne Kopytoff, "Apple: The
First \$700 Billion Company," *Fortune,* February 10, 2015, http://
fortune.com/2015/02/10/apple-the-first-700-billion-company/.

204   *In 1907 alone, 3,242 miners died:* MSHA, "Coal Fatalities for 1900
Through 2014," US Department of Labor, accessed January 9, 2016,
www.msha.gov/stats/centurystats/coalstats.asp.

205   *drew up such an oath:* Emanuel Derman and Paul Wilmott,
"The Financial Modeler's Manifesto," January 7, 2009,
www.uio.no/studier/emner/sv/oekonomi/ECON4135/h09/
undervisningsmateriale/FinancialModelersManifesto.pdf.

206   *FindFamilyResources:* FindFamilyResources website, accessed
January 9, 2016, http://findfamilyresources.com/.

208 *If you plot year-to-year scores on a chart:* Gary Rubinstein, "Analyzing Released NYC Value-Added Data Part 2," *Gary Rubinstein's Blog*, February 28, 2012, http://garyrubinstein.teachforus .org/2012/02/28/analyzing-released-nyc-value-added-data-part-2/.

210 *as the computer scientist Cynthia Dwork has noted:* Claire Cain Miller, "Algorithms and Bias: Q. and A. with Cynthia Dwork," *New York Times*, August 10, 2015, www.nytimes.com/2015/08/11/upshot/ algorithms-and-bias-q-and-a-with-cynthia-dwork.html.

210 *Web Transparency and Accountability Project:* Elizabeth Dwoskin, "How Social Bias Creeps into Web Technology," *Wall Street Journal*, August 21, 2015, www.wsj.com/articles/computers-are-showing-their -biases-and-tech-firms-are-concerned-1440102894.

211 *Message Machine:* Jeff Larson, "Message Machine Starts Providing Answers," *Pro Publica*, October 18, 2012, www.propublica.org/article/ message-machine-starts-providing-answers.

212 *Fair Credit Reporting Act:* Federal Trade Commission, "Fair Credit Reporting Act," 15 USC § 1681 et seq., FTC website, www.ftc.gov/ enforcement/rules/rulemaking-regulatory-reform-proceedings/fair -credit-reporting-act.

212 *Equal Credit Opportunity Act:* Federal Trade Commission, "Your Equal Credit Opportunity Rights," FTC website, www.consumer.ftc .gov/articles/0347-your-equal-credit-opportunity-rights.

213 *Americans with Disabilities Act:* US Department of Justice, Civil Rights Division, "Information and Technical Assistance on the Americans with Disabilities Act," Americans with Disabilities Act website, www.ada.gov/.

213 *Health Insurance Portability and Accountability Act:* US Department of Labor, "The Health Insurance Portability and Accountability Act," November 2015, www.dol.gov/ebsa/newsroom/ fshipaa.html.

213 *the European model:* L-Soft, "Opt-In Laws in North America and Europe," Lsoft.com, www.lsoft.com/resources/optinlaws.asp.

214 *illegal to sell user data:* Elizabeth Dwoskin, "EU Data-Privacy Law Raises Daunting Prospects for U.S. Companies," *Wall Street Journal*,

December 16, 2015, www.wsj.com/articles/eu-data-privacy-law-raises
-daunting-prospects-for-us-companies-1450306033.

214   *the number of homeless people in the city*: Meghan Henry, Alvaro
Cortes, Azim Shivji, and Katherine Buck, "The 2014 Annual
Homeless Assessment Report (AHAR) to Congress," US Department
of Housing and Urban Development, October 2014, www
.hudexchange.info/resources/documents/2014-AHAR-Part1.pdf.

215   *wean families from Section* 8: Giselle Routhier, "Mayor
Bloomberg's Revolving Door of Homelessness," *Safety Net*, Spring
2012, www.coalitionforthehomeless.org/mayor-bloombergs-revolving
-door-of-homelessness/.

216   *Made in a Free World:* Issie Lapowsky, "The Next Big Thing You
Missed: Software That Helps Businesses Rid Their Supply Chains
of Slave Labor," *Wired*, February 3, 2015, www.wired.com/2015/02/
frdm/.

217   *Eckerd, a child and family services nonprofit*: Darian Woods,
"Who Will Seize the Child Abuse Prediction Market?," *Chronicle
for Social Change*, May 28, 2015, https://chronicleofsocialchange.org/
featured/who-will-seize-the-child-abuse-prediction-market/10861.

217   **Boston Globe:** Michael Levenson, "Can Analytics Help Fix the
DCF?," *Boston Globe*, November 7, 2015, www.bostonglobe
.com/2015/11/07/childwelfare-bostonglobe-com/AZ2kZ7ziiP8c
BMOite2KKP/story.html.

INDEX